Christoph Gluck

GLUCK

by

ALFRED EINSTEIN

Translated by ERIC BLOM

With music examples in the text

McGraw-Hill Book Company

New York • St. Louis • San Francisco • Düsseldorf

Mexico • Montreal • Panama • Rio de Janeiro • Toronto

First published 1936

First McGraw-Hill Paperback Edition, 1972
07-019530-7

1 2 3 4 5 6 7 8 9 MU MU 7 9 8 7 6 5 4 3 2

TO MY ENGLISH FRIENDS

ERIC BLOM

RICHARD CAPELL

H. C. AND HESTER COLLES

EDWARD J. DENT

EDWIN EVANS

A. H. FOX STRANGWAYS

WILLIAM GLOCK

SCOTT GODDARD

DYNELEY HUSSEY

ROBERT L. JACOBS

WILLIAM MCNAUGHT

MARION M. SCOTT

J. A. WESTRUP

BERYL DE ZOETE

CONTENTS

vii

Contents

Gluck's imagination is immense. The confines of all national music are thus too narrow for him: out of Italian and French music, out of that of every people, he has made a music that is his own; or rather, he has sought in nature all the sounds of true expression and conquered them for himself.

J. A. Hiller, *Wöchentliche Nachrichten*
(24th October 1768).

EXPOSITION

Is it true, the pronouncement of worthy Johann Adam Hiller, which serves as motto for the present appreciation of Christoph Willibald Gluck? Does it not merely reflect a free and keen mind of the second half of the eighteenth century, a mind that saw in Rousseau's 'return to nature' a panacea for every political and aesthetic ill of the time? Does Gluck really stand above all nations? Is it not wildly unseasonable—or again perhaps all too topical—at a time when nationalism is taking on paroxysmal forms, to take under observation a great musician who belongs to Italian, French and German musical history alike, and whom in the earlier days of this paroxysm Czech national pride also claimed for its own?

The question is difficult even for one who is not inclined to regard the occurrence of Slavonic rhythms and Viennese tunes in Gluck's music as an awkward racial problem, but believes that such rhythms and melodic blossoms simply pleased Gluck, just as Italian *canzonette* and French *chansons* too captivated his ear. It is not easy to say whether Gluck was international or German, Italian or French, for he was an opera composer, and in fact exclusively an opera composer, even though he may occasionally have entered the domains of church music, instrumental composition or song. And German opera did not yet exist at that time, or existed no longer, since it is not necessary to consider whether the operas with German words, which enjoyed a short florescence at the smaller North German courts and had a middle-class settlement in Hamburg at the turn of the seventeenth century, should be called *German* operas and not rather a hybrid, an offshoot, a bastard form of French and Italian opera. At the beginning of Gluck's career in any case Italian and French opera alone were established, and if he wished to make his way as operatic composer at all, his only choice lay between the writing of Italian and French opera.

He did both, one after the other. Although a German, he first wrote Italian, then French operas—two types the conditions of which

I

were precisely determined and strictly separated from each other.
Nor did he ever alter these conditions. Even his reformed Italian
opera is still Italian opera; even the opera with which he engaged
in the supposed contest against the tradition of Lulli and Rameau
in Paris is still French opera, in style and not only in language.
Not till the end of his life did stronger national tendencies awaken
in him. 'I have now grown very old, and have squandered the
best powers of my mind upon the French nation, regardless of which
I feel an inward impulse to make something for my own nation yet,'
he wrote on 10th February 1780 to Duke Carl August, the Maecenas
of Goethe and Schiller in Weimar. But what kind of German
opera could he have 'made'? No German poet, not even Goethe
or Schiller, and least of all Wieland, would have been capable of
supplying him with the subject and the text he required. There
was no German opera in the grand style to set him up again. It
is part of his 'international' and personal greatness to have in his
turn set up German opera indirectly, by way of his Italian and
French works.

No less difficult to determine than his position above or among
the nations is his place in musical history. It has been said of him
as the reformer of opera that he bore a Janus head: that he pointed
back to the primitive beginnings of opera at the end of the sixteenth
century, with its striving after simplicity, grandeur and dignity, its
endeavour to recall the ideals of antique drama; but that he also
pointed forward into the future, to the whole work of Richard
Wagner, whose principles, they say, he had anticipated in many
particulars. All of which amounts at best to a pretty *bon mot*.
Just as Wagner is separated from Gluck, of whose reforms he shows
an utter lack of understanding in his writings, or Gluck is separated
from Wagner by a whole aesthetic world, so Gluck had not the
remotest experience of the Florentine choral opera. He is a child
of the eighteenth century, explicable only by reference to the eighteenth
century. The presuppositions and effects of his art are almost entirely
delimited by that century. Instead of assigning him to this or that
nation, instead of determining his value for the history of opera, let
us rather show how he came to be Gluck, and who that Gluck was.

CHAPTER I

DEVELOPMENT

ORIGINS

DISPUTES about Gluck begin as soon as questions of the place and time of his birth are raised; indeed, even his name furnishes material for them. In the second quarter of the nineteenth century the opinion prevailed that Gluck was born on 25th March 1700, at Neustadt on the Waldnaab, and bore the baptismal names of Johann Christoph, like one of Johann Sebastian Bach's uncles. Then for a long time the parochial village of Weidenwang claimed the glory of having given birth to him. The truth is, however, that he came into the world at the neighbouring village of Erasbach, near Beilngries, on 2nd July 1714, and was merely christened at Weidenwang. Both places are in the Upper Palatinate, near the small town of Berching between Nuremberg and Ratisbon, about equidistant from those cities. All the same, Gluck may not be called an Upper Palatine and thus turned into a Bavarian composer. His father, Alexander Johannes Gluck, was born about 1681 at Neustadt on the Waldnaab, not far from Weiden, which two hundred years later became Max Reger's birthplace. This was close to the Bohemian frontier, and he was the second son of one Johann Adam Gluck (1650–1722), who had been court huntsman to Prince Sagan and a citizen of Neustadt. But Neustadt at that time did not belong to Bavaria: it was the capital of Sternstein, a county of the realm exalted to the rank of principality, belonging to the Prince of Lobkowitz, Duke of Raudnitz and Sagan, and not restored to Bavaria until 1806, when Napoleon conferred a kingship on the Elector Max Joseph. Gluck's father as well as his grandfather was thus subject to Prince Lobkowitz, a circumstance that explains why all the children of Johann Adam Gluck

3

with whose destiny we are familiar gravitated towards the east, to the patrimonial dominions of Bohemia. A stepbrother of Alexander, Leopold Gluck, became a forester in Hungary; another, Georg Christoph Gluck, court huntsman at Raudnitz; a third, Johann Christoph, went first of all to Ratisbon, and his later career is shrouded in darkness.

Gluck's own brothers and sisters too—all younger than he, for he was the first-born—went eastward without exception. Franz became a head forester in Bohemia, Karl chief huntsman at Baumgarten in Lower Austria, Alexander an official in Vienna, and his youngest sister married a captain of the imperial hussars. Gluck's father himself, Alexander Johannes, soon returned to his homeland, the Bohemian dominions. It is easy to explain how he came to live so far westward, in the middle of the Upper Palatinate. He was what we should nowadays call an official in occupied territory. As a young man he had been attached as huntsman to Prince Eugene of Savoy and had clearly been appointed forester at Erasbach during the occupation of Bavaria by the Austrians after the battle of Höchstädt (1704), which had had so unhappy an issue for the Elector Max Emanuel. This was presumably before 1708, until which year Bavaria remained under Austrian administration. He built himself a house and married—unfortunately we know only the baptismal name of Gluck's mother (Walpurga) and nothing else whatever about her. But when, after the peace of Nijmwegen in 1714, Max Emanuel returned to Bavaria, Gluck's father did not long remain in Bavarian electoral service, but went back to the imperial dominions of Bohemia in August 1717, to the foot of the Erzgebirge.

Christoph Willibald was then just three years of age. Father Gluck, who seems to have been an enterprising and energetic man, had settled down so firmly in Bavaria that the process of his removal took some considerable time. He was in charge of the forestry (and the toll) not only of Erasbach, but also of the wealthy monasteries of Seligporten and Plankstetten; he was on good terms not only with the Count Palatine von der Hauben, who had superseded the imperial occupation of the Upper Palatinate in 1708, but also with

4

the authorities of the Bavarian electoral government, which returned in 1714. It is from him that Christoph Willibald must have inherited the characteristics of energy, of 'economy' (i.e. close-fistedness), of a 'political head'—as they still say in Bavaria—which is a faculty of recognizing and exploiting a situation with instinctive quickness. From the father, too, came his pugnacity or vehemence, for we find among the documents in the forestry archives of Neumarkt, under 2nd and 10th September 1716, traces of a trial of Alexander Gluck for 'disrespectful speech.' With the church Gluck's father was on good terms, for his name as well as that of Gluck's mother is among those who established early Mass in the church of Erasbach.

CHILDHOOD AND YOUTH

Alexander Gluck first went as ranger for Count Kaunitz to Neuschloss near Böhmisch Leipa: a good distance to the north-east, beyond the Elbe. There young Gluck came to know not only the woods, but also a lake. In 1722 Alexander became head forester to Count Kinsky at Böhmisch Kamnitz. Two years later he is said to have taken a similar post at the residence of the Duchess of Tuscany at Reichstadt; but this is extremely questionable. At any rate, in 1725 he was back at Kamnitz and later became head forester to Prince Lobkowitz at Eisenberg. Young Gluck was not always in the paternal forest home or ranging about the woods as his father's childish assistant, but went to school at Kamnitz and at Albersdorf near Komotau at an early age. (At Eisenberg he cannot have gone to school, since there was none.) That he first came in contact with music at these schools is certain. We know from a hundred testimonies that Bohemia was then the most musical country in Europe and that, particularly in the elementary schools, children were taught not only the first principles of singing, but also the playing of instruments.

Whether music began to determine Gluck's fate in these early years; what plans his father had for him; whether the biographer's favourite struggle over the choice of a profession was waged between father and son—of all that we know nothing. It has so far been taken for granted that the father must have recognized special gifts in his son and would not have sent him to the Jesuits at Komotau had he intended him for a forester. Unfortunately, however, a course of education at Komotau has not only never been proved, but is extremely doubtful. Thus, considering our lack of reliable sources of information, it may be preferable not to ask what Gluck *learnt,* but what he *was* and what idiosyncrasies he had inherited: the will-power and toughness of a youth grown up in the woodlands as the son of a forester and huntsman, a presence of mind equal to any unforeseen situation, a sharp eye and a sure hand.

Supposing that the Komotau chapter of life were authenticated, something like the following might be said:

Concerning those years in the Jesuit College, the years of puberty between thirteen and eighteen which are decisive in the life of a genius, all that is recorded is the assertion that he received organ and clavier tuition there. But then these aspects of musical education should have left their traces on his later life. The change from the freedom of home to the discipline of a religious educational institution must have affected Gluck tremendously, for every Jesuit pupil was mercilessly torn from his family. The principles of Jesuitic upbringing ought to have made more visible impressions on Gluck's life and work, and he must have become not only a good Latinist in that school, but also a good logician. But he was only the latter, and in the eighteenth century clearness of thought and smartness in polemic were no longer exclusively confined to the teaching of the Jesuits. He would not only have become acquainted with all kinds of church music at divine service, but would have taken part in the frequent saints' festivals and scholastic celebrations, which were unthinkable without music and culminated in the performance of Latin school plays — in other words, real operas. It would be pleasant to imagine him as having sought compensation in music whenever he felt oppressed by the rigour of studies and examinations, by religious observances, by the unavoidable penitential sermons and by the catechism. No less pleasant would it be to conclude from the peculiarities of the scholastic drama cultivated by the

Jesuits, which revelled in violent emotions and extreme pathos, disdaining neither tragic crises nor tragic endings,[1] that Gluck must here have received his first ideas of operatic reform; that in Komotau was planted the first seed of his later tragic conception of the *opera seria*; that here the soil was prepared from which sprang the 'more serious' traits in his early operas, and in which the germs of the ideas of Durazzo and Calzabigi were to thrive so fruitfully.

As it is, all such conclusions and observations must be regarded as very doubtful indeed. The roll of pupils kept by the old Jesuit college at Komotau has been preserved, and in it may be found, it is true, the name of Franz Gluck of Eisenberg, but not that of Christoph Willibald, his great elder brother. Let us therefore calmly confess that we are groping in impenetrable darkness where young Gluck's so-called years of maturing are in question. The strongest proof against his having been a pupil at Komotau is the information given by one of his biographers, Schmid, that he worked at Latin in his fifties, for if anything was to be learnt from the Jesuit fathers, it was a thorough command of that tongue. One single fact might be adduced as not arguing against Komotau, namely that Gluck never wielded the German language with absolute ease in writing. The Jesuits deliberately neglected it, and we know of the Viennese poet Michael Denis, a younger contemporary of Gluck's and himself a Jesuit, that at the age of eighteen he still did not know German correctly.

Gluck lived to witness the dissolution of the Jesuit order (1773) —with what feelings? He had become a man of the world, an 'independent spirit,' as they said in those days, and Joseph II's deed of violence hardly filled him with the pain and indignation which other just men of the time felt. It is not without significance that he let the event pass without a word of comment.

PRAGUE

In 1732 Gluck went to Prague and is said to have entered the university as a student. Again we have not the least knowledge

[1] See Vladimir Helfert, *Die Jesuiten-Kollegien der Böhmischen Provinz zur Zeit des jungen Gluck (Festschrift für Johannes Wolf)*. (Berlin, 1929.)

of what he studied there and what aims he pursued. We have merely his own word for the fact that he studied 'as it was the custom to study there at that time,' which does not sound exactly appreciative. A tradition that 'besides German, he also cultivated French and Italian' may be dismissed as anything but credible, for these subjects were not in the curriculum of a university. The truth seems to be, once again, that he had nothing whatever to do with the university, but was disinclined to admit this candidly later on.

Only one thing is certain: music attracted him more and more irresistibly at that period. He sang and appears to have played not only the violin, but preferably the violoncello. It may be supposed that he simply earned his daily bread by music and played whatever instrument happened to be required. He knocked about the fairs in the neighbourhood of Prague; he performed with the Prague church choirs, notably that of the Tein church and also that of St. James, where—not until 1735, it is true—Bohuslav Černohorsky was chapel master. An important name, this, for if Gluck really was his pupil, then Černohorsky gave him an *Italian* training and personally directed him towards Italy. A Franciscan monk, he had once been *regens chori* at the 'Santo' in Padua and organist at the convent church of Assisi. His nickname was 'il padre boemo,' as later on Hasse's was to be 'il caro Sassone.' He not only boasts Gluck as his pupil, but Tartini also. It was under him that Gluck had an opportunity to become familiar with the strict and with a less strict church style. However, Gluck doubtless devoted himself more assiduously to instrumental music in Prague and may thus have come into contact with opera at the houses of princely and aristocratic patrons.

What kind of opera this was can be estimated only in general. Prague was in this respect a branch of Vienna. What may be asserted with fair certainty is the impossibility of Gluck's *not* becoming acquainted with the work of Johann Adolf Hasse, who was at that time the ruler of the Italian (and with it the German) operatic stage as the chief exponent of the so-called second Neapolitan school, i.e. of a generation of dramatic musicians who forced the operatic ideal

8

of Alessandro Scarlatti, which was already concert-like, still farther towards concert conditions. There has surely never been a more prolific composer of opera (Hasse wrote over a hundred operas and set many of Metastasio's librettos three times and more) who was at the same time more of a pure musician, although needless to say he too sedulously wrote *recitativi accompagnati* and disdained none of the conventional 'dramatic' expedients, indeed now and again led an aria directly into a recitative. But as a rule he merely filled the given formulas of opera with refined and opulent music in which the singer shines and the orchestra furnishes delicate or saturated colours. About the *problems* of opera Hasse never troubled to think, nor did he dare to criticize any of Metastasio's librettos. He was Metastasio's musical counterpart: a willing court purveyor for Vienna, Dresden and the more or less aristocratic public of the Venetian theatres. And if Gluck was unable to escape his influence in the matter of the construction, melodic formation and florid decoration of the aria, he must nevertheless have been conscious of a secret opposition against Hasse from the beginning. We shall see that the 'Italian' arias in his first operas, which come nearest to the manner of Hasse, differ from it by their greater energy—their squareness or roughness, one might say—by their stronger thematic contrasts and by shorter and syllabically melodic middle sections (for Hasse was unable to sacrifice coloratura even there). Gluck had quite another, much more vehement nature than the mild, gentle, harmonious Hasse.

VIENNA

It was only natural for Gluck to leave Prague for Vienna. What chiefly decided him, however, seems to have been a domestic incentive, for he became chamber musician to Prince Ferdinand Philipp Lobkowitz, his father's youthful employer. This shows, incidentally, that any possible conflict between the claims of some professional study and music had by that time been decided in favour of the latter. It was high time, for Gluck was now twenty-two, an age at which musicians of a less sluggish temperament had long won

9

their spurs. It was the year in which Pergolesi, only four years
older than Gluck and famous all over Italy, lay down to die, thus
making the beginnings of a European reputation. A slow development, a gradual maturing, a cultivation of his talent by energy and
thoughtfulness—all this is characteristic of Gluck.

In Vienna he became acquainted with Italian opera in its most
lavish form and at a turning-point of its local history. If he had arrived
there by 13th February 1736, he may have heard the festival opera
performed to celebrate the wedding of Maria Theresa with Stephen
Francis, Duke of Lorraine: the *Achille in Sciro* of Antonio Caldara.
Operas by the same composer were *Ciro riconosciuto,* performed on
28th August, and *Temistocle,* given on 4th November, the name-day
of the Emperor Charles VI. There is no denying that the music
of these last ostentatious operas by old Caldara, who died that same
year, made an impression on Gluck. Vienna, with Caldara as
vice-*Capellmeister* and the famous Johann Joseph Fux as first *Capellmeister,* was at that time a stronghold—let us not say of reaction, since
there was no such thing in the eighteenth century except in Paris,
but of an older conception of the aria, a relic of the seventeenth
century which elsewhere had long been replaced by a less 'contra-
puntally' behaved aria form with less lively basses, a more monumental
build and more extravagant concessions to the singer. As a young
man—in his Milan days—Gluck gave up this 'polar' relationship
of voice and bass parts, concentrating all the expression in the vocal
line; but he retained the formal construction of Caldara's aria. And
Gluck now for the first time made the acquaintance of a poet who
was to become fateful for him, as he became for the poet. The
librettos of his first three operas were by Pietro Metastasio, who
seven years before had been appointed imperial court poet in Vienna
in succession to Apostolo Zeno.

ZENO AND METASTASIO

Zeno and Metastasio are the two 'reformers' of the Italian opera
libretto, which, after a beginning with 'a search of the soul after
the land of the Greeks,' had degenerated in the course of the seven-

teenth century into an absurd, unbridled caricature of dramatic poetry, mainly under the influence of a freakish species of Spanish drama. This degeneration is easily explained by any one who knows the order of precedence given to the separate arts in the 'complete art-work' of the opera of the time. The most important element was that of stage machinery, which together with scenic painting conjured up technical marvels before a pampered audience. Then came the musician, who had to write for the gratification of the *primi uomini* and *prime donne,* and was thus little more than a menial. But the most pitiable slave was the librettist, who was expected to please *everybody.*

One thing, however, opera certainly was in the seventeenth century, even in its grossest deformities: *it was opera*—opera that admitted the miraculous, the fantastic, the improbable, and yet made it seem true. It is from these features that the two 'classics' of the operatic libretto, Apostolo Zeno and Pietro Metastasio, delivered the *dramma per musica.* Both set in the place of a bad operatic convention another that was scarcely less bad, but merely 'purified' and more tasteful.

Zeno (1668–1750), a man of honourable character descended from a noble Venetian family, and of comprehensive scholarship and wide reading, was actually an archaeologist. His contemporaries attributed to him the merit of being 'the father and creator of the new melodrama and oratorio, being the first to banish the impossible from the stage by basing the action on the probable, the serious, the heroic and the didactic.' He threw comic characters and situations overboard and chose only 'historical' subjects. It follows that opera—the *dramma per musica*—split into two sections from its core, for the better Zeno's dialogues became, the more incongruous were the arias with which his stereotyped form brought every scene to a close. Zeno is thus, if not the father and creator of a new melodrama, unquestionably that of the 'exit-aria.' Which hardly consoles one for the fact that he rarely wrote good dramatic dialogues. Finely chiselled and richly sententious ones—yes; but good ones—no. He wrote a *Hamlet* (*Ambleto*) in which the scene between mother and son remotely suggests Shakespeare, but which on the whole is a clumsy farrago of intrigue; he turned out a *Cato Fabbrizio,* a scene in which might have served Lessing as a model for his *Emilia Galotti*; nor is an *Ifigenia in Aulide,* rich in amorous episodes and complications, missing among his fifty librettos, written partly in collaboration with Pariati, the second imperial court poet. If his unruly precursors worked under the influence of a picturesque Spanish drama, he came under that of the chivalric and courtly French species, the drama of Corneille and lesser men. His merits are purely negative. He banished mythology and fantasy from the opera, thus purging and rationalizing it; but while he removed excrescences, he attacked the very core of its life. Tyrants and villains were often the heroes in seventeenth-century opera; in his the tyrant is as a rule only a foil for the virtuous hero, and it is no rare occurence for him to turn into a model of forgiving and under-standing highmindedness himself. There is nothing but external complication and external solution; no guilt and no catharsis. Passion is unknown; there is only rhetoric. Phrases take the place of gentle emotion, and in the aria we find metaphors doing duty for true feeling.

Metastasio (1698–1782) is distinguished from Zeno only by the quality, not by the nature of his talent. His fame was established as early as 1724, when he came forward with his *Didone abbandonata* —a Dido who seeks to keep her Aeneas, among other things, by the expedient of flirting with the Moorish king Jarba, and who surprises one by nothing so much as the fact that she really throws herself into the fire at the end. True, this is a work of great charm in versifica-tion, containing some dramatic situations and showing a theatrical adroitness.

For more than fifty years Metastasio lived in Vienna, honoured and extolled, a model of domestic virtue, an ideal of personal amiability, an object of universal fame, providing the imperial family with courtly librettos, each of which was received with rapture for its elegance, ease and singableness, and composed by twenty or by fifty musicians. His dialogue is shorter than Zeno's, his arias are more euphonious, his metres more manifold, his phrases less forced.

Metastasio is that happy poet whose work everybody may read with pleasure: men, because they find therein true descriptions of originals, who actually live among them; women, because no other poet shows them more clearly than he the extraordinary power of beauty and the influence of their sex.

Of this praise from Arteaga, who wrote a history of opera, only the second half is approximately true. Metastasio's dramas swarm with impossible heroes of magnanimity and renunciation and their doings (the climax is reached, as in Zeno, when in *Temistocle* the Persian king Xerxes turns from a tyrant into an admirer of patriotic virtue); with heroic sons and daughters; with intriguers and conspirators, who are invariably pardoned; with attempts at suicide as invariably frustrated. All the subjects of history become courtly tales in Metastasio's hands, tales in which some noble-minded ruler or other is mirrored. His mastery shows itself in attractive details, not in the general trend of the operatic action. The generation succeeding him had already discovered this, as may be judged from the following passage in the appendix to Sulzer's *Allgemeine Theorie der Künste*:[1] 'His greatest merit lies in his improvement of style, in a loftier, more correct and animated language, and a certain lyrical turn of mind, in which he vastly surpasses his predecessors.'

Gluck was later to embody the most thoroughgoing antithesis to Metastasio's operatic ideal. Meanwhile he was as yet far from that. The unknown and unrenowned chamber musician of Prince Lobkowitz cannot but have cherished the same feelings of veneration and admiration for the famous *poeta cesareo* as the rest of the world. He too was for a long time yet to regard the Metastasian libretto as desirable material for his music, material he began by accepting without question.

What the Vienna of about 1736 may have offered young Gluck in the way of musical experiences it is difficult to estimate. The air was already, as in the youth of Haydn and Mozart, filled with music, both popular and artistic. From the court to the humble inn, music was always to be heard.

In the Lobkowitz palace one evening Gluck appeared, both as

[1] Leipzig, 1794; vol. III, i, p. 144.

singer and player, it is said, before a guest from Milan, Prince Francesco Saverio Melzi, who, with the permission of his patron, took him to Italy as his chamber musician. He was a curious man who held the appointment of administrator-general of the post in Lombardy and in 1746 became involved in Countess Borromeo's conspiracy against Maria Theresa. To have left Vienna at that very moment proved one of those fortunate accidents which were to recur more than once in the course of Gluck's life. The Turkish war broke out, the three generals of the imperial army, Baron Seckendorf, the Archduke Francis Stephen and Prince Hildburg-hausen (whom we shall meet again later), went to experience the most spectacular defeats in Croatia, to which others succeeded under new command, until the disgraceful peace of Belgrade brought the war to a conclusion. The same year, 1740, saw the death of Charles VI, the accession of Maria Theresa—and of Frederick the Great, which meant new complications and the beginning of the Silesian wars. Viennese court music decayed; opera was silent. The imperial court poet that year wrote scarcely anything but small *divertimenti* and *azioni teatrali* in addition to his oratorio of *Isacco*. It was as well to be in Milan, and not in Vienna.

MILAN — SAMMARTINI

In Milan Gluck completed his education for a composer as a pupil, and later a friend, of Giovanni Battista Sammartini, who was some thirteen or fourteen years older than he.

It is noteworthy that Sammartini was only incidentally a composer of opera. We know but two works for the stage by him, and one of them does not seem to have appeared until the composer had come into contact with Gluck. Sammartini was first and foremost an instrumental composer, one of the first representatives of the new symphonic tendencies, of a type of symphony that had freed itself from the thematic shackles of the *concerto grosso* and aimed at a lighter, freer, more natural and unfettered, not to say *buffo*-like style. He had the misfortune to have been saddled with obloquy by one of the great masters: Haydn once very violently disclaimed any connection with him and stigmatized him as a 'scrawler,' contrary to the generally accepted opinion. It is well known that Mysliveček, when he and the youthful Mozart listened to symphonies by Sammartini in Milan in 1770, exclaimed: 'I have found the father of Haydn's style!'

Disregarding Haydn's attitude towards Sammartini, we are bound to regard the latter as being as epoch-making a master for northern Italy as Pergolesi was for Naples, although the greater part of his output—he did not die until 1775—fell into the years subsequent to his relations with Gluck. A modern composer himself, he made Gluck too into a modern musician, and certainly by way of an instrumental style at first. In 1746 Gluck published in London a set of six trio Sonatas—his only wholly instrumental work— which we may be sure were not written in London at that time, but during the Milan period. They are in that new style which first asserted itself in the trio sonatas of Pergolesi, and affinities with similar works of Sammartini's are obvious. This style consists in a new thematic formation that may be described negatively as 'anti-contrapuntal' and positively as a *buffo* manner— the kind of melody that obtained in the *opera buffa*: short-winded, skittish and with dialogue-like contrasts instead of thematic imitations in quick movements, and full of sentiment without solemnity in the slow ones. A new world of expression unfolded itself which had scarcely anything in common with the 'anonymity' and the elegiac character of the older classical sonata.

Those who wish to ascertain Gluck's 'modernity' and Sammartini's influence on him in symphonic writing should look up the *sinfonia* in G major for strings and two horns which forms an introduction to the *Ipermestra* of 1744, and which Gluck evidently performed again as a concert symphony at Venice in 1746.[1] The egg-shells of the *concerto grosso* are still visible; but they are broken, and a chicken emerges which cannot be called anything but *buffo*-like. Every note is made to sit in its right place and a subtle function of crossing is performed by the second violin (see page 16). In the *andante*, in E minor, an even more strikingly new expression

[1] Edited by Hans Gál. (Universal Edition, No. 10,648, 1934.)

15

takes the place of the old classical solemnity or serenity: an intimacy of tone that betrays itself particularly by almost agitated dynamic changes. No other than that 'scrawler,' that 'imbrattacarte' of a Sammartini could have suggested anything of the kind to Gluck.

But opera, too, must have played its part in the intellectual exchange

between Gluck and Sammartini. It is certainly not by accident that Sammartini brought out his second opera, *L'Agrippina, moglie di Tiberio,* in the Carnival of 1743, a work in which the construction of the arias and their melodic cut corresponds entirely with that of Gluck's first operas. Master and pupil, side by side and in collaboration, discussed and acquired their means of technical handling. Not that either of them won absolute technical mastery, or perhaps even strove for it. It must be pointed out here and now, as it will have to be again later on, that in the sense of the great artistry of men like Bach or Mozart or Brahms, Gluck never had any more *ability* than Sammartini himself, and in that sense Haydn's unkind epithet remains justified. In the decisive years of his youth Gluck went through no severe schooling; he is a musical savage who breaks with the utmost unconcern through the thickets of technical practice.

When Handel heard Gluck's opera, *La caduta de' giganti*, he opined that Gluck understood counterpoint about as much or as little as his (Handel's) cook, Waltz. But if Gluck had understood a little more about counterpoint, it is possible that he would have been able to write neither *Orfeo* nor *Alceste*, nor the two *Iphigeneias*, and Handel's mastery in counterpoint has not prevented his operas from being one and all forgotten. A genius is not only not hindered by his defects, but makes them part of his virtues. Gluck became a reformer or revolutionary of opera perhaps for the very reason that he had not the same amount of 'ability' and was not so richly and perfectly endowed in a scholastic sense as Hasse or Jommelli or Porpora, who had an eye on music pure and simple and not on music drama.

How closely Gluck felt himself to be linked to Sammartini may be judged from the fact that for the serenata, *Le nozze d' Ercole e d' Ebe*, produced at a Dresden wedding in 1747, he simply borrowed an *allegro* from one of Sammartini's symphonies, making only small cuts and alterations; and he permitted himself the same kind of thing for the second of the two introductions to his *Contesa de' numi* at Copenhagen in 1749. No doubt, instead of a 'link,' one might equally well speak of a sovereign habit of freebooting, of which Gluck was guilty as late as 1756, in an aria of *Antigono*. In any case, all this proves that Gluck's personal style was the same as Sammartini's, or that at any rate he felt it to be so and was sure that his hearers would never notice anything.

It is desirable to be more closely acquainted with the operas Gluck heard during those years in Milan. As early as 26th December 1737 he came across a book of Metastasio's he was himself to compose fifteen years later: *La clemenza di Tito*, with music by the otherwise as good as unknown Giovanni Maria Marchi. In January 1738 Giovanni Battista Lampugnani, himself a Milanese, who had already in 1736 furnished the Teatro Ducale with an *Ezio* and an *Antigono,* followed them up with an *Angelica.* On 26th December appeared another Milanese, Giuseppe Fernando Brivio, with a *Merope,* and in 1739 with a *Didone abbandonata* and an *Incostanza delusa.* In 1740 the Neapolitan Leonardo Leo introduced his *Scipione nelle Spagne.* The death of Charles VI in October imposed national mourning even on the province of Lombardy, and only on 26th December 1741 was the Teatro Ducale reopened with Gluck's *Artaserse.* Of all the composers of these Milan operas Leo was the oldest, the most important and the most modern. He must have shown Gluck something that differed from the operatic type indigenous to Milan.

THE FIRST OPERAS

No less desirable would it be to study Gluck's first opera in connection with these impressions of his and to determine how they reacted upon him, whether he submitted to their influence or resisted it. Unhappily, however, only two arias in the second act of *Artaserse* are preserved, and all the rest of the score is irretrievably lost. One is an aria expressive of indignation and reproach ('Mi scacci sdegnato,' E major), flung by an unjustly treated son in the face of a more than dubious father: a violent, not to say heated piece consistently kept to the single expression of anger. The other, given to a female character ('Se del fiume altera l'onda,' F major), is one of those unfortunate similes of Metastasio's: the vacillating state of one who is torn by two opposed duties is compared to the perplexity of a farmer whose fields are flooded on both banks of an overflowing torrent—he cannot run to one side without leaving the other undefended. Gluck therefore contents himself with an energetic description of the furiously onrushing waters, to which the voice supplies a simple commentary, renouncing all bravura. And what is the good of analysing separate arias when their position in the whole organism is not known, when the connecting recitatives are lost in which the tempo of the drama and the composer's dramatic energy finds expression? We shall be able to conclude from later works that Gluck did not by any means endeavour to transcend convention in the recitative. As it is, we are left with the bare fact that he too set *Artaserse* to music, as a hundred other composers did—Hasse and Vinci at first (1731) and men like Jommelli, Galuppi and Cimarosa later. It was one of Metastasio's weakest 'political' pieces, dealing with love and magnanimity, filled with an array of linguistically enchanting arias, which still served Mozart in his youth for his first essays in aria form.

Gluck was as yet anything but a 'reformer.' He simply set a favourite operatic subject to music, whether with greater energy or freedom than his forerunners it is hardly possible to tell any longer; whether with downright insistence on his rights as a dramatist in the face of the singers and their arrogance—Giuseppe Appiani and Caterina Aschieri are mentioned as principals—is more than questionable. The anecdotes connected with the first performances of *Artaserse* need not be recounted: they are clearly inventions such as must needs always accompany a composer's early efforts, and it is scarcely likely that Gluck would have jeopardized the success of his first work by extravagances of behaviour. One thing only is certain: the opera did have a success and at once earned Gluck the commission—the *scrittura*—for further operas. In the space of three and a half years, from the end of 1741 to the beginning of 1745, he wrote no less than ten: *Artaserse* (Milan, 1741); *Demetrio,* also called *Cleonice* (Venice, Teatro San Samuele, Ascension 1742); *Demofoonte* (Milan, 26th December 1742); *Tigrane* (Crema, autumn 1743); *Arsace* (one act, Milan, December 1743); *Sofonisba,* also called *Siface* (Milan, 13th January 1744, dedicated to a military member of the Lobkowitz family, Georg Christian); *La finta schiava* (a few arias only, Venice, spring 1744); *Ipermestra* (Venice, October 1744); *Poro* (after Metastasio's *Alessandro nelle Indie,* Turin, 26th December 1744); and *Ippolito* or *Fedra* (Milan, 31st January 1745).

Of these operas a single one has been preserved complete, with all the recitatives, fortunately what is probably the most valuable of all—*Ipermestra*. Of *Demetrio,* the second, six arias have come down to us, three of them assigned to the title part. Of the third, *Demofoonte,* we have all the arias, but the recitatives and overture have disappeared.

The work shows particularly clearly how ruthlessly young Gluck already interfered with Metastasio's drama, on which Calzabigi was later to exercise his devastating criticism. *Demetrio* was evidently a great success, for it was repeated at Reggio in 1743, at Bologna in 1744 (cruelly mutilated both times) and again in Milan as late as 1747. Of *Tigrane,* produced at Crema during the autumn fair of 1743, the text of which goes back to an old libretto by Francesco Silvani dating from 1691, twelve arias are preserved, while of the pasticcio of *Arsace,* for which Gluck composed the first act, we have eight. The most regrettable loss is that of *Sofonisba,* a grand piece of work with truly passionate situations in spite of the tasteless disfigurement of its action by a happy ending, of which we possess but twelve musical numbers. The words of the recitatives again come from a libretto of old Silvani's, whereas most of the arias are borrowed from the works of Metastasio. Of *Poro* and *Ippolito* there remain only two and eight arias respectively. Finally, there are still nine 'symphonies,' i.e. overtures, preserved in parts, but to which of the early operas each of them belongs is unfortunately not known.

Incomplete as this material no doubt is, it suffices to afford us a picture of Gluck as a beginner in operatic composition. If it is considered that this young foreigner enjoyed success next to rivals and exemplars like Hasse, Vinci and Leo, that success must have been due to some peculiarity, since Italy was at that time as full as ever of minor composers of average gifts. The explanation is doubtless that while Gluck was far from 'revolutionary,' indeed not even intent on 'reform,' while he by no means swam against the stream, but wrote congenially for his singers, among whom some of the greatest were already at his disposal (Carestini, for instance), he yet attracted attention by the energy and the modern melody of his arias. This 'modernity' is the same as that of the instrumental music: into the aria of the *opera seria* there penetrated, for all its conventionality, a greater melodic freedom, a more unfettered expression, which assigned a more important function to the orchestra as well.

That, for the time being, is all. One must beware of believing that Gluck had a new operatic ideal in mind so soon, or indeed that he even envisaged it from afar. Purely as a musician he is much less adventurous than such a man as Domenico Scarlatti, who has left us separate arias of the greatest originality. Gluck—we can see it in *Ipermestra*—does not yet treat the *recitativo secco* more freely, strikingly and dramatically than any of his contemporaries. He is still far from suspecting that the *accompagnato*, the recitative supported by the orchestra, in which the drama gathers force before an impassioned aria, might become the point of departure for the clinching of whole scenes. It does not occur to him to tamper with the hallowed form of the aria with its principal section, its middle part with a more or less contrasting metre or key, and its return to the first portion. Indeed, his construction of the principal section has a stiffness that is particularly noticeable; only the middle parts often attract attention by exciting modulations and strong metrical contrasts. For him too the words of an aria are never more than an excuse for music, and music means to him nothing so much as the exhibition of the singer. The main section of the aria by far exceeds the middle part in length, and in bravura when florid figuration is used, since the singers needed it, he knew, for a brilliant 'exit.' Now and again it is enriched in colour by the use of oboe, flutes, bassoon, horns and—very rarely—trumpets. The texture is poor: the voice part goes with the violins, the viola rarely detaches itself from the basses, the second fiddle runs parallel to the first. Just at a pinch one may speak of three-part writing. It is all a rather coarse *al fresco* style calculated to make theatrical effects at a distance.

Again, in the *ritornelli* and the *sinfonia* (overture) of *Ipermestra* everything is stiff and constrained. We are a long way as yet from any instrumental interplay, from 'filigree work,' from a lightening or transparency of the musical fabric. Still, one quality is to be discerned in most of these arias, and it explains Gluck's success: manliness, melodic decision, precise and forcible rhythm. Here was no namby-pamby musician, but rather a 'barbarian.' Hasse still further softened the Neapolitans' suavity; Gluck, within the framework of Italianism, sounded a note of his own. In these very first Milan operas, many an aria was enriched by a peculiar accompanying rhythm in the strings, the connection between an *accompagnato* and the opening of an aria would become closer and more dramatic, and the formal scheme might be departed from in favour of a freer and more personally felt expression. It is not too much to say that this young Gluck—or Kluk, as they called him—was an Italian opera composer who knew his somewhat rough trade, who had no 'chamber-musical' ambitions, but turned out stageworthy operas without many scruples and above all without the least aesthetic reasoning, all the while beginning to show some character; and a composer to whom, significantly enough, sombre and agitated themes appealed more than courtly and pastoral ones.

Thus we have early confirmation of the observation Padre Martini made in the spring of 1777 in a letter to the Neapolitan ambassador in Paris, Marchese Caraccioli. Every composer, he put it, showed some special disposition in his art, and Gluck leant more towards the tragic and wild (*fiero*) than the gentle and delicate. And so it came about that Gluck was able to take numbers from these youthful operas, from *Demofoonte* and *Tigrane*—numbers containing expressions of energy, be it noted—and transfer them without much alteration into so late a work as *Alceste* without perpetrating any conspicuous solecism in style.

LONDON

In the autumn of 1745 Gluck accompanied Prince Lobkowitz to London, at the invitation of Lord Middlesex, who directed the Italian Opera there. The war dragged itself threateningly into Lombardy, and Milan was soon to fall for a short time into the hands of the allied Spaniards and French. It might be said that this journey meant nothing more than a migration from one Italian operatic province to another, for England was at that time, where opera was concerned, a country importing Italian singers and such works as they required. But while engaged in this great undertaking, which at that time meant almost a world journey, Gluck for the first time visited Paris on the way, where he may have made the acquaintance of Jean-Philippe Rameau, the last great master of French opera, who after a lengthy pause had reappeared that year with a new work: *Les fêtes de Polymnie.* A curious coincidence is that Ranieri Calzabigi, Gluck's later collaborator, produced his first libretto in Naples at that time, a *componimento drammatico* entitled *L'impero dell' universo, diviso con Giove,* performed at the marriage of the Dauphin with the Infanta Maria Teresa on 5th August 1745. No less remarkable is the fact that at the celebration of the same event in Paris on 5th September a ballet-opera in five acts appeared: *Jupiter vainqueuer des Titans.* If Gluck heard it, we may suppose that it yielded him the subject for the work with which he introduced himself to London on 7th January 1746: *La caduta de' giganti,* although this is contra-dicted by the supposition that it was dictated by political considera-tions. The Italian Opera had been closed owing to the Jacobite rebellion and Lord Middlesex seems to have obtained permission to reopen it with an opera by Gluck only by choosing a plot in which the victory of the Duke of Cumberland at Culloden was symbolized by that of Jupiter over the rebellious giants.

It was done in the most vapid manner. The Abbate Francesco Vanneschi, an obscure poet, patched up a libretto in which Jupiter, apart from his obligatory contest against the giants, becomes the rival of the war-god Mars by engaging in a petty love struggle with the gods' messenger Iris, which arouses the justified jealousy of Juno. This work in two acts—not three—is not a real opera, but somewhat in the nature of the *licenze* or *serenate drammatiche* performed on special occasions at continental courts. Jupiter and Mars are male sopranos, and the giants Titan and Briareus are likewise trebles, the latter being moreover represented by a lady. That Gluck was ready to compose such tasteless nonsense on coming to a country that was strange to him is a proof of how far he was as yet from any artistic and 'diplo-matic' maturity. In his haste he made the task doubly easy for himself by having new texts fitted to old arias borrowed from *Tigrane, Ipermestra* and *Sofonisba.* Of the six numbers preserved in a publication by Walsh only one appears to have been composed *ad hoc.*

The piece was repeated no more than five times after the first performance—a clear case of failure. Handel, who had written

Messiah four years earlier, who had *Samson, Semele* (what a glorious opera!), *Hercules, Belshazzar* and the *Occasional Oratorio* behind him, and was now preparing to compose *Judas Maccabaeus,* evidently criticized Gluck's capabilities far more trenchantly than Burney had the courage to let us know. Which did not prevent Gluck from calling upon Handel, nor the latter from receiving him kindly and offering him good advice.

In any case Gluck was not discouraged, or else Lord Middlesex did not lose confidence in him. In March he composed another opera for the King's Theatre, Haymarket: *Artamene*—or rather he did not compose it, not having much time, but again adapted older arias from *Demofoonte, Tigrane* and *Sofonisba* to a libretto originally written by Bartolommeo Vitturi for Tommaso Albinoni (Venice, 1740) and arranged by Francesco Vanneschi for London. The subject this time was a story of love and intrigue enacted in India. Walsh again engraved six favourite arias, one of which, 'Rasserena il mesto ciglio,' stands out by reason of its depth of feeling and melodic beauty. Gluck sang it to Dr. Burney in Vienna as late as 1772. Four of the others are on the graceful side.

On 25th March, in place of a performance of *Artamene,* Gluck gave a concert with Handel. All the six singers who formed the cast of his opera, of whom Angelo Monticelli was the most distinguished, took part. Handel had three arias from *Alexander's Feast* and *Samson* sung, and played one of his concertos; Gluck was represented by the 'symphony' and arias from *La caduta de' giganti.* On Monday, 14th April, he intended to give a concert for his own benefit at 'Mr. Hickford's Great Room in Brewer Street'; but it did not take place until the 23rd at the little theatre in Haymarket. He there appeared as a performer on the musical glasses, an instrument known already in the seventeenth century and exhibited all over England by an Irishman, Richard Pockrich, in 1744. Gluck produced a variety of his own, promising 'a concerto upon twenty-six drinking-glasses tuned with spring-water, accompanied with the whole band, being a new instrument of his own invention; upon which he performs whatever may be done on a violin or harpsichord and therefore hopes to satisfy the curious, as well as the lovers of music.' Had he perhaps kept his head above water with inventions of this sort in Prague? Feats of skill we no longer admire any-where but in a variety theatre were regarded as perfectly worthy of the concert-room in the eighteenth century, and we know that a few years later, in Copenhagen, Gluck was still exhibiting this instrument, singular as it may seem to think of the composer of *Alceste* stroking twenty-six wine-glasses with his fingers.

A second concert, or a repetition of the first, is said to have taken place on 30th April. At a benefit concert of Thomas Augustine Arne Gluck's 'Rasserena' was sung, which points to friendly relations with the most important English composer of the eighteenth century, the singer of 'Rule, Britannia!', who at the time of Gluck's sojourn in London was employed as composer at Vauxhall Gardens and had just produced new music for the masque in Shakespeare's *Tempest* for a revival of that play.

In November 1746, apparently after Gluck's departure from London, occurred the publication by Simpson of the six trio Sonatas supposed to have been composed in Milan and already briefly referred to: 'Six Sonatas for two Violins & a Thorough Bass composed by Sr. Gluck, Composer to the Opera.' To these must be added a seventh, preserved only in manuscript. Their general character has been described earlier. Differing in key (C major, G minor, A major, B flat major, E flat major, F major), they are all alike in construction. At the opening there is always an *andante* or *largo,* at the end invariably a *minuetto,* with an *allegro* or *presto* in the middle. The mixture of *sonata da chiesa* and *sonata da camera* of the preceding epoch of Corelli is just discernible still, though already far removed. Much the same is true of the contents of the movements. The *allegro* of the second Sonata contains a *giga,* which, however, is marked by burlesque traits; the *andante* of the third recalls the old classical style, but must needs bear the expressive direction of *amabile.* The *largo* of the first begins with direct reminders of Pergolesi and the *allegro* of the fourth shows equally direct references to that second great transformer of style, Domenico Scarlatti. Then the *allegro* of the third unites Pergolesi and Scarlatti in the spirit of a true *buffo* style:

SIX SONATAS 1746

It is tolerably clear that although he did not suffer a fiasco in London, Gluck's success there was not what he had expected. He would hardly have left England had he been able to secure as firm a footing there as Carl Friedrich Abel or Johann Christian Bach did later. The comparison with J. C. Bach is particularly indicated, for a decade and a half after Gluck he too came from Milan in much the same way, to maintain his position at the Italian Opera until his death.

But what did London mean to Gluck? The most important

event for him was unquestionably his acquaintance with Handel and with some of his works. Still, the effects of this acquaintance have been immoderately exaggerated. Handel's opera was dead, and deservedly so. He invested in his stage works, supplied as employee of an aristocratic clique, a wealth of imperishably and overpoweringly beautiful music; he wrote a series of arias in which the emotional content of a situation is most movingly expressed; but he never thought about the dramatic meaning of opera as a whole, of opera as such, or at any rate did not feel inclined to tamper with its traditional form. Gluck, the creator of the *Alceste* of 1767, never committed a dramatic outrage similar to that of Handel, the creator of an *Alceste*, or rather an *Admeto*, of 1727. The title itself is an absurdity. Admetus, torn between two operatic princesses—his wife, whose jealousy forces her to assume male disguise, and an earlier mistress, Antigona—is in reality the male soprano Senesino between two hostile prima donnas, Faustina Bordoni and Francesca Cuzzoni. Handel was never more thoroughly the subordinate of prima donnas than here, in spite of his supposed tyranny over them. As operatic composer he did not influence Gluck at all. Moreover, his influence as composer of oratorio on Gluck's work did not show itself immediately, but only, if ever, much later and as it were in a transformed, sublimated way. For that the species of Italian opera and English oratorio were kept much too rigidly distinct. When Burney visited Gluck on 2nd September 1772, the latter confessed to him that England had induced him to apply himself to the study of nature for his dramatic compositions. If that was not a mere compliment—and Gluck was not the man to pay compliments—it still does not mean that it was Handel who urged him to study nature. Had it been so, Gluck would certainly not have neglected to tell Burney on that occasion. Burney himself tries to give an explanation of Gluck's remark:

He then studied the English taste; remarked particularly what the audience seemed most to feel; and finding that plainness and simplicity had the greatest effect upon them, he has, ever since that time, endeavoured to write for the voice, more in the natural tones of the human affections and passions, than to flatter the lovers of deep science or difficult execution.

27

It seems, however, as though Burney had somewhat exaggerated the importance this London visit had for Gluck. Be that as it may, the effects of that observation of English taste did not, at any rate, come about immediately, but took a long time to manifest itself. If the verdict is true that Gluck did not know more of counterpoint than Handel's cook, Waltz, this only goes to show—as Sir Donald Tovey indicates in a brilliant essay on Gluck[1]—the antithesis between two generations: a superannuated one for which polyphony is still a treasured possession, and a young, modern one seeking new means of expression.

TRAVELLING CONDUCTOR

It is generally supposed that Gluck left London towards the end of 1746 and went to Hamburg, where the so-called 'German' opera had by that time suffered an inglorious collapse and operatic require-ments had since been supplied by travelling Italian companies. One of these, belonging to Pietro Mingotti—another was under the direc-tion of the impresario Giovanni Battista Locatelli—was then carrying out a lengthy season in Hamburg. Mingotti's first conductor was Paolo Scalabrini, who in the years immediately before Gluck's arrival had supplied the opera house on the Gänsemarkt with pasticcios. Under or next to him Gluck was engaged as conductor and composer, perhaps also incidentally as singer. But the remark-able fact must not be overlooked that at Graz, during the Carnival of 1746, Pietro Mingotti's brother Angelo produced a pasticcio, *La finta schiava,* in which Gluck was represented by several arias. However, it would be going too far to take this for an excuse to make Gluck into Angelo Mingotti's conductor, and to shift back his departure from London into the early summer of 1746.

About the time of the Easter fair of 1747 the brothers Mingotti united their companies in Leipzig, where among other operas they performed Scalabrini's *Demetrio* and *Merope* and gave a concert at which 'arias by a great *maître* from Italy, sung with great applause

[1] *The Heritage of Music,* vol. ii, p. 75. (1934.) What Tovey says about Metastasio is as erroneous as possible.

by the opera singers Signor Canini and Signora Forcellini, here present' were to be heard. It would be altogether misjudging Gluck's influence and position at this time if he were to be taken for this 'great *maître*.' This is proved by the fact that he played no leading part at the famous celebrations that took place on the occasion of the sumptuous double wedding between members of the Saxon and Bavarian royal houses. These festivities, in honour of the marriages of the Elector Max Joseph of Bavaria with Maria Anna, daughter of the Elector Frederick Augustus II of Saxony, and of the Saxon electoral Prince Frederick Christian to the Bavarian Princess Maria Antonia Walpurga, who was well known as a composer, lasted from 10th June to 3rd July. Needless to say, the Saxon court musicians took the major share. Hasse composed the festival opera proper for 14th June, *La Sparta generosa (Archidamia),* to a libretto by Giovanni Claudio Pasquini. But Pietro Mingotti came to Dresden as early as May with his people and opened the operatic festivities at the small theatre in the Zwinger with Paolo Scalabrini's *Didone* (10th June), which he repeated on the 19th, letting the same composer's *Merope* follow on the 25th. On the 28th the whole court moved to the castle of Pillnitz, where Johann Georg Schürer's *Galatea* was given the very same night on an open-air stage, succeeded on the 29th by Gluck's serenata of *Le nozze d' Ercole e d' Ebe,* the first of those occasional festival pieces of which he was later to write a whole string. It was given only a single performance. Gluck received, 'for clearance,' 412 thaler and 12 groschen, and curiously enough the documents call him 'the singer Christoph Gluck.'

Only four singers were employed in this festival opera: Settimio Canini (Jupiter), who was well known to Gluck, having already played parts in *Tigrane* and *Sofonisba*; the famous Regina Mingotti, the impresario's wife (Hercules); Giustina Turcotti (Hebe), a somewhat dated celebrity at that time; and Giacinta Forcellini (Juno). The libretto was not new, but had been composed three years earlier for Venice by Nicolo Porpora. Only a *licenza* [1] was added to it for

---

[1] The *licenza* was a topical aria, generally in praise of the patron of the moment, introduced into a new opera or written for the revival of an old one.

the special occasion. It is a lamentable production: Hercules refuses the seat offered him by Jupiter on Olympus because he fears the hatred of Juno; but Juno herself acts as procuress by showing him Hebe in the shape of the shepherdess Eurilla, with whom, of course, Hercules falls in love at sight, and equally of course he enters the Olympic court with pleasure when his mistress turns out to be a goddess. A musician, to compose anything of the kind, had still to be stuck fast in the operatic conventions of the time, indeed could not have thought of the constitution of opera as a dramatic work of art at all. And this was the same Gluck who, twenty-five years later, was to confine the function of music to 'the furtherance of poetry, the strengthening of emotion and of interest in the action, without interrupting the latter and weakening it by superfluous decoration.'

Gluck, then, once again took things easy here. Only two-thirds of the work were newly composed by him: two arias were taken from *Artamene,* one each from *Sofonisba* and *Ippolito,* for which he wrote new middle sections. The aria 'Rasserena,' from *Artamene,* here put into the mouth of Juno, again attracts attention by its simple beauty in this new framework. A portion of the overture, if not the whole, he borrowed calmly from Sammartini, as already mentioned; and if the *andante* of the 'symphony,' with its oboe solo, is likewise taken from Sammartini, then Gluck owes him not only that violin figure which receives its highest sublimation in the overture to *Iphigénie en Aulide,* but also a 'pastoral' type of music.

In the newly composed numbers he conformed altogether to the tone of the courtly festival play. He went out of his way to be light, amiable, graceful, to write the most handsome coloratura for Hercules, or rather for Regina Mingotti; he composed a duet for the conclusion of the first act in which Hercules and Hebe alternated with the instruments in cooing like amorous doves, and the shepherd Hercules is given an agitated note only in an *accompagnato* where he searches the groves of Arcadia for his lost shepherdess. The aria of the *licenza,* also introduced by an *accompagnato,* undisguisedly recalls Pergolesi. Most charming and popular is the final chorus of the second act. On the whole, however, the Gluck who was to be himself such a Hercules later on is armed with anything but a bludgeon in this festival play; much rather with a shepherd's staff.

Pietro Mingotti returned to Leipzig from Dresden. Gluck himself, it is supposed, on hearing of the death of his father in September 1747, visited his home in order to secure his share in the heritage at Hammer, near Brüx. He is said to have sold it at the beginning of 1748. Alexander Gluck had left him a freehold, the Neuschänke near Hammer, to which belonged the lease of two houses as well as an inn and a butcher's shop. Thence he went to Vienna. We know that on 4th May the imperial family was present at a rehearsal of his *Semiramide riconosciuta,* which was produced at the celebration of the empress's birthday on 14th May. The commission to set a book by Metastasio for such a festive occasion in Vienna proves that Gluck's reputation as a composer of Italian opera was by this time well established. This was the first great success of his life.

What it was that prevented him from making the most of this Viennese triumph we can only surmise. Perhaps one may be allowed to suspect that it was no triumph. On looking through the score one is in the end quite confused by so much heated or stoked-up recitative, such a pell-mell mixture of emptiness and significance (shown already by the *sinfonia*), by the unwieldiness or mediocrity of the arias, in which convention and truth alternate, and by such an ingenuous and uncritical attitude towards Metastasio's monstrous comedy of intrigue and disguise, in which the heroine (whose part was sung by Tesi) appears now as lover, now as national hero, and always in trousers. Gluck's arias here are a collection of irregular bars and concertizing passages in the older Viennese or Neapolitan style. Never was Gluck more baroque than in this opera, and it is not improbable that the imperial family, used to the smoothness of Hasse, were shocked by such an excess of roughness. Moreover, Gluck made the singers' task as difficult as possible here.

In September 1748 at the latest Gluck again joined Mingotti's company, in Hamburg, and this time as conductor in the place of Scalabrini. A Hamburg newspaper of 3rd October says:

This past week the opera of *Arsace* was performed here with the greatest approval of all connoisseurs, and we gladly confess never to have seen so excellent a company assembled, four of the most glorious voices in the whole of Italy being met here almost side by side. Next to the famous Madame Turcotti and Signor Casati, Madame Bircherin (Marianne Pircker) and Madame Pompeati, from London, as well as the great virtuoso, Herr von Hager, from Vienna, have been engaged. Herr Gluck, so well known to the art of tone, is now conductor in the place of Signor Scalabrini, who has entered the Danish royal service.

We know, too, the rest of the company's repertory: the *opere serie* were Hasse's *Clemenza di Tito* and Scalabrini's *Bajazet*; there were also the intermezzi of *La furba e lo sciocco, Grullo e Moschetta, La serva padrona* —no doubt Pergolesi's little masterpiece—and *Il pittore*. It is important to know what Gluck conducted in Hamburg, for the year 1748 marks a decisive turn in his career, a turn towards something richer, more grandiose and more purposeful. The Dresden *Nozze* and the *Semiramide* are the last works he wrote, so to speak, in a state of innocence.

We may persue Gluck's further fortunes in Marianne Pircker's correspondence with her husband in London; indeed we owe to it a very 'intimate' piece of information. November had not run its course when Gluck, with Mingotti and his company, embarked for Copenhagen, where he arrived, after a very disagreeable crossing, on the 23rd or 24th. On the 26th the rehearsals for *Bajazet* were already in full swing, and on 4th December the royal family attended a performance. Gluck conducted neither the one nor the other. He was ill, and unhappily not merely seasick. He had formed an intimacy in Hamburg with the *buffo* singer Gaspera Becheroni, the mistress of Wick, the former English resident there, and evidently carried off a memento in the shape of a disease from which he recovered but slowly. (Marianne Pircker called her rival by a most unequivocal name.) The fact is not to be glossed over, more especially because it most pointedly explains Gluck's later childlessness.

He had time to compose the serenata, *La contesa de' numi,* for performance as a festival play at the reappearance of the queen, the consort of Frederic V, after the birth of an heir to the throne. The rehearsals began in the middle of February, but as the queen took her time over her delivery, the performance did not take place until 9th April. In the meantime Gluck played his glass harmonica again at Charlottenborg, probably on 12th March at the court dinner and on other occasions. 23rd April closed the season, in which, unlike that of Hamburg, *opera seria* vastly predominated. The works given were, apart from *Bajazet,* a *Temistocle* by an unknown composer, *Artaserse* and *Didone abbandonata,* both by Scalabrini, *Orazio, Arsace* and, as the only intermezzo, *Le gelosie fra Grullo e Moschetta.*

The *Contesa de' numi* is still no great achievement for Gluck the music-dramatist. Metastasio's text, originally written for the celebration of the birth of the French dauphin, was accommodated to Danish conditions by simply assembling the quarrelling gods and goddesses by the Great Belt instead of on the banks of the Seine. The stress of the work is thrown wholly on the florid arias, such as the extremely brilliant ones of Fortuna ('Se vorrà fidarsi all' onde') or the warlike ones of Mars. The concerted piece at the end of the second part, which draws upon all the six voices, is pastoral in tone. The whole is a court production showing little ambition, and it is easy to understand that it gave little satisfaction to the 'retired royal Danish chapel-master,' Johann Adolf Scheibe, who had already thoroughly reasoned out 'the possibility and nature of good vocal pieces,' had composed an opera, *Thusnelde* (1749), according to these principles, and is sure to have looked upon Gluck, the Italianate operatic musician, with disdain. It is not very likely that Gluck met Scheibe, as has been supposed,[1] and received suggestions from him.

Mingotti probably went to Holland from Copenhagen. Whether Gluck went with him we do not know. It is possible that he may have got into touch with the rival of the Mingotti brothers, Giovanni Battista Locatelli; at any rate Locatelli and his company performed Gluck's *Ezio* in Prague in 1750 and at Leipzig the following year, as well as *Issipile* in Prague in 1752. A hint that Gluck may really

[1] Cf. Angul Hammerich, *Gluck und Scheibe in Kopenhagen* (*Festschrift für H. Kretzschmar*). (Leipzig, 1918.)

have been in the Netherlands may be found in the fact that an engraver and publisher of Liége was the first on the Continent to bring out arias of his. Benoît Andrez in 1758 began to publish a journal entitled *L'Écho,* the first year of which contained an aria from the *Rè pastore* of 1756, and that in full score. A second aria from the same opera appeared in the *Écho* of 1766. It is significant that Andrez calls Gluck 'un célèbre maître de musique italien.'

HOME IN VIENNA

If the tales of Gluck's engagement and marriage be accepted without question, he asked for the hand of Marianne, elder daughter of the merchant and banker Joseph Pergin (or Perg) in Vienna, before the Prague production of *Ezio,* and was refused by her father. About the same time, during the Carnival of 1750, when Gluck was in Prague, Joseph Pergin must have died. The story that Gluck, on hearing of this, 'hurried back' to Vienna from Italy is manifestly a fable. Some of Gluck's biographers take the view that in 1750 he produced a first version in three acts of his *Telemacco* in Rome; but in the summer and autumn Rome had no opera whatever, and no libretto, no fragment of a score of this legendary first version is preserved. The fact is that it never existed.

Marianne's mother appears to have looked favourably upon the marriage. Gluck's wedding with Marianne Pergin took place on 15th September 1750, and it brought him a considerable dowry. Henceforth he was to be relieved of all economic cares, which was not without its influence on his character, for good and for ill, but never made him into an average citizen, for it only strengthened the independence of the artist in him. He could from now on afford to decline all compromise, both personal and artistic. From the time of his marriage he never composed anything that did not correspond to his taste and character.

With *Ezio* Gluck composed the drama of Metastasio which, first performed in Rome with music by Auletta in 1728, had done most to open up the poet's path to Vienna. It was set to music dozens of times, among others by Porpora (1728), Hasse (1730), Jommelli

(1741), C. H. Graun (1755) and Anfossi (1778). It was a great success, for Locatelli brought the work to Leipzig in 1751, although greatly changed and watered down by contributions from other hands. And it is, in fact, one of the strongest and most valuable works Gluck wrote after the Milan operas and before his acquaint-ance with Count Durazzo, for he made special efforts for the Prague public, which was exacting and intelligent already in those days.

Gluck's life during the year 1751 is shrouded in complete dark-ness; but one could scarcely go wrong in supposing that he spent it quietly in Vienna with his young wife, calmly waiting for things to come. (His silence was possibly not unconnected with the presence of Niccolò Jommelli in Vienna—Jommelli, who had taken root on the imperial stage there in 1749 with a German version of his *Merope,* based on Zeno's libretto, and who was a formidable rival.) They came with a new commission from Locatelli to write an opera for Prague for the Carnival of 1752, Metastasio's *Issipile,* with Caterina Fumagalli in the principal part. Unhappily four arias are all that is preserved of it.

While its performances went on, another important *scrittura* came his way in March 1752: to write a festival opera to be performed on the name-day of Charles III of Naples at the San Carlo Theatre there. The impresario, Don Diego Tufarelli, spoke of him with the greatest respect as 'il famoso Kluk che risiede in Praga in Boemia' and looked forward to 'a music of an entirely different and unheard-of style,' since the composer was 'new to this place [Naples] and exceed-ingly well versed in his craft.' The libretto chosen for him had been the *Arsace* of Antonio Salvi, of which, years ago in Milan, he had already composed one act; but Gluck refused it and demanded, 'for urgent reasons and with energetic emphasis,' Metastasio's *Clemenza di Tito,* although this libretto was already intended for another festive occasion in Naples. He had his way, and arrived at Naples with his wife in August 1752. The first performance was on 4th November. The famous male soprano Caffarelli sang the part of Sextus. Gluck had once again borrowed from himself: the first and last movements of the 'symphony' came from *Ezio,* two arias from the same opera and two others from *Le Nozze d' Ercole e d' Ebe,* of which one had already occurred in *Sofonisba*. In the libretto Gluck made no essential changes; but forty years later Mozart, thanks partly to the composer of *Alceste* and the *Iphigeneias*, felt it to be outmoded and had it re-modelled by Mazzola into a great dramatic choral opera.

One of the arias of Sextus, 'Se mai senti spirarti nel volto'—which Gluck used again in his *Iphigénie en Tauride* twenty-seven years later, where it became one of his most famous numbers, 'O malheureuse Iphigénie'—aroused a dispute among the Neapolitan composers, in the provocation of which envy of the *divo boemo* and his success doubt-less had a share. A harmonic transition of the orchestra under the sustained part of the soprano was regarded as incorrect. The decision of the aged Francesco Durante was sought (who, by the way, had written harmonically far more daring things), and he is reported to have said: 'I shall not decide whether this note is correct or not. All I can say is that, had I written it, I should regard myself as a great man!'

Concerning some episodes in Gluck's life and some traits of his character after his return from Naples we are informed by Ditters-dorf's autobiography, written, it is true, nearly fifty years after the events it describes and edited for the press by another hand, but containing no untruths or distortions wittingly sat down. Young Dittersdorf—he was only thirteen years of age at the time—played the violin as soloist in the orchestra of Prince Joseph Friedrich von Sachsen-Hildburghausen, imperial field-marshal and master-general of the ordnance, who, under the direction of the court composer Giuseppe Bonno, gave a concert once a week and matinées three times a week in his palace (now the Prince Auersperg Palace). The attractions at these concerts were Bonno's singing pupils, Mesdemoiselles Catarina Scharrer, a contralto, and Therese Teiber, and above all the Florentine Vittoria Tesi, one of the greatest singers, not only of Vienna, but of the time, and still, at an advancing age, 'the foremost actress of the century.'

When Gluck returned to Vienna in December 1752,

the prince already knew from his correspondent what a success this worthy man had earned in Italy [says Dittersdorf]. This same correspondent had, a few weeks before, sent the prince a score of the well-known aria, 'Se mai senti spirarti sul volto,' whereby Gluck had created such a sensation throughout Italy. The prince had it performed by Mademoiselle [Therese] Heinisch, a celebrated chamber singer in Vienna, and it was universally admired. The natural consequence of this was that the prince became eager to know Gluck personally. This was brought about by Bonno, who presented him to the prince.

Gluck was a jovial man in his relations with others and, outside his profession, was well read and had a knowledge of the world; he thus soon became a family friend at the prince's. At the academies [as concerts were called] . . . Gluck led the violins. On rehearsal and concert days the prince's band was reinforced by a considerable number of the choicest orchestral players; so that it was no wonder if our academies were recognized all over Vienna as the best. . . .

Gluck let the prince copy many of his compositions, both symphonies and arias, and each piece from the pen of this honourable composer was a new and delectable feast for our ears.

Gluck received not only the title of princely *Capellmeister,* but also a commission. In the autumn of 1754 the prince had invited the Empress Maria Theresa and her consort to spend a fortnight at Schlosshof, a palace that had been built for Prince Eugene of Savoy, and this visit was to be made particularly brilliant by several operatic representations. Bonno took on the composition of Metastasio's *L'isola disabitata* and *Il vero omaggio,* and Gluck that of *Le Cinesi (The Chinese Ladies),* a little *trattenimento drammatico* Metastasio had written for the imperial ladies in 1735 and to which he added a male part for the Schlosshof performance, perhaps at Gluck's request.

This was the first subject treated by Gluck that was not tragic, although it is by no means an *opera buffa,* but rather a comedy in rococo style, with a peculiar note added to its action by the Chinese disguise. Three merry Chinese girls, gathered together on a fine summer's day, are bored to death, when the forbidden appearance of the brother of the eldest of them, who needless to say is in love with the youngest, brings life into the party. The intruder is at first to be shown the door, but presently it is decided that it would be more prudent to keep him there until dark and to pass the time with representations of fictitious parts and scenes. Not Chinese scenes, of course. Lisinga, the eldest of the ladies, enacts Andromache,

37

from whose breast her son is torn by grim Pyrrhus: *recitativo accompagnato* for Tesi's contralto, a wild aria in B minor in the grandest tragic style, consisting almost exclusively of interjections. The intruder does not merely act, but expresses his true feelings as a languishing shepherd in a very florid minuet, whereupon his beloved rejects him rather resolutely in the guise of the shepherdess Lycoris. The second of the young women chooses the part of a French coquette at her dressing-table, and Gluck's turn of phrase in the *buffo* style is too rare not to be quoted for its melody:

The proximity of *La serva padrona* and its many successors is felt. But it never comes to a real *buffo* scene at the conclusion: the *opera buffa,* one of the ladies declares, leads too easily to a dangerous caricature of one's dear neighbour, and so a concluding vocal *ballo* is agreed upon, again in 3–4 time and very pretty and graceful. The most remarkable thing in this little work is the recitative. This quick-flowing dialogue, light as a shuttlecock, was composed in the purest *buffo* manner by Gluck, who in this respect at least might have vied with Galuppi or Paisiello or Piccinni, if he had cared. The *sinfonia* in three movements, too, is agile, mobile, weightless— a genuine Italian *buffo* symphony. It is a sign of the disregard into which Gluck has fallen that this charming work has not been resuscitated long ago, for it deserves to be at least as much as Mozart's *Schauspieldirektor,* which belongs to the same species, but which it greatly excels in refinement and grace of action.

The performance, given on 24th September 1754, is described for us by Dittersdorf. The scenic setting as well as the musical and dramatic achievement of the singers—the ladies Heinisch, Starzer and Tesi and the able tenor Joseph Friberth—must have had an enchanting finish.   The work was repeated on 17th April 1755 in the theatre next the Burg in Vienna, but, because Tesi was not there to appear in it, the impression was less favourable.   Being in one act and not filling a whole evening, it was probably supplemented by a *ballo* composed by Starzer, which became the principal piece of the evening.

But the performance of *Le Cinesi* before the imperial couple and their court had more important consequences for Gluck.   Before the end of 1754 the new intendant of the Viennese theatres, Count Durazzo, engaged him as *Capellmeister* with an annual salary of 2,000 florins, and his task was to compose 'theatrical and chamber-musical matters' for the court.   If the sum is correctly given, the esteem in which Gluck was held may be judged by a comparison with the salary of the court chapel-master, Georg Reutter, who had only 1,200 florins.   Otherwise Gluck's position was not clear, as we may tell from an action that arose between him and Reutter (1760–1) over the question of their duties.   Durazzo declared that Gluck had for the last six years been 'engaged by contract to compose theatre and academy music,' while the court authorities asserted that they had not the least knowledge of anything of the kind.   Gluck might have been given the title of Court Composer, but his acting as conductor could only be regarded as a usurpation.   And indeed he had, under the patronage of Durazzo, not only conducted his own works, but assumed the direction of others.

DURAZZO

The acquaintance with Durazzo meant for Gluck a new stage in his artistic development.   This curious man, Giacomo Conte Durazzo, who deserves a place of honour in every history of music and was unquestionably the most gifted of all the 'gentleman-managers,' came from an old Genoese noble family that had given several doges to the republic.   His elder brother Marcello, among others, was to be Doge of Genoa in 1767–9.   He himself was three years younger than Gluck and had been called to Vienna by

Count Kaunitz as Genoese ambassador in 1750, before long playing an important social part in the capital by his marriage with a Countess Ungnad, 'the most beautiful woman in Vienna.' He had great literary culture, took a particular interest in operatic problems and adapted Quinault's *Armide* to the Italian taste. In 1753 he was therefore given to Count Franz Esterházy, who held the supreme command of the imperial theatres, as assistant, and when Esterházy retired in June 1754, he assumed undivided sway over Viennese theatrical affairs, and held it, in spite of growing hostility against him, for the next ten years. All our sympathy is on his side, and it is increased by the recollection that, as Austrian ambassador to Venice, he furthered the appearance of the young Mozart in 1771. He survived Gluck, for he did not die until 15th October 1794, in Venice.

We cannot tell whether purely aesthetic inclinations and disinclinations, or personal ones as well, induced Durazzo to make a secret stand against the Metastasian operatic ideal. We shall learn through Calzabigi that Gluck did not like Metastasio, and we may read in the correspondence of Metastasio with Farinelli [1] how the imperial court poet judged Gluck: 'Wonderfully fiery, but mad.' The sober, harmonious poet found Gluck's temperament too stormy, too unreasonable, too impatient of restraint. Enough: Durazzo did not side with Metastasio, Hasse and Giuseppe Scarlatti, but with Gluck, Hilverding and Angiolini. He promoted whatever endangered the conventions of the *opera seria*; he became interested in the *opéra comique* and at the end of 1759 took steps to approach Favart, one of the three directors of the Opéra-Comique in Paris, with the avowed intention of creating a purified and more elevated species of comic opera. He was the soul, the initiator of a reformed *opera seria* and dramatic ballet. As intendant he did not favour economies, being a man of ideas and passionately attached to his cause. His fall was brought about by a vile intrigue on the part of his protégé, Dancourt, by the disingenuousness of Joseph II and by the philistinism of Maria Theresa, who hated him and thought his broad-mindedness too broad.

[1] 8th November 1751.

The first commission Gluck was offered in his capacity of theatre composer was for an out-and-out courtly work: the *componimento drammatico pastorale a due voci,* Metastasio's *La danza,* which was to precede a court ball at the palace of Laxenburg. It is one of those rococo pastoral scenes, like a picture by Albani. Caterina Gabrielli, who had replaced Tesi at the repetition of *Le Cinesi* in Vienna, sang the shepherdess, the tenor Joseph Friberth the shepherd. This work, too, performed before their imperial majesties on 5th May 1755, was repeated on the 13th at the Burgtheater on the eve of the empress's birthday, for the delectation of her faithful Viennese. Here again Gluck's pastoral piece served as introduction to a ballet by Starzer. It contains, apart from the 'symphony,' only four arias and a *duetto finale,* which is remarkable for the fact that the repeat of the first section is made plausible by a recitative. Otherwise Gluck relieved the tedium of composing the arias by animating the orchestra with a fair amount of colour: English horns, plucked double basses, a bassoon with *staccato* figuration, sustained horns, and so on. In the aria with horns ('Che ciascun per te sospiri') he let the following blunder occur to him:

LA DANZA 1755

which he repeats half a dozen times in order to make us thoroughly believe in it at last. He could show a sovereign unconcern in such matters.

'L'INNOCENZA GIUSTIFICATA'

Gluck's collaboration with Durazzo, and with it his activity as reformer of the opera, begins with *L'innocenza giustificata,* performed on 8th December 1755 at the theatre in the Hofburg for the birthday of Francis I. Its description as a *festa teatrale* is misleading. Here is no longer an 'opera,' that is to say, no longer a conventional spectacle with music to flatter the vanity of singers, but a musical drama; no longer the play of amorous intrigue, but genuine dramatic passion. No less deceptive is the preface that is prefixed to the libretto. To all appearances it is an obeisance before Metastasio: 'The author of this little drama did not intend to bring a new work to light; he merely endeavoured to devise an action suited to the public's justified admiration for the illustrious author, who wrote all the arias in this piece at various times.' In reality *L'innocenza giustificata* was a declaration of war against Metastasio, whose operatic ideals it defies at every turn.

La Borde's *Essai sur la musique* makes it still clearer who was the author of the text, i.e. the action or, more exactly still, the recitatives: Count Durazzo himself. These recitatives are comparatively short and full of passion; the work is in one act and complete in itself; and above all it introduces the dramatic chorus into its final scene, a chorus no longer satisfied with a decorative or purely musical share, but taking a decisive part in the action. The only old-fashioned thing about it is the title: we should call the work *The Vestal*, and it is in fact under this name that Gasparo Spontini, the last of the Gluckians, composed the subject seventy years later. Not only that, but when Gluck revised the work in the summer of 1768, between *Alceste* and *Paride ed Elena*, he did actually change its title to *La Vestale*.

Briefly told, this is the story: The gods are angered against Rome. Both the senate and the people believe that the guilt lies with the vestal Claudia, who has had the misfortune to let the sacred fire go out and at whose sisterly relations with the knight Flavius they take offence. In vain does the high priestess Flaminia vouch for her innocence and purity: the consul Valerius pronounces her sentence of death in the senate's name. Then a miracle happens: the boat which is to bring the image of the Phrygian Great Mother to the banks of the Tiber cannot be made to stir by any human agency. Claudia launches it by her prayer, and the people, who had threateningly demanded her death — as later the Achaeans demand that of the Aulidian Iphigeneia—jubilantly acknowledge her innocence in concert with the soloists.

These soloists number no more than four. There is no intrigue, no plot, neither love nor jealousy, neither conspiracy nor magnanimity. It is all a simple *azione drammatica,* impaired only by the facts that, through the arias, Durazzo still remains tied to Metastasio, that Caterina Gabrielli sang the part of the vestal and that each of the four soloists had to be obliged with arias such as those, for instance, in which the consul Valerius declares that

> Quercia annosa sull' erte pendici
> Fra 'l contrasto de' venti nemici
> Più robusta, più salda si fa.

> (The ancient oak, clinging to a slope,
> The more it is opposed by hostile winds,
> Becomes the more robust and staunch.)

which is dramatically as superfluous as possible, however temperamentally it may have been composed by Gluck. Then a good deal was sacrificed to the vocal virtuosity of Gabrielli in two of the arias, though the sacrifice, it is true, allowed of a melodic beauty and an instrumental wealth such as Gluck was later consciously to deny himself. The second especially, that in G major, 'La meritata palma,' beginning softly with a sustained D in the oboe and making a concerto-like use of oboes, horns, bassoons, violins and viola, has a brilliancy that really cannot be compared to anything but the great aria of Constanze in Mozart's *Elopement.* On the other hand the aria to which Claudia performs her miracle, 'Ah rivolgi o casta diva,' accompanied only by plucked violins and basses, is a model of simplicity and a direct anticipation of the entreaties of Orpheus, accompanied by the harp, in the scene with the Furies. And the aria in which the death-doomed vestal feels the touch of a divine ray, 'Fiamma ignota nell' alma mi scende,' is one of Gluck's grandest inspirations, with its muted violins and horns making a muffled entry and then becoming radiant (see page 44). Claudia sings this number, which cannot be called an aria or a *cavata* or given any other conventional name, since it takes on a grandiose shape suited to the situation; but she does not sing it to the end, for she is interrupted by Flavio, who rushes on the stage

Gluck

and announces the miracle. A few of the arias lack a *ritornello*; others have no middle section. That Durazzo considers not only his own dramatic intentions but also the lyric requirements of the musician is proved by the glorious farewell duet between Claudia and Flavio, with the climax of which the one-act piece is divided into two parts.

Durazzo is the father of the idea of the Gluckian reformed opera. It was he who first saw in Gluck the fit and proper person to defeat the Metastasian operatic ideal. The advance beyond Durazzo which Calzabigi made together with Gluck seven years later is merely the abandonment of historical subjects, of the drama of ancient Rome, in favour of the purely human, the mythological and the legendary. It was the same heightening or purifying that may be observed in Wagner's choice of subjects: *Orfeo* stands in much the same relation to *L'innocenza giustificata* as *Lohengrin* does to *Rienzi*.

MINOR RIVALS

This negation and defeat of the Mestastasian operatic ideal is the real achievement of Gluck and his associates. Attempts have been made to prove, by analysis of the operas of a few of Gluck's precursors and contemporaries, that the 'reform of the opera' did not fall ready-made from heaven, but was conditioned by the times. The assertion is perfectly just; still, the decisive step was not taken by Niccolò Jommelli, by Tommaso Traetta, by Francesco di Majo, by Davidde Perez or by G. C. Wagenseil, although as 'musicians' they probably all of them surpass Gluck.

The eldest among them was Jommelli. Very conventional and hardly the equal of Hasse at first, at the end of his career dismissed by young Mozart as outmoded and all too 'learned,' Jommelli disintegrated the Neapolitan aria from the inside, so to speak: by broken, sometimes almost nervous melody, by violent dramatic intensification of the accents and piling-up of orchestral means, by the transformation of the 'concertizing' principle into a 'polyphonic' one, in so far as it may be said that his courtly age knew polyphony. But he only achieved a baroque effect inside the accustomed framework of opera without ever finding the Archimedean point outside its conventions. Above all, it has not been proved, nor is it demonstrable, that Gluck esteemed and imitated him.

It is otherwise with Traetta, whom Gluck knew very well, having himself conducted his operas, and with Majo, who perhaps lacked nothing but a longer span of life for his great gifts to grow to historically significant proportions. Majo recognized already that the real hindrance to dramatic effect lay in the formalism of arias written for the singer's sake. He shortens the *da capo* by omitting its first half; he sometimes plunges *in medias res* by cutting out the orchestral *ritornello*; altogether he prefers the shorter form of the cavatina to that of the aria—and indeed he is a melodist of the first water, capable of writing long-drawn and tender lines of the most sensitive *cantilena*. Majo, like Traetta, wrote an *Ifigenia in Tauride* long before Gluck, though it still remained pure Italian opera.

Traetta went farther. His life (1727–79) fell wholly within that of Gluck, and he did not begin to produce operas until ten years after the latter. To survey his output is to be struck by its appearance of similarity to that of Gluck, if one disregards the fact that Traetta wrote a few *opere buffe* and did not handle the French *opéra comique*; but there are among his *opere serie,* apart from a mass of pieces by or influenced by Metastasio, a few which point to a French provenance and some showing a tragic, 'Hellenic,' antique content: a *Sofonisba* of 1762 for Mannheim, an *Ifigenia in Tauride* of 1763 for Vienna, an *Antigona* of 1772 for St. Petersburg. It has been claimed that this *Iphigeneia* had been performed in Vienna as early as 1758; but this is not to be reconciled with Traetta's biography and only literary testimonies exist, for the libretto of 1763 alone is extant. That Traetta was connected with Vienna earlier is certain: he composed an *Armida* for it, the libretto of which, based on Quinault, was due to no other than Count Durazzo, the versification alone being by Migliavacca. It was produced on 3rd January 1761. Thus we see connecting threads running between Traetta and Gluck everywhere.

The fortunate incident in Traetta's destiny was his appointment to the Bourbon court of Parma, the court of Don Filippo, Infante

of Spain, whose eldest daughter became the consort of Joseph II.
The operatic conditions at that court were very similar to those in
'opera-reformatory' Vienna, save that the duke did not, like the
Viennese court, wish to have the modish *opéra comique* transplanted
root and branch, but the Parisian lyrical grand opera, though transformed by an Italian guise. The intendant Du Tillet, a Frenchman,
was Count Durazzo's counterpart at Parma; Calzabigi's was the
poet Carlo Innocenzio Frugoni, known, although not always honour-
ably, to every branch of Italian literary history. In 1758, the year of
Traetta's appointment, Frugoni translated Rameau's *Castor et Pollux*
into Italian, a work Traetta himself composed later (1760) *alla francese,*
that is, with choruses and ballets, under the title of *I Tindaridi.*
Before that (1759) he had produced *Ippolito ed Aricia,* likewise in
Frugoni's translation, in five acts and after Rameau. The *Tindaridi*
went to the Vienna Burgtheater in 1760, and it is impossible to
think that Gluck did not hear the work. Traetta later fell out with
Frugoni and associated with Marco Coltellini, the friend and
countryman of Calzabigi, who made him his successor in
Vienna. Coltellini furnished the librettos of *Ifigenia in Aulide* and
Antigona.

The operatic tendencies of Parma may be gathered from a letter
written by a Count Paradisi to Count Algarotti on 21st July 1758.
'I went to the opera at Parma,' he says, 'where I found many things
entirely to my satisfaction . . . the way seemed to me open for a
renewal of the miracles of that art which the Greeks so much
prized.' A renewal, then, of music-drama in the spirit of the
ancients.

Were Traetta and his assistants, Frugoni and Coltellini (to whom
Mattia Verazi was joined in the case of *Sofonisba*) the men to create
a 'Greek' opera? No doubt their tendencies were the same as those
of Calzabigi and Gluck. But we have only to compare the libretto
of his *Iphigeneia* with Euripides and with that written by Guillard for
Gluck to become aware of the compromises Coltellini made with
the *opera seria.* He cannot do without a companion for Iphigeneia,
named Dori, to engage her in dialogues and sing an aria of compas-
sion; what is worse is that Iphigeneia herself is saddled with the task

of stabbing the tyrant Thoas. So after all it is only a new *framework* once again, with choral and dance scenes, which Coltellini offered Traetta. The composer filled it like the splendid 'melodist' he was, and a few of his arias show a direct link with Johann Christian Bach, not to say with Mozart. But Traetta was of too conciliatory a nature, a defect from which even Goethe said he himself suffered as a dramatist. His contralto Orestes sings beautiful contralto music in his moments of extreme torture; his Furies are tractable and, above all, they sing too long. That Traetta influenced Gluck musically is certain: he helped and encouraged him in the introduction of chorus and dance into *opera seria*; but he had not the good fortune to come across a Calzabigi, and he would not have been the person to make of such fortune what was made of it by the manly Gluck, less richly endowed with music, but far more with character. Traetta's later operas, *Sofonisba* and *Antigona,* significant as they often are, hardly count any longer as suggestions and incitements for Gluck.

It is only among Gluck's Viennese contemporaries that we find a musician who far excelled his colleagues, such as Bonno, Reutter and Predieri, not merely as instrumental composer, but also as a man of the theatre: Georg Christoph Wagenseil. In 1750 Wagenseil took part in a pasticcio entitled *Euridice,* a *favola pastorale* to which he contributed an important scene that was the core of the drama: Orpheus's farewell to his fellow-mourners, his conquest of the demons in Hades and the joyful duet of the reunited pair. He shaped all this into a single scene divided into many sections and yet unified, consisting of recitative, chorus, aria and duet. Formally it is interesting and astonishing enough, but formally only. Hades appears to let Eurydice go free in the end only because Orpheus would otherwise have to sing his *arioso* for the fourth time: these choruses are wanting in power of characterization, in emotional and musical tension and release. Other operas of Wagenseil's doubtless offered Gluck many a stimulating idea in certain details; but he again was clearly not the great and strong personality with whom Durazzo could have realized his plans.

RELAPSES IN ROME AND VIENNA

The *Innocenza giustificata* did not prevent Gluck from composing, during the next two months, another libretto by Metastasio, and taking it over neck and crop, so to speak. It was *Antigono,* first set to music by Hasse for Dresden in 1744. Gluck was a political realist who did not care to jeopardize his success by untimely audacities. He composed *Antigono* for the Teatro Argentina in Rome, where it was produced on 9th February 1756. (A fortnight earlier Wolfgang Amadeus Mozart was born at Salzburg.) The *scrittura* presumably came to him through Prince Hildburghausen, for Gluck is mentioned in the libretto only as his *Capellmeister,* while his post of imperial composer remains unnoticed. He was more than ever intent on using arias from earlier works, the earliest being *Ezio*; the 'symphony' he simply took from the *Innocenza.* The libretto was once again a court piece: Princess Berenicestands between the king, Antigonus, and his son, Prince Demetrius, and once more a comedy of mis-understanding and magnanimity unfolds itself and leads to a happy conclusion.

After the performance of *Antigono* Gluck received, it is said, the Order of the Golden Spur from Pope Benedict XIV, 'a serene, comfortable man,' as Goethe calls him. This is unlikely, since he did not use the title of 'Cavaliere' until 1757. It was the same order, not regarded as particularly distinguished by the eighteenth century, which the boy Mozart received in 1771 and which earned him so much ridicule at Augsburg in 1778 that he never again made use of such a questionable distinction. Gluck, on the other hand, made the most of it, and because he was not an insignificant youth, like Mozart, but an imposing man of the world, nobody dared to make fun of the 'Cavaliere' or 'Chevalier,' a title Giacomo Casanova too regarded as so agreeable and so advantageous to his success in the world.

Into these Roman weeks falls Gluck's acquaintance or encounter with Johann Winckelmann, whose ideal conception of the antique he was later to realize in the domain of opera—or so his contemporaries thought. But Winckelmann, who according to his own affirmation 'had begun to live only in Italy,' in other words, in the contemplation of the antique, was but the exponent of a European mood of the time, a time that regarded a purified antiquity, an antiquity seen in the light of its own century, as the only possible manifestation of art. There is nothing to show whether Gluck knew Winckelmann's writings and, if so, at what period; but this is in any case of little importance, since Winckelmann's influence affected all men of genius, including those who were unconscious of it. However, the transition and clarification of the operatic subject shown by Gluck's development between the *Innocenza* and *Orfeo* is purely Winckelmannian in spirit. Nevertheless, if Winckelmann's influence on Gluck is compared with that exercised by him on, let us say, Rafael Mengs and other representatives of plaster antiques, one cannot help feeling grateful that music was incapable of directly reflecting his purist enthusiasm.

If Gluck's relapse into the Metastasian manner, the relapse from the *Innocenza* to *Antigono,* is just comprehensible because it was a question of supplying an opera for Rome, to be played on strange territory, it is hard to understand the decline from the *Innocenza* to *Il Rè pastore,* which was again written for Vienna and once more for the birthday of the Emperor Francis, being produced on 8th December 1756. Metastasio had written the libretto in 1751 for a performance by four ladies and a gentleman of the court at Schönbrunn. The music was by Giuseppe Bonno, who earned Metastasio's endless praise for it. Young Mozart—if Mozart at twenty may still be called young—composed the same text in 1775, without wasting much thought on the dramatic content of the little work, as a festival piece for a son of the emperor whom Gluck celebrated. It meant nothing more to him than a *festa teatrale,* a *serenata,* to be set to music in a lavish, concertizing style. But Gluck too, the coming reformer, made a thoroughly courtly setting of this play of polite disguise, affected innocence, highmindedness and faithful love. There is much beautiful and carefully fashioned music in the work, but not a single feature that exceeds the most conventional of conventions. Only two of the arias begin without a *ritornello*; the first act closes with a rather commonplace duet, the second with an uncommonly

stiff quartet for the four sopranos (the noble-minded king of the Macedonians alone is given a tenor voice, which once blares into a march accompanied by trumpets and drums), and the last with a short and indifferent concerted piece. Two *recitativi accompagnati* remain unattended by arias. Once only, when the shepherdess Elisa expresses her consternation, does Gluck write an aria with changing tempos and rich in pauses, beginning beautifully as on page 51. The stress on the ninth will show how well Gluck was able to combine a surprising emotional force with the greatest beauty of the melodic line. This same third act contains yet another astonishing piece, astonishing because it is given to a secondary character, Agenor:

> Sol può dir come si trova
> Un' amante in questo stato,

A minor, *andante non molto,* with solo parts for bassoons, horns and cellos answering to the suppressed pain of the noble and resigned lover with an equally noble, full-toned lament. Yet on the whole the work is no more than the response to a command from the throne of which Gluck acquitted himself with decency.

THE OPÉRA COMIQUE

The events of 1757 in Gluck's life are again wrapped in complete obscurity. The Seven Years War evidently precluded, first of all, any and every court occasion in the wonted sumptuous style. Only with the marriage of the Archduke Joseph, the later emperor, did a reflection of the former brightness return.

The war must also have been partly responsible for the fact that Gluck, in order to have something to do, occupied himself with a more modest form of art than that of the *opera seria*: the *opéra comique.* In May 1752 a French company of actors, engaged by imperial command by the impresario Hébert, had begun to give performances of comedies that much delighted the courtiers and the nobility. This company soon began to cultivate French comedy with music as well, the *opéra comique,* which had originally taken the form of parodies of French grand opera, but was soon converted into a national rival of the Italian *opera buffa,* from which, it is true, it was distinguished by spoken dialogue and by greater musical simplicity. Not until the German *Singspiel* arose—a species of which Mozart's *Elopement* is the crowning example—was the musical wealth of the *opera buffa* linked up with the outward form of the *opéra comique.*

Was it due merely to external circumstances that Gluck, the 'Italian' opera composer, was never to be permitted to write an *opera buffa,* but was to be led to the *opéra comique?* At first nothing more was required than to impart a new attraction to these pieces by the addition of 'airs nouveaux' for their revivals. With the first of these *opéras comiques,* which Count Durazzo obtained through the offices of Count Starhemberg and later (after 1760) through the playwright Favart in Paris, Gluck seems to have had little to do except as conductor and dramatist, though he can hardly have left any of them quite untouched. Among the earliest were Favart's *Le Déguisement pastoral* (Schönbrunn, 1756), first performed in Paris in 1744 with old tunes to which Favart's verses were fitted; *Les Amours champêtres* (Schönbrunn, 1755), Paris, 1751; Favart's *Tircis et Doristée* (Laxenburg, 1756), a charming parody of Lulli's *Acis et Galatée,* Paris, 1752; *Le Chinois poli en France* (Laxenburg, 1756), Paris, 1754; *Le Diable à quatre* (Laxenburg, 1759), Paris, 1756. What Gluck's share in the adaptation for Vienna of these modest one-act plays was is uncertain; but a little number like the first ariette in *Le Diable à quatre,* whether composed by him or not, or only adapted (the song has in fact been ascribed to Ciampi), is certainly worthy of him. The poor little beaten wife is here seen running breathlessly on to the stage, and the melody not only paints the situation, but at the same time outlines her character (see page 54).

It would seem as though the primitive musical additions to these ballad operas were not regarded as adequate to the pampered musical tastes of the Viennese court after all. Gluck had to step into the breach. Thus in *L'Isle de Merlin,* performed on 3rd October 1758 at Schönbrunn on the eve of the emperor's name-day, only a small selection of the songs was old, and twenty-two numbers were newly composed by Gluck. The piece, by Le Sage and d'Orneval, was very old, for it had been given as early as 1718 at the Théâtre de la

Gluck

LE DIABLE A QUATRE 1759 Ariette No. 1   ?Ciampi

Oui, Oui, je veux en sor-tir J'en ju-re l'in-ju-re ne peut se soutenir, je ne le puis souffrir. Oui, Oui, c'est trop longtemps souffrir c'est trop longtemps souffrir à moi des coups je ne puis le souffrir etc.

54

Foire Saint-Laurent under the title of *Le Monde renversé*, and revived
at the Théâtre Saint-Germain in 1753. To the same year, 1758,
probably the period of the carnival, belongs *La Fausse Esclave*, an *opéra
comique* in two acts, played at the Saint-Germain the preceding year
as *La Fausse Aventurière*. Gluck apparently composed all the vocal
numbers anew.

To these succeeded, on 3rd October 1759 at Schönbrunn, *L'Arbre
enchanté*, the book by P.-L. Moline, the subject the familiar story
from Boccaccio, which here serves to fool an old man and make
a sentimental young couple happy. Unfortunately Moline cannot
do without a *deus ex machina* even in such a simple case. Not only
before their imperial majesties, but also before the Elector Palatine
Carl Theodor, *La Cythère assiégée* was performed in 1759, first in
Vienna and then at Schwetzingen. The libretto was printed at
Mannheim and there were twenty-six new vocal pieces by Gluck.
The elector is said to have rewarded him for the entertainment with
a hogshead of good Rhine wine, which we may be sure was quite to
Gluck's taste. Favart's book is once again the purest rococo, the
dramatic counterpart of Boucher's paintings. The Scythians besiege
Cythera, abandoned by Venus, but are soon themselves made
captive by the amiable nymphs.

L'Ivrogne corrigé, performed in 1760, leads us back into real life.
Anseaume took his story from *The Drunkard in Hell*, one of La
Fontaine's fables. In *Le Cadi dupé*, 1761, where the book by Le
Monnier is based on a tale from the *Arabian Nights*, Gluck's music
took the place of Monsigny's, with which the little work had been
given at the Théâtre de la Foire Saint-Laurent on 4th February 1761.
Durazzo informed his 'agent' Favart on 12th December 1761 that
Gluck's substitute ' a eu toute la réussite imaginable.'

It is astonishing with what refinement and taste Gluck kept within
the confines of a definite style in supplementing and rewriting these
unassuming little pieces. The composer of Italian *opera seria,* so much
engaged with heroes and heroines, is to be recognized only in the
ease with which he acquitted himself of his musical task. He is
here concerned with stupid, mean, or grumbling old men, shy pairs
of lovers, roguish girls, merry lads, beatific drunkards—all of whom

are characterized in a masterly way by delicate strokes, and from among many conventionalities emerge little melodic blossoms, tiny melodic piquancies of the utmost charm. The spirit which Rousseau called 'the return to nature' is to be perceived everywhere; in the orchestra nature's ways are painted by means of figuration and tone-colour.

'LA RENCONTRE IMPRÉVUE' ('THE PILGRIMS TO MECCA')

A special place among these small comic operas is occupied by *La Fausse Esclave* and *Le Cadi dupé* because, with their Oriental subjects, they prepare the way for Gluck's greatest *opéra comique*: *La Rencontre imprévue*. This falls into a new period of his labours, appearing a year later than *Orfeo,* without which it would assuredly not have grown so far beyond all the laws of style and the dimensions of the species. All the same, as the crowning conclusion of Gluck's occupation with the *opéra comique,* it must be discussed here and now. Gluck did not disdain its small forerunners, for he took up both *L'Arbre enchanté* and *La Cythère assiégée* again for production in Paris later on; but he confined his revisions of these delightful trifles solely to some alterations in point of size, and so *La Rencontre imprévue* remains his last, best and, when all is said, only comic opera.

The title is modest: '*La Rencontre imprévue,* comédie en trois actes melée d'ariettes, tirée de l'ancien Théâtre de la Foire par Mr Dancourt, Comédien de Leurs Majestés Impériales et Apostoliques.' The original play, again by Le Sage and d'Orneval, had first appeared, with the title of *Les Pèlerins de la Mecque,* at the Saint-Laurent. It had to be thoroughly altered, and behind the choice both of the piece and the adapter stood once again Durazzo, who wrote to Favart on 19th November 1763:

I have just had *Les Pèlerins de la Mecque* by the late M. Le Sage arranged; I had all that is licentious suppressed and only what is noble and comic left, so far as it could be fitted together. I do not doubt but that this poem, arranged in this manner for the present taste of the nation, will make its effect, especially as it is supported by music composed by the sieur Gluck, a man indisputably unique in his line.

It is clear that Dancourt, a comedian whose successes in the Prussian capital had earned him the name of 'the Berlin harlequin,' and who had gone to Vienna in 1762, was nothing more than the count's hack. Durazzo's ambition went far beyond providing an amusement for Vienna: he was anxious to bestow something upon the 'nation'! But the French nation—for no other could have been meant—did not seize the gift. The work reached the stage of Brussels two years after its first performance in Vienna (January 1764), though evidently thanks to Dancourt's personal exertions alone; the Paris Comédie Italienne followed only in 1790 with an adaptation by Soulié. The echoes it awakened in Germany were all the greater, however. After a performance at Frankfort in 1770, in a German translation, it was repeated countless times by the *Singspiel* companies in every town, and to Vienna *Die Pilger von Mekka* returned in 1776 as a German *Singspiel*. Six years later followed Mozart's *Elopement,* the spirit and subject and colouring of which is simply unthinkable without Gluck's precedent. Mozart paid Gluck a tribute that was no more than his due when he honoured him by taking an air from the opera, 'Les hommes pieusement' ('Unser dummer Pöbel meint'), as a theme for varia- tions. Gluck went to hear Mozart's 'academy' on 23rd March 1783, and in honour of the illustrious visitor Mozart improvised this, his finest set of variations—the finest because the Gluck theme is the best he ever chose.

Nobody has yet taken the trouble to compare the Durazzo-Dan- court libretto with the old model, printed in 1731 in the fourth volume published by the Théâtre de la Foire. The dramatic object was to ennoble the action, which sets a high-principled pair of lovers in the centre and admits only character parts, but no longer a harlequin. The musical object was to fill the French comic opera with Italian matter. Italian forms, the concerted pieces and finales of *opera buffa,* were not wanted. The air in minuet time ('Maîtres des cœurs, achève ton ouvrage') sung by Rézia, the heroine, for example, has a tuneful amplitude and a tenderness of the melodic line that was unheard-of in *opéra comique*; and as unheard-of was the sharpness and downrightness with which the character of the dervish is drawn: its realism is so grandiose that it becomes style again. The crazy painter in the play, Vertigo, points to Italy: I find in a Venetian *opera buffa* by Buini and Galuppi (1747), *Il protettore alla moda,* a 'Monsù Voragine.' It offends us to-day to see a poor lunatic as the pivot of comedy; but the eighteenth century saw nothing unpleasant in this, and Gluck at least used a few of the painter's arias to give us some of his most astonishing descriptions of nature or tone-paintings. There he comes in touch again with a French inclination towards the descriptive; in fact the fusion of the spirit of the *opéra comique* with the Italian style is nowhere more evident than in these airs. One who was present at the first performance, Count Zinzendorf, therefore lays stress on the 'Italian taste' of the music to this work, the length and weak planning of which, by the way, he by no means unjustly censors.

THE DRAMATIC BALLET: 'DON JUAN'

In dealing with *La Rencontre imprévue,* Gluck's programmatic *opéra comique,* we have anticipated his development. We now revert to 1761, the year preceding *Orfeo,* when his dramatic ballet, *Don Juan,* was produced at the theatre near the Kärnthnerthor, a work which, although different in kind from *Orfeo,* was nevertheless an approach to it.

The dramatic ballet, the drama expressed by the dance, was a protest against the senseless or merely sensuous succession of ballet numbers, the *divertissement de danse,* much as Gluck's reformed opera is a protest against the senseless or sensuous *opera seria.* The originator of the dramatic ballet was J. G. Noverre (1727–1810), who was an admirer of Rameau, in whose operas he discovered scenes of characteristic choreographic art. We need but think of the scene of the Furies in *Castor et Pollux* to recognize in it the purest realization of hundreds of similar scenes in earlier operas and the model for hundreds more in later works. Noverre must already in his youth have conceived the idea of connecting such choreographic scenes into a unified danced drama. In 1745 he appeared as solo dancer in Berlin, where he may have suggested a dramatic ballet in one act,

Graun's *Pigmalion*. In 1747 he returned to Paris, visiting London in 1755, where he became acquainted with the art, the expressive power, the dumb-show of David Garrick, with whom he entered into personal relations. Retired to the provincial city of Lyons in 1757-9, he devised a new system of dramatic dance, and in 1760 appeared the first edition of his *Lettre sur la danse et sur les ballets*.

The later events in Noverre's life need not be recounted here. It is clear that there is an immediate connection between the appearance of his book and that of Gluck's *Don Juan*, and that Durazzo's circle read the manifesto of a new art with ardent eagerness. Noverre's demands are those generally made of art and of life at the time: the 'return to nature,' expression in place of 'style,' vitality and truth instead of symmetry, 'live painting of the passions, manners, customs, ceremonies and costumes of all the peoples on earth.' To achieve that no mere ballet-masters would do; it required a dramatic poet and affecting subjects—and the most affecting were tragic ones. The new ballet was the equal of the drama, indeed it excelled it by its power to gather up the action into a few scenes loaded, as it were, with events. The task of the music was to underline this action, which could no longer content itself with neutral ballet numbers. The composer was to be the servant of the dancing-master, the dance-poet, the dance-dramatist.

In the spirit of this reform Gluck wrote his *Don Juan*, the scenario for which was supplied by the imperial ballet-master Gasparo Angiolini, who based it on Molière's *Festin de pierre*, not without enlarging in his libretto on programmatic features, in order to ascribe the priority of invention of the dramatic ballet to the Viennese stage and to his teacher, Hilverding. But we have an important witness to Noverre's priority: Calzabigi. He said in a letter to Vittorio Alfieri:

In 1762, when *Medea, The Death of Hercules*, and other pantomimes of Noverre's were already performed at Stuttgart, *Il convitato di pietra*, a work of Angiolini's, took the stage in Vienna. Gluck wrote the music for it and I the French programme, in which, by way of introduction, I made some brief remarks concerning the pantomimic art of the ancients.

Calzabigi merely made a slight error in his date, for *Le Festin de pierre* had been performed on 17th October 1761, at the Burg-theater. The work is not yet thorough-going 'expression': the *accompagnato,* which the melodrama finds the courage to employ only ten years later, is as yet missing. Everything is still enacted in 'closed,' stylized forms. But these forms are strong and expres-

DON JUAN 1761

sive enough already. Above all, everything is of a striking brevity and plasticity that establishes itself at once in the wild and martial 'symphony,' which seems to be laden with premonitions of disaster.

Dramatically, Angiolini's scenario is clumsy. Act I: Don Juan serenades Elvira; the commandant intervenes and is killed in a duel. Act II: Feast in Don Juan's house; the stone guest appears, the company flees, and the statue invites the murderer to return his visit. Act III: Cemetery; the commandant leaves his stone pedestal, demands Don Juan's conversion and reform, and consigns the impenitent sinner to hell. The fault lies in the anticipation of the stone guest's appearance as early as the second act. For compensation, however, this visitor from another world intrudes into a noisy festivity, and the effects of his knocking, his approach, his appearance among a multitude, their flight and their return, were tempting to a good ballet-master.

Gluck's music is a masterpiece. What is perhaps most admirable about his mastery is that he did not allow himself to be drawn into naturalism. Even the dignity and poise of the commandant is adapted to the dance, even Don Juan's impudence is stylized. But note how accurately it is painted. Gluck suggests in the space of sixteen bars a derisively whistling urchin (see page 60).

Never was his melodic invention richer and rounder. Nothing more perfect can be imagined than the proud and luxuriant gavotte with which the dance festivity in Don Juan's house opens:

DON JUAN 1761   Archi Fl Corni

Mozart knew Gluck's *Don Juan* very well. Jahn long ago drew attention to the identity of the fandango in the third act of *Figaro* with that in *Don Juan* (No. 19 in the score). However, this melody might have been taken by Mozart from a dance tune well known in

Vienna. The impression of Gluck's *Don Juan* on him goes deeper and reappears on the surface out of subterranean shafts. Don Juan's serenade to Elvira in Gluck's work:

not only lent its colour to Pedrillo's serenade in *The Elopement,* but is also the source of the theme for the variations of the D minor string Quartet—one of the most uncanny, tragic, desolate and terrifying movements in Mozart.

With its principal number, the great ballet of the Furies, *Don Juan* points directly towards *Orfeo.* Gluck simply took over this grandiose piece for the incidental music between the first and second acts of the French version of that work. It has remote ancestors: the chaconnes in the operas of Lulli; but it is new by reason of its inexorable rhythm, its wild dynamics and figurations, the other-worldly air it breathes. No other composer of the time was capable of writing anything of the kind. Bach and Handel were both dead, and Gluck commanded the field as a new, revolutionary spirit free from stylistic scruples and from the strict rules that were supposed to govern the mastery of the artist's craftsmanship.

The period of Gluck's *opéra comique,* of the great dramatic ballet and the preparations for *Orfeo,* was marked by one single relapse into *opera seria*. It was *Tetide,* a serenata for the wedding of the heir to the throne, Joseph, and Princess Isabella of Parma—a marriage of short duration, for Isabella died three years after the wedding, in November 1763. Hasse linked himself with Metastasio by composing the *festa teatrale* of *Alcide al bivio,* a piece in one act 'alluding to the sure signs of a generous disposition shown from the earliest days of his adolescence by the great prince for whom it is written . . .' How sumptuously would not this marriage have been celebrated in more peaceful times? But it took place at the very height of the Silesian war. Three years before our Prince Hilburghausen had already ingloriously lost the Battle of Rossbach to Frederick the Great, and was now on the point of dissolving his orchestra, with which Gluck had had so much to do.

The book of Gluck's serenata was not written by Metastasio, but by the Saxon ambassadorial councillor and court poet Gianambrosio Migliavacca—a thoroughly unpoetical name. It is the usual dramatic adulation in the Metastasian style, except that this time Apollo, Mars, Hymen, Venus and Pallas Athene quarrel over the distinction of rendering pedagogic services to Achilles on his marriage with Deidamia and being allowed to present them with the choicest gifts, with mother Thetis acting as judge. There is an introductory and a concluding chorus with solos, a quartet as conclusion of the first part, a richly florid duet and a series of ample and finely coloured arias, of which those for Thetis (Caterina Gabrielli) are the most lavish, and one for the otherwise so sagacious Pallas is the most warlike ('No, nuovi oltraggi ormai'). Gluck rarely wrote a work in which he was so dependent on the singers, and he had thus scarcely ever been less Gluckian than such a short time before the appearance of *Orfeo.*

CHAPTER II

THE 'REFORM' OF ITALIAN OPERA

CALZABIGI

FROM the dispute with old *Capellmeister* Reutter it may be deduced that Count Durazzo, Gluck and Angiolini had entered into a relationship in the operatic activities of Vienna which we should nowadays call a clique, to which, moreover, the Duke of Braganza, Count Philipp and the dancer Mlle Bodin (or Geoffroi) belonged, and which secretly opposed the imperial court poet—for it would have been a sheer impossibility to attack openly a man like Metastasio, so blameless in his private life, so honoured by the court and so much the spoilt darling of the whole literary and musical world. In 1761 a man came to Vienna who was at last to bring about the realization of that clique's artistic aims: Ranieri Calzabigi. He was also called de Calzabigi, whether with his consent or not, and his name some-times took the French turn of Calsabigi; but he was ennobled in much the same way as his very good acquaintance, Giacomo Casa-nova, Chevalier de Seingalt. In truth he had been born as the son of simple citizens of Leghorn, in 1714, the same year as Gluck, and it is sufficiently curious that the paths of these two contemporaries did not cross until so late, when they were nearly fifty.

Casanova characterized Calzabigi most aptly: 'Well aware of the main chance [*grand calculateur*], versed in financial operations, familiar with the commerce of all nations, learned in history, *bel esprit,* poet and great lover of women.' In short, he was an adventurer like Casanova himself, and perhaps even more astute, worldly and talented. His youth is obscure, but he undoubtedly enjoyed a classical education. In the forties we find him in Naples, where he wrote his first libretto in 1745, *L'impero dell' universo,* a *festa teatrale* for the festivities held on the occasion of the dauphin's marriage with the Spanish infanta, which had to be celebrated in Naples too. It was a palpable, unblushing imitation of Metastasio's *La contesa de' numi,* set to music by Gennaro Manna. Calzabigi was already an Arcadian, and as such bore the name of Liburno Drepanio. In 1747 he wrote a second, similar work for the celebration of Prince Filippo's birth, *Il sogno d'Olimpia,* performed at the San Carlo; and he sent it, together with a canzonetta, to Metastasio, who returned a friendly and encouraging answer. About 1750 he must have got to Paris, presumably with a younger brother, Antonio Maria. He did not let his relations with Metastasio cool; indeed he even succeeded in persuading the cautious poet to agree to a complete Paris edition of his works, which was published after many delays by the widow of Quilleau, provided with a preface by Calzabigi, a *Dissertazione su le poesie drammatiche del sig. Abate Pietro Metastasio,* which described Metastasio's librettos as perfect tragedies—a eulogy not altogether without an admixture of malice any more than Nietzsche's panegyric of *Richard Wagner in Bayreuth* was later on. Arteaga, Calzabigi's enemy, was quite right when he called the latter a cunning flatterer, 'not unlike that Greek painter who painted King Antigonus of Macedonia in profile in order that his squint might not be perceived.' For all that, the *Dissertazione* was still retained in the third edition of Metastasio's works, brought out by the poet himself, and as late as 1786, when the contest round the court poet was nearly at its end, J. A. Hiller, the cantor at St. Thomas's in Leipzig, translated it into German.

His literary occupation with Metastasio was by no means Calzabigi's chief pursuit in Paris. He knew how to secure the good graces of Madame de Pompadour. Under her protection he established a lottery with his brother in 1757, admitting Casanova as a partner with a smaller share, a venture that can only be called a financial operation of the most questionable kind. (However, Frederick the Great himself did not disdain to make use of Calzabigi's brother in order to fill his royal coffers with the aid of a similar transaction.) It is said that both the brothers were shortly afterwards expelled from Paris, which is quite likely. They turned to Brussels, whence Calzabigi came to Vienna as 'Consigliere alla Camera dei

Conti dei paesi inferiori,' that is, as chamber councillor to the exchequer. He introduced himself there by a *Mémoire sur l'arrange-ment de la Chambre des Comptes* (15th February 1761). He received a salary of 2,000 florins and soon became the right hand of Prince Kaunitz.

It is plain that Gluck's new helper, who was, in fact, not a mere assistant, but rather the obstetrician of the new operatic reform, was anything but a paragon of virtue. Further details of his career are still to confirm this. He was a child of his time and 'a man with all his contradictions.' He combated the Italian vice of gambling by lottery, yet at the end of his life devised new lottery schemes for the kingdom of Naples; he blamed the Italians for their want of patriotism and drew—with one small interruption—a pension from the house of Habsburg until his death. It was he, not Gluck, who condemned the system of eunuch singers:

In France castration would be regarded as a crime . . . with us it is practised everywhere to our honour and very great profit. Fathers and mothers expose their little sons to this cruel but lucrative operation . . . a pretty trade, truly, worthy indeed of the inventive Italians.

He admired Shakespeare, 'the English Aeschylus,' and translated Milton, Gray and Thomson; but he never forsook his classicist ideals.

Calzabigi himself described how *Orfeo* came into being, and there is not the slightest reason to doubt the truth of his narrative:

The then intendant of the spectacles of the imperial court, Count Durazzo, believed that Calzabigi (who had shortly before come to Vienna with some reputation as a poet) might have some opera books in his desk, and invited him to dispose of them to him. Calzabigi was obliged to accede to the request of a man of such weight. He wrote *Orfeo* . . . and chose Gluck to set it to music. Every one in Vienna knows that the imperial poet, Metastasio, belittled Gluck, and that the feeling was mutual; for Gluck thought little of Metastasio's meticulous dramas. He was of opinion that this high-flown poetry and these neatly manufactured characters had nothing that was great and elevated to offer to music. . . . Gluck hated those meek political, philosophical and moral views of Metastasio's, his metaphors, his garrulous little passions, his geometrically devised word-plays. Gluck liked emotions captured from simple nature, mighty passions at boiling-point and at the climax of their outbreak, loud theatrical tumults. The imperial poet, on the other hand, took delight in ingenious flowers of speech, which he liked to present in the form of antitheses, in amorous disputes, in academic discourses, in petty characters one and all full of lovelorn affectation. The minds of these two were diametrically opposed to each other.

It seems to me that this exposition reveals the facts quite clearly and that any question as to the relative importance of Gluck and Calzabigi is superfluous. Durazzo is the driving power of operatic reform, of the antagonism to Metastasio, which Gluck shares. Calzabigi, the aesthete and literary man, gives shape to the new operatic ideal: he supplies the subjects and the texts. Gluck's music imparts to the subjects and texts solidity and immortality. Only, without Calzabigi Gluck would never have become what he did become. Calzabigi's merits simply cannot be exaggerated: he it was who gave the decisive impulse by supplying the subjects in their proper form. All the same, it was Gluck who gave these subjects life and endurance. Later, after *Paride ed Elena,* he no longer needed Calzabigi (whom, to tell the truth, he treated in the basest manner), and wrote masterpieces in collaboration with other librettists. Calzabigi's later librettos, *Le Danaidi, Elvira, Elfrida,* were condemned to ineffectiveness without Gluck. But the latter himself, in a letter written in 1781 to the editor of the *Mercure de France,* quite honestly granted the chief merits of the reform to his librettist:

I should reproach myself even more grievously if I consented to let the invention of the new style of Italian opera be attributed to me, the success of which has justified the attempt: it is to M. Calzabigi that the principal merit belongs; and if my music has had some success, I think it my duty to recognize that I am beholden for it to him, since it was he who enabled me to develop the resources of my art. This author, full of genius and of talent, followed a path with which few Italians are acquainted in his poems of *Orphée, Alceste* and *Pâris.* These works are full of those well-managed situations, those terrible and pathetic features, which hold out to the composer the means of expressing great passions and creating energetic and touching music. How much soever of talent a composer may have, he will never produce any but mediocre music, if the poet does not awaken in him that enthusiasm without which the productions of all the arts are but feeble and drooping.

Which Calzabigi sums up as follows, not without rancour, in a letter (to which we shall have to revert) of 25th June 1784 to this same editor of the *Mercure de France*:

. . . if M. Gluck has been the creator of dramatic music, he did not create it out of nothing. I furnished him with the material, or with chaos, if you like; we thus share the honour of this creation.

But the musical shaping of *Orfeo* too was influenced by Calzabigi. It went even as far as the declamation:

. . . M. Gluck not pronouncing our language well, it would have been impossible for him to declaim several verses in succession. I read him my *Orphée* and declaimed several pieces to him repeatedly, drawing his attention to the inflections I put into my delivery, the suspensions, the slowness, the quickness, the tone of voice, now stressed, now subdued and glossed over, which I desired him to make use of in his composition. I begged him at the same time to banish *i passaggi, le cadenze, i ritornelli* and all the Gothick, barbarous and extravagant things that have been introduced into our music.

It would, of course, be ridiculous to pretend that Gluck, who had spent years of his life in Italy and in the company of Italian singers, and who had composed hundreds of Italian recitatives and arias, could not accent the Italian language properly. Calzabigi is nevertheless right. (It must not be forgotten that he wrote all this during Gluck's lifetime, and that Gluck would certainly have contradicted him, if he had been able to do so.) Calzabigi, in the printed copies of *Orfeo* in both editions of his complete works (1774 and 1793), made marginal notes giving directions to the actors concerning the declamation, and it is to be noticed that Gluck literally observed these glosses in his recitatives. True, he filled these recitatives with an unheardof dramatic and psychological significance that far surpasses mere 'correctness.' What is much more important in *Orfeo* than these details, is his shaping of the recitative as such by composing it straight through, which, as it was understood at the time, means the complete replacement of the *recitativo secco* by the *recitativo accompagnato*. Where had this already been done? In

French opera, by Lulli and Rameau. It was not Gluck's flying visit to Paris in 1747 which became important for *Orfeo,* but Calzabigi's sojourn of several years there; and as regards style *Orfeo* has less in common with Gluck's own *Innocenza giustificata* than, let us say, with Rameau's *Castor et Pollux.*

When Calzabigi wrote his *Dissertazione* on Metastasio in 1755, he had secretly done with the imperial court poet for a long time, which, if it does no honour to his character, at least speaks well for his judgment. His exposition of Quinault's and Lulli's operatic ideal shows that he recognized its faults; but he knew its advantages too and came to this conclusion:

. . . if in the end the same ground-plan could be reconciled with the exigencies of truth; if once purely human actions were to unfold themselves to the exclusion of pagan divinities and all that smacks of the devil and of magic; in short all that is beyond things within the control of human beings, there is no doubt that a delightful whole would result from the interplay of a large chorus, the dance and a scenic action where poetry and music are united in a masterly manner . . . the poet and the composer must constantly bear in mind the famous precept of Horace: 'Denique sit quodvis, simplex dumtaxat et unum.'[1]

Well, this Horatian verse is the device at the head of *Orfeo* and of *Alceste.*

'ORFEO ED EURIDICE'

Let it not be thought that the libretto of *Orfeo* is a masterpiece. It is not that even in the Calzabigian sense itself. Among Calzabigi's reformatory notions is a protest against the 'happy ending,' the ridiculous 'matrimoniale catastrofe' which the courts and the public

[1] '. . . qualora però al piano medesimo si adattasse il puro verisimile; qualora azioni puramente umane sopra di esso si ordissero con allontarne il divino del Paganesimo, e il diabolico, e il cabalistico; in una parola tutto ciò che eccede il potere che all' umanità si attribuisce, non v' ha dubbio che dal coro numeroso, dal ballo, dalla scena maestrevolmente unita colla poesia, e colla musica un tutto sommamente dilettevole risultar non dovesse . . . con aversi sempre in mira dal Poeta e dal compositor della musica il famoso precetto d'Orazio: denique sit quodvis simplex dumtaxat et unum.'

expected. In Metastasio's *Didone* the death of the heroine was tolerated, for a knowledge of Virgil and the classicist conscience of the time drew the line, after all, at making a happy bridal pair of Dido and Aeneas. People reconciled themselves to the catastrophe because there was a grand stage effect—the conflagration of Carthage. But when in 1728 Metastasio wished to give his *Catone in Utica* the only possible tragic conclusion, he was forced by the operatic conventions to alter that close, and he never again dared to revolt against this fashion. But *Orfeo* too, which begins as a tragic opera, ends like a *festa teatrale,* with the god Cupid as *deux ex machina,* and that in spite of the fact that a tragic termination, with the death of Orpheus at the hands of the Thracian Corybantes, is inevitably demanded by the subject. To motivate such a tragedy, however, would have been to penetrate into mythical depths which far transcended the understanding of the eighteenth century. Let not the date of the first performance of *Orfeo,* 5th October 1762, be forgotten. It was the name-day of the Emperor Francis, a day on which it would have been impossible to produce a piece with a tragic ending. Even *Orfeo* is in this respect a court opera, concluding with a ballet and a jubilant chorus:

> Trionfi Amore
> E il mondo intiero
> Serva all' impero
> Della beltà.

To this festive close corresponds the *sinfonia* which Gluck, according to the custom of the day, did not compose first, but last (as was still Mozart's habit), and the light, conventional tone of which has occasioned so much astonishment and regret. It is new only in that it discards the second and third movements of the Neapolitan operatic 'symphony.' The drama of Orpheus begins only with the rise of the curtain.

It was part of Calzabigi's principles to let the action of an opera develop, not in dialogues, but in pictures. There is no exposition in *Orfeo,* no wedding festivity, no messenger's account of Eurydice's death, such as we find them in earlier Orpheus operas that are famous: in the librettos of Rinuccini (Caccini and Peri) and Alessandro

Striggio (Monteverdi). Eurydice is dead, and we stand with Orpheus at the mound of her grave, with a crowd of shepherds and nymphs gathered round him: one of those *tombeaux* so much favoured by French opera, such as Rameau set at the beginning of his *Castor et Pollux*. But this funeral ceremony in *Orfeo* is the most impressive and unforgettable in the whole history of opera, because it is the simplest and richest.

A choral lament in gloomy C minor, a sacrificial celebration, is interrupted by the grief-stricken accent of the bereaved husband, who calls Eurydice's name: it is plangent, sometimes piercing in its melodic formation, but made solemn in colour by the use of trombones and cornets, and by this contrast in the expression of sorrow it is lifted into the realm of *drama*.

Orpheus wishes to be left alone. He sends the chorus away:

> Basta, basta, o compagni,
> Il vostro lutto
> Aggrava il mio.

And now follows a *ballo,* musically speaking a 'trio' to the choral movements that frame it, in E flat major:

ORFEO ED EURIDICE 1762
Larghetto
Archi.

But this is much more than an 'exeunt' for the chorus, and it has not only a musical function: it is a consolation and transfiguration, a deeply affecting spiritual reflection of heaven such as may on occasion illumine the most cruel pain; and, seen historically, it is the first and at the same time the ripest fruit of the alliance between Noverre's mimed drama and opera.

Orpheus is alone and sings a strophic song—a song, not an aria —in a clear, pure F major; and he sings it in his clear, pure male contralto, for the first impersonator of Orpheus, Gaetano Guadagni, was a *castrato*. It is indeed one of Gluck's greatest notions to have made a eunuch's voice the vehicle for the part of Orpheus—just as it is one of his most deplorable compromises to have rewritten the part for a tenor for the Paris performance twelve years later. For his Orpheus is not merely a plaintive human being, but also a symbol of the singer's most exalted art, transcending all that is personal wherever it finds expression in regular forms. Thus Orpheus's lament on having his wife torn from him is no wild outburst of woe, but a reflection of his loss seen in nature's acoustical mirror

—the echo. Note how delicately the three strophes of this plaint, interrupted by a short recitative, are heightened each time by means of figuration and the colour of wind instruments. The echo orchestra on the stage consists of strings and the primitively natural chalumeau. It would seem as though Gluck had been aware that Calzabigi had modelled these three strophes on some hexameters from Virgil's *Georgics*.

In a new recitative despair and defiance break out afresh. Then Cupid appears to show him the way, telling him of the condition on which he may recover the lost one from Acheron. Cupid's aria is one of the proofs of the independence of Gluck's characteriza-tion (the other being the part of Eurydice): his god of love is no neutral phantom, but a domineering, pitiless boy who plays with men, gods and demi-gods, and almost capriciously brings about the reunion of the pair at the end.

The second act, with its contrast between Hades and Elysium, has always been rightly regarded as a masterpiece of opera in general and of Gluck in particular. It is an almost unimaginable fusion of antique plasticity and simplicity with the most subtly vibrating paintings of the human soul. The approach of a mortal throws the majestic underworld into a threatening agitation; nothing of the kind had happened since Hercules had torn the wife of Admetus from the powers of darkness. Hercules had succeeded by his half-godlike power; Orpheus wins by song, by sound, by music. He strikes plain chords from his lyre and sings in simple, touching tones; his first attempt is interrupted again and again by a terrifying 'No!' that seems invincible; but renewed and heightened onsets soften the spirits of Hades themselves; they weary, they lie down to sleep, they yield a free path. The whole proceeding is depicted by chorus, song and dance with an incomparable scenic grip; but at the same time it seems to mirror itself in the soul of Orpheus like a dream-picture. It is surpassed in spiritual sensitiveness only by the scene in Elysium that succeeds it—a scenic contrast as strong and quite as legitimate as that of the first act of *Tannhäuser*, for instance. There is a 'roundelay' of blessed spirits for strings with two flutes floating above the melody which nobody who has once heard it can ever forget. There is Orpheus on those celestial heights:

Che puro ciel! Che chiaro sol!

a recitative limned into the orchestral painting of an unearthly landscape: an oboe solo with murmuring strings, a limitless expanse, a strangeness, an endless bliss and endless melancholy—a dream once more passing before Orpheus's inward vision (see pages 75-81):

It is hardly to be believed that this piece, which seems to be so inevitably invented for this incident and breathes the very poetry of nature, is to be traced back to an aria in the earlier operas of *Ezio* and *Antigono*. As in a dream, again, during the gentle song and slow-pacing dance of the blessed spirits, Orpheus finds his wife; it is as if her hand fell inadvertently and of itself into his own. Then the chorus finds some words that prove Calzabigi to have been something of a poet after all:

Torna, o bella, al tuo consorte,
Che non vuol che più diviso
Sia di te pietoso il ciel.

The third act, in which the catastrophe occurs, has been found weaker than the first two, both textually and musically. But, save for the happy ending, this is by no means true. Gluck was obliged to condense the whole characterization of Eurydice into a duet and an aria expressing all her hesitation, her bewilderment at Orpheus's apparent coldness, her reproaches. We have to resign ourselves to the fact that Calzabigi and Gluck saw their heroine as by no means an 'ideal' spouse, but quite realistically as a violent one, full of passion and blinded by jealousy, and that they fashioned her accordingly. Look at the splendid copper engraving that adorns the 1764 Paris edition of the score of *Orfeo* and was surely not made without consultation with the poet and the composer: it represents the moment of greatest tension between the couple: Orpheus turning away full of pain; Eurydice, an imperious and glorious woman, in the attitude and with the gestures of an angry Juno. Those who see the duet and the aria in this light will not regard these two numbers as frigidly

'Orfeo ed Euridice'

Gluck

'Orfeo ed Euridice'

continued

77

Gluck

continued

'Orfeo ed Euridice'

intellectual, but as cutting and disquieting. And they achieve their purpose: Orpheus turns to look at Eurydice, and her soul flies for the second time to the nether world.

The most famous and most disputed number of the whole opera follows—Orpheus's aria:

> Che farò senza Euridice,
> Dove andrò senza il mio ben?

Critics have thought it strange that Orpheus should at this ineffable moment sing an aria at all, and that *this* aria should be in C major and might as well express the opposite meaning. But let a phrase of Goethe's be remembered as explaining everything:

> And although man be stricken dumb in woe,
> A god did grant me words to tell my sorrow.[1]

It is devoid of pathos because, as has been finely said, it transcends all expression. Only the singer is left to speak here, and to speak as purely and perhaps as inflexibly as possible. If this aria were out of place, how comes it that nobody is able to resist its beauty and its effect? Only in the recitative that follows are words found again by a man who wishes to die, and who with this very resolution calls upon the intervention of the gods and draws down Cupid to his side again. Whereupon the *festa teatrale* with chorus and elaborate ballet comes into its own.

To anticipate, Gluck revised *Orfeo* in 1774 for the Paris stage, thus sacrificing some important features of the Vienna version, notably the logically justified assigning of the principal part to a male alto. But it could not be said that he failed, on the other hand, to enrich and deepen the Vienna version. Wonderful as the orchestration cf 1762 is, the experience of another twelve years led to new strokes cf genius, as in the use of the trumpet, which in the earlier version played its conventional part in the 'symphony' alone. He disturbed the admirably devised key relationship of the Viennese *Orfeo* here and there for the sake of that unfortunate tenor voice; he gave Cupid a

---

[1] *Torquato Tasso,* V. v.:

> 'Und wenn der Mensch in seiner Qual verstummt,
> Gab mir ein Gott, zu sagen was ich leide.'

superfluous aria in the first act; but the scene at the gates of Hades and that in Elysium are vastly superior in breadth and abundance in the Paris version, by reason of the addition, as transitional music, of the dance of the Furies from *Don Juan,* the new orientation of the tonality towards D minor, and a song for Eurydice with choral refrains of the most lovely melodic invention. Anyone who wishes to stage *Orfeo ed Euridice* nowadays should not keep wholly to the Vienna or to the Paris version, but will have to attempt to fashion the ideal form of the work out of both.

Orfeo ed Euridice marked an epoch not only in Gluck's work, but in the whole of operatic history. Here for the first time is an opera without *recitativo secco* (which therefore also banished the accompanying cembalo almost completely and required only a *conductor*); here for the first time was a work so closely grown together with its text that it was unique and could not be composed again. When Ferdinando Bertoni did this all the same and made a new setting of Calzabigi's libretto, he did so with many apologies and deplored the fact that he had to go without the poet's advice. But Calzabigi would have withheld that advice in any case, for he believed in a definitive and unrepeatably apt composition of a poetic theme. *Orfeo ed Euridice* was written for Gluck, and for no other. How different from Metastasio, whose librettos were set to music anything from twenty to a hundred times! An opera at last whose manner of performance required the composer's supervision, the first opera that culminated in the musician's labour!

The spectators soon became aware of the importance of such an event. Not at once, though: the first performance did not receive the full approbation of the court and the courtiers, who indulged in niggling criticism according to their wont, and Gluck was at once ready to impute the fault to his collaborator. But before long the work gained recognition, as could be judged from the satisfaction of the empress, who after the third performance presented Gluck with a snuffbox filled with ducats. There were negative signs of success, too, for no scene in the whole of operatic history has been more often parodied than Orpheus's intrusion into the nether world, the wittiest travesty being Paisiello's *Socrate immaginario.* Wherever a comic underworld was put upon the stage, *opera buffa* made its music to it out of a parody of the scenes of the Furies. But the strongest proof of how much the work meant to its contemporaries is the publication of the score in Paris, in March 1764. '*Orfeo* is the first dramatic work in the Italian language that had been published since 1639,' said Wotquenne, for Paris had so far regarded only the operas of Lulli, of his successors and of Rameau as worthy of being perpetuated in print. A single exception was Handel's operas, which Wotquenne overlooked, probably because they were intended for the English, not for the European market.

'IL TRIONFO DI CLELIA'

After *Orfeo* Gluck became guilty of another relapse into the old operatic system that has frequently surprised and troubled his biographers. He composed, for the opening of the new theatre at Bologna, *Il trionfo di Clelia*, 'dal celebre Signor Abbate Pietro Metastasio poeta cesareo.' If only it had at least not been Metastasio! Yet it is perfectly understandable that Gluck did not continue his 'reforms' just then, a continuation dependent on the existence of a new kind of poem, on a stage like the imperial stage and a public like the Viennese public. Gluck was a realist and fond of money. He wrote an opera for the Bolognese more or less as they wanted it. The commission from Bologna had most likely come to him through Antonio Galli-Bibbiena, a Bolognese, who was imperial architect and had built the new theatre.

About Gluck's journey to Bologna and his sojourn there we are once more informed by Dittersdorf's dictated autobiography, based, it is true, on recollections going back nearly forty years. Gluck asked the young violinist, who was then twenty-four, whether he would care to go to Italy with him, on condition that he should contribute half the travelling expenses and pay for his food out of his own pocket.

'With no end of pleasure!' I answered with the greatest enthusiasm, which a man like Gluck, who knew my love of art as well as my whole circumstances, ought to have prized above everything. 'But,' I added sadly, 'I have not the money to do so.' 'Ah,' Gluck answered, cold and alienated. 'In that case, of course, nothing can come of the matter.'

Something did come of it, all the same, for a few of Dittersdorf's well-wishers made him a present of the money for the journey; and Dittersdorf describes most attractively how they first went to Venice with the prima donna Chiara Marini and her mother; how he and Gluck took it in turns to play the part of gallant travelling companion; how they stayed there a week; how Gluck finished the composition of his opera after their arrival in Bologna, delivering the first act at the end of ten days after devoting the morning to work and the afternoon to social amenities; how they paid their visits to Padre Martini, the greatest musical oracle of the age, and to old Farinelli, the greatest singer of the preceding generation. The return journey was made by way of Parma, where they heard a performance of Johann Christian Bach's *Catone in Utica* (the work was already two years old), and they appear to have reached Vienna quickly through Mantua, Trieste and Klagenfurt. Even if the whole of Dittersdorf's story should not be quite true, we may be certain that he sketches an accurate portrait of Gluck for us: a downright, jovial cavalier, averse to none of the pleasures of life, least of all to those of the table, prudent, energetic and imposing—an autocrat. It is much the same picture as a later travelling companion of Gluck's, Johann Christian von Mannlich, drew for us during the Paris period.

On 14th May 1763 the first performance of *Il trionfo di Clelia* was given. According to Dittersdorf

it pleased immensely, notwithstanding that it was not by a long way performed as the composer had imagined it. Much as the Italian orchestras were praised, Gluck was thoroughly dissatisfied with them. Seventeen full rehearsals were held, and yet the performance lacked the team-work and precision to which the Viennese orchestra had accustomed us from the first.

The truth is that the work was a failure, reflected not only by the poor box-office returns—the twenty-eight performances brought in only 63,867 lire, so that each of the theatre's fifty-six guarantors had to pay more than 50 zecchini (412 lire)—but also in the dialect of the streets of Bologna:

Dman al part al Cluch
El va per Triest;
Ch' al faga ben prest,
Perchè l' è un gran Mameluch.

(To-morrow departs Gluck,
He goes by way of Trieste;
Let him be quick about it,
For he is a great Mameluke.)

Were the Bolognese right in their judgment? The libretto could certainly not have shocked them. Metastasio had once again made a heroine the centre of the action because the libretto had been performed a year earlier, with Hasse's music, for the heroic and 'happily issued confinement of her royal highness, the Archduchess Isabella' in Vienna, and for a poetic reflection of an archducal childbed nothing less would suffice, needless to say, than a Roman heroine, the opponent of the Etruscan King Porsenna, who, however, could not be saddled with any unpleasant traits, being, after all, the ancestor of the Tuscan branch of the imperial family.

The libretto accordingly bristles with 'heroic deeds,' the most splendid being a sporting achievement on the part of Clelia, who swims across the swollen Tiber on horseback, which is the more astonishing because she otherwise plays more of a diplomatic or intriguing part as ambassadress-extraordinary in the camp of the Etruscan king. The latter vies with her in magnanimity, as her lover Horatius does in patriotism and the traitor Tarquinius in scheming. Both traitor and lover sing soprano, while King Porsenna at any rate is a tenor. The part of Clelia was given to a distinguished singer, Antonia Maria Girelli-Aguilar. A somewhat more modest but still exacting subsidiary part, that of Larissa, was sung by Cecilia Grassi, later the wife and the widow of Johann Christian Bach in London.

Such a book could not have been composed with a view to 'reform,' and nothing is more fit to prove that Gluck counted for nothing as 'regenerator' of the opera without a suitable poet than *Il trionfo di Clelia,* though again the poet counted for nothing without Gluck. Here Gluck made the success of his opera wholly dependent on the singer once more. There are arias at each fall of the curtain, for the short *coro finale* of the last act is sung when the public is already leaving its boxes, applauding Horatius for his heroic bravura aria:

IL TRIONFO DI CLELIA 1763

De fol · go · ri di Gio · ve Ro · ma pu - gnan · do al lam · po

Scarcely one aria of the three chief parts is free from extravagant coloratura. For Clelia's aria that concludes the first act the creator of *Orfeo* writes, among other things, the following passage:

IL TRÌONFO DI CLELIA 1763

pro - tè

Porsenna too, who is an insufferable prig, has a few florid arias that might, as it were, be called great arias of state. But there are also some accompanied recitatives of dramatic intensity, a warlike march that is among Gluck's great instrumental pieces, a lovely, richly accompanied duet for Clelia and Horatius (Act ii, scene ii) and, by way of an exception, a magnificent and perfectly free aria for the heroine (Act ii, scene vii):

Above all, however, *Il trionfo di Clelia* shows Gluck on the topmost heights of his melodic mastery, his songfulness. This is supported by an instrumentation producing the most refined and transparent sounds, although Gluck's resources are not especially abundant, being confined to flutes, oboes, bassoons, horns, trumpets and drums besides the strings, which alone suffice him for many of the arias. But he divides the violas, separates the cellos from the double basses, writes concerto-like solos for the violins—the finest occurs in the aria that opens the third act—and it is not difficult to understand that the orchestra of Bologna, unaccustomed to tasks of that kind, could not easily satisfy him.

The most simple and sustained cantilenas are the real climaxes of this score. One of them is generally known, for Gluck used it in *La Rencontre imprévue* and recalled it in *Iphigénie en Aulide,* where it reappears as the 'Menuet gracieux, 7e air' in the ballet diversion shortly before the end of the opera. In the *Trionfo di Clelia* it is sung by Larissa as a *tempo di minuetto* (Act II, scene ii), and it is this melody which clings to the memory as the strongest impression of the work:

IL TRIONFO DI CLELIA 1763

Ah, ri - tor - na e - tà ___ dell' o - ro _ al - la ter - ra abbando na - ta, _ se non fo sti - ma - gi - na ta nel ___ so - gnar _ fe - li - ci - tà, etc.

And that in spite of the fact that Metastasio has been shown to be sufficiently wide of the mark with his linguistically enchanting presentation of a fair dream and his assurance in the middle portion of the aria that

> Non è ver, quel dolce stato
> Non fuggì, non fu sognato;
> Ben lo sente ogni innocente
> Nella sua tranquillità.

> ('Tis not true, this happy seeming
> Has not fled, 'twas more than dreaming;
> All who're candid understand it
> In their tranquil peace of mind.)

MINOR WORKS; 'TELEMACCO'—'SEMIRAMIDE'

Il trionfo di Clelia and other works show that the five years that lay between *Orfeo ed Euridice* and *Alceste*—Gluck's greatest and purest work—were occupied by inward preparation; but an inward preparation such as is often found in creative men: they occupy themselves apparently with all sorts of trifles, tidy up their study, read novels, catch butterflies, concern themselves with irrelevances, and yet in their heart of hearts undistractedly pursue their aim. In Gluck's case, however, these 'trifles' include a representative work like *La Rencontre imprévue*. One of the obstacles in his career was doubtless the dismissal of Count Durazzo from his post as intendant. Durazzo left Vienna in 1764 and went as ambassador to Venice. His successor was Count Wenzel Sporck. Gluck, too, resigned his appointment in March 1764, to be succeeded by Florian Gassmann. Fortunately for musical history Calzabigi did not at once fall a victim to the intrigues that brought about these changes. One of Gluck's last activities under Durazzo's auspices was a revival of the *Ezio* of 1750, apparently unaltered, in December 1763.

Although Joseph II was involved in the dismissal of Durazzo—the first blunder in the musical politics of this doctrinaire and unperceptive monarch, who was nothing more than a crowned bureaucrat—*Orfeo* was at one time said to have been performed as the festival opera at his coronation at Frankfort-on-Main on 3rd April 1764, with the Viennese cast. This, however, is incorrect. Gluck's only contribution to the festivities was a *bravura* aria for Guadagni, preserved in a German translation as 'Die Hoffnung schwillt in meinem Herzen.' It is a heroic piece, full of force, ornamentation and superficiality. Later on Gluck incorporated it in the Paris version of *Orfeo*. For a long time it was suspected that he had borrowed it from Bertoni. who did not come before the public with his own *Orfeo* until 1776. Earlier in the year 1764 Gluck paid a short visit to Paris in connection with the publication of the score of *Orfeo*, which was issued in April. We know that he visited the engraver Wille on 2nd March in the company of Durazzo and on the 9th in that of Coltellini.

The year 1765 sees Gluck in connection not only with Calzabigi and Metastasio, but also with Coltellini, the later successor of those two. For the first time Metastasio wrote a piece specially for Gluck, a little festival play, *Il Parnasso confuso,* performed on 24th January at Schönbrunn by four archduchesses—the eldest aged twenty-three, the youngest thirteen—with the Archduke Joseph at the cembalo, for the wedding of this same Joseph, now King of the Romans, with Maria Josepha of Bavaria, his second consort. The libretto was not only printed twice in Vienna, but appeared also in Rome and Milan. Nine archduchesses not being available, the court of the Muses consisted of only three ladies: Melpomene, Erato and Euterpe. Like the composer in the prologue to Strauss's *Ariadne,* they are agitated beyond measure by Apollo's command to celebrate the wedding on the very next day. They take counsel together in six arias and a duet, the younger of the exalted actresses being spared any great exertions. Gluck lavished a few of his finest melodies, including two in minuet time, as well as his choicest scoring on this piece.

For the end of the year a similar commission came his way. Again the text was by Metastasio, again it was set for the four exalted singers. The piece was an *azione teatrale* entitled *La corona,* intended for the name-day of the Emperor Francis on 8th December. But Francis I died on 18th August, and so this festival play was never performed. This time Apollo transforms himself into the huntsman Meleager and the trio of Muses turn into Atalanta and two other hunting nymphs; the wreath, contested between those who aim at slaying the wild Calydonian boar, is awarded to neither, but, needless to say, offered to the imperial birthday-child. Gluck again wrote six arias and a duet, but added a *tutti* by way of a conclusion. In accordance with the subject arias in martial 4–4 rhythm predominate this time; the *tutti* alone is pastoral in tone. A repeated call of warning from the huntresses, into which the hunting horn is sounded, is worthy of note, but on the whole this occasional piece cannot be said to add a laurel leaf to Gluck's 'wreath.'

Between these two court compositions stand two enigmatic works. One is *Telemacco o sia L'isola di Circe,* an *opera seria*; the other a new mimed drama, *Semiramide.* Earlier Gluck research assumed for a long time that *Telemacco* had appeared already in 1750, a supposition that has caused much speculation, as a hundred 'post-reformatory' features simply could not be made compatible with so early a date. What puzzles us is rather that the work came between *Orfeo* and *Alceste.* The choice of the subject is in itself curious, for it is a romantic-operatic subject of the seventeenth, the pre-Metastasian century. The libretto goes back to an elderly *dramma per musica* by Carlo Sigismondo Capeci, performed in Rome with Alessandro Scarlatti's music in 1718. Its revision for Gluck was made by Marco Coltellini, the countryman of Calzabigi, whose dramatic ideas he shared. Here, however, he made no use of those ideas, unless one likes to regard his adoption of two acts, generally permitted only to the *opera buffa,* as a progressive innovation.

Dramatically nothing clumsier can well be imagined. The two acts are so disconnected that the opera could be terminated after the first without damage and given a title indicating the successful search after Ulysses. The second would then be called by some name suggesting 'the successful departure and the rage of the abandoned Circe.' As regards its subject, *Telemacco* is a strange forerunner of *Armide.* The valiant Telemachus, with the aid of an oracular sentence, frees his father from the seductive chains of Circe, who has transformed Ulysses's companions not into swine, but into trees, and has held Penelope's virtuous husband in thrall for seven years without being able to win his love. A nice Greek girl of unknown origin, Asteria, makes the approach to the island easier for Telemachus, who in his search after his mysteriously vanished father is aided by Prince Meriones, son of King Idomeneus of Crete, whom he has picked up on his voyage from Ithaca to the island of Ogygia. Circe is com-pelled to release Ulysses, and at the end of the first act Telemachus discovers his father after sundry hindrances and anxieties. But Circe does not throw in her hand so soon. In the second act she conjures up the spirits of hell, who show Telemachus the death of his mother in a dream, a manœuvre on the part of the sorceress which the astute Ulysses is clever enough to see through at once. Yet he himself causes his son renewed perplexities by refusing, for dynastic reasons, to let Asteria leave with them, or indeed so much as to take her into the secret of their clandestinely planned departure. Fortunately Asteria turns out just in time to be the sister of Meriones and thus a Cretan princess. The boat is launched successfully and nothing is left for Circe but to curse the obstinate conqueror of Troy and to transform her magic island into a desert, in spite of the protestations of her flower-maidens.

The music to this work is quite as devoid of unity as its book. It is not by any means a relapse: *Orfeo* had been written once and for all, and a compromise with earlier practices was no longer possible. Even a consideration of the singers or the public, such as *Il trionfo di Clelia* had still shown, was now out of the question. The *secco* recitative is ready to flow into an *accompagnato* at any moment, and the latter almost predominates in quantity as well; the *da capo* is used only in two or three instances; *ritornelli,* where they occur at all, are as short as possible. The ballet plays a very subordinate and stric.ly dramatic part; the chorus, on the other hand, a correspondingly great one, with a variety of combinations and functions. The most curious things are the concerted pieces: a quartet at the close of the first act and two trios in the second. The quartet begins where the father embraces the son who has found and delivered him:

an ensemble in several sections in which, to tell the truth, Circe and Meriones should give much more decided expression to the difference of their feelings from those of Telemachus and Ulysses. This quartet and the equally gentle and melodious trios are nevertheless the closest approach Gluck ever made to *opera buffa*. The following might be by Mozart:

Besides such numbers there is an oracle (although a much less monumental one as yet than that in *Alceste*), an agitated 'messenger's speech' about the magic forest from Meriones, Circe's invocation of Hades, and a dozen more of strong and unconventional notions side by side with conventionalities of sometimes captivating melody. It is therefore not to be wondered at if Gluck singled out this half-and-half work particularly as an arsenal for future use. He quoted from it in *Armide* (the 'symphony'), in *Alceste* (the introductory chorus), in *Iphigénie en Tauride* and in the Paris version of *La Cythère assiégée*. The most striking of the borrowed passages is the supplicating question of Telemachus in the first act:

seconded impressively by the chorus. It is to take on a mighty significance on the lips of Agamemnon, and thus to become immortal.

Even greater riddles than those of *Telemacco* are presented by the ballet of *Semiramide*. Only one score is preserved, 'put together from many pieces from *Armida* and above all from the two *Iphigeneias,* and thus clearly not written until towards 1785,' as Wotquenne opines, ranging the work accordingly among the doubtful compositions. The truth is that, on the contrary, all these numbers are taken from the ballet of 1765. Calzabigi mentions in a letter to Count Alfieri (1784) his *Dissertation sur les ballets pantomimes des Anciens,* which was printed in 1765, in Vienna, by Johann Thomas de Trattnern, and copies of which are very rare. The artistic exemplification of his theories was evidently *Semiramide,* for the action of which Calzabigi followed the tragedy of Voltaire. It can hardly be doubted that he was the author of this work, and not Angiolini, as it is said in some sources. Angiolini was clearly only the stage-manager and dancing-master engaged for its performance. He nevertheless maintained that he was also the composer of the work. A 'Semiramide, Ballo Tragico, diviso in cinque (!) atti,' was given, as I learn from a libretto in the Liceo Musicale of Bologna, on the occasion of a performance of Paisiello's *Andromeda* at Milan in 1774, and there is a strip of paper pasted into the libretto (!) informing us that 'La Musica dei Balli è dello stesso Sig. Gasparo Angiolini.'

Is it not perhaps a question of two different works? At any rate Gluck's *Semiramide* is in three acts, like *Don Juan*, and it shows the same brevity and forceful condensation. The work opens with the unquiet dream of the murderess of her husband, the accompanying music for which is to return in the second *Iphigeneia* where Orestes dreams of the Erinyes; it includes an incident of the writing hand, as in *Belshazzar*; it ends with the queen's struggle with the spirit of the dead Ninus, the matricide by Ninias and the heroine's death-dance.

The effect of this spectacle was greater than could have been imagined. The tragedy itself, though so many times represented by excellent actors at the same theatre, never called forth so much interest, never infused so much terror and pity into the souls of the spectators. The first appearance of the ghost of Ninus appalled them. The dancing actress who represented Semiramis [her name was Nancy and she was a pupil of Noverre's at Stuttgart], when later she fought with the shade with vivid motions and varied gestures, showing horror, made the audience tremble and weep; and they were obliged to turn their gaze elsewhere in order to find distraction.

Does it not read like the description of an 'expressive dancer' of to-day?

The counterpart to *Semiramide,* only with a happy ending this time, is the ballet *L'orfano della China*, again arranged from a tragedy of Voltaire's and staged by Angiolini. The performance probably took place in 1766. The subject had also been treated by Metastasio, for did it not culminate in an act of magnanimity? The faithful mandarin Zamti offers his own son as a sacrifice in order to save the heir to the Chinese throne, when Genghis Khan and his Tartars capture Peking. What interested Gluck, as it had interested Handel in *Belshazzar* and Gluck himself later in *Paride ed Elena* or in *Iphigénie en Tauride,* was the contrast of varied characters and peoples, in this case that between the civilized Chinese and the barbarous Tartars. A noisily scored march even bears the expression *barbaro e maestoso* as a direction for its performance, like Bartók's *Allegro barbaro* about the year 1920. The height is reached in a *vivace*:

L'ORFANO DELLA CHINA 1766

The refined Chinese are characterized not only by a 'humane' polish of melody, but also by a silvery scheme of tone-colour and an archaic treatment of the scales.

The last episodic work between *Orfeo ed Euridice* and *Alceste* was *Il prologo*—a prologue because it was composed in anticipation of the renewed visits to the Teatro della Pergola in Florence of Maria Luisa, Grand Duchess of Tuscany, after a hoped-for happy confinement. This event evidently came to pass on 22nd February 1767. The libretto was by the illustrious *bailo* (magistrate or prefect) Lorenzo Ottavio del Rosso. It brings but one person on the stage, a Jupiter who sings soprano—represented by the *castrato* Giacomo Veroli—and who, among an assembly of choral divinities, is given an enormously long solo scene in which he welcomes and praises the new scion and heaps prophetic blessings on his head. No singer of to-day could cope with this fatiguing scene.

The 'symphony' and the chorus that is linked to it Gluck took from his *Rè pastore,* and there follow only three arias and recitatives with arias and choral responses, all, with one exception, in a festive C major, with concertizing instruments emerging from the rich orchestral background. Gluck conducted, at Florence, apart from his own work, the *Ifigenia in Tauride* by Tommaso Traetta, which had received its first performance at Schönbrunn on 4th October 1763. Its book was due to a Tuscan and grand-ducal subject, our Marco Coltellini. This significant work plays a more than merely superficial part in Gluck's career.

THE MANIFESTO OF THE 'DRAMMA PER MUSICA'

To this Grand Duke of Tuscany, Peter Leopold, who later, after the death of Joseph II, was to become emperor under the name of Leopold II, was dedicated the score of *Alceste,* published, like that of *Orfeo,* two years after the first performance, which took place on 16th December 1767 (exactly three years before the birth of Beethoven). It was printed in Vienna (1769), not in Paris. The score of *Orfeo* had contained no dedication or preface, whereas that of *Alceste* bore a dedication in Italian that is at the same time in the nature of a programme and was, of course, written by Calzabigi, the librettist, although it was signed by Gluck. It is the document of the accom- plished revolution in operatic history, or rather the reinstatement of opera on the throne of its earlier dignity. The history of opera begins with a kind of artistic conspiracy: the Florentine *camerata* took it into their heads to call antique tragedy back to life again and created the *dramma per musica.* Gluck too called his *Alceste* a *tragedia in musica,* and in his dedication found such flattering words for the illustrious city that had given rise to the musical drama that here again one suspects premeditation. The dedication has been reproduced hun- dreds of times, generally very faultily, and it is so important that it must not be omitted here:

YOUR ROYAL HIGHNESS,

When I undertook to write the music for *Alceste,* I resolved to divest it entirely of all those abuses, introduced into it either by the mistaken vanity of singers or by the too great complaisance of composers, which have so long disfigured Italian opera and made of the most splendid and most beautiful of spectacles the most ridiculous and wearisome. I have striven to restrict music to its true office of serving poetry by means of expression and by following the situations of the story, without interrupting the action or stifling it with a useless superfluity of ornaments; and I believed that it should do this in the same way as telling colours affect a correct and well-ordered drawing, by a well-assorted contrast of light and shade, which serves to animate the figures without altering their contours. Thus I did not wish to arrest an actor in the greatest heat of dialogue in order to wait for a tiresome *ritornello*, nor to hold him up in the middle of a word on a vowel favourable to his voice, nor to make display of the agility of his fine voice in some long-drawn passage, nor to wait while the orchestra gives him time to recover his breath for a cadenza. I did not think it my duty to pass quickly over the second section of an aria of which the words are perhaps the most impassioned and important, in order to repeat regularly four times over those of the first part, and to finish the aria where its sense may perhaps not end for the convenience of the singer who wishes to show that he can capriciously vary a passage in a number of guises; in short, I have sought to abolish all the abuses against which good sense and reason have long cried out in vain.

I have felt that the overture ought to apprise the spectators of the nature of the action that is to be represented and to form, so to speak, its argument; that the concerted instruments should be introduced in proportion to the interest and the intensity of the words, and not leave that sharp contrast between the aria and the recitative in the dialogue, so as not to break a period unreasonably nor wantonly disturb the force and heat of the action.

Furthermore, I believed that my greatest labour should be devoted to seeking a beautiful simplicity, and I have avoided making displays of difficulty at the expense of clearness; nor did I judge it desirable to discover novelties if it was not naturally suggested by the situation and the expression; and there is no rule which I have not thought it right to set aside willingly for the sake of an intended effect.

Such are my principles. By good fortune my designs were wonderfully furthered by the libretto, in which the celebrated author, devising a new dramatic scheme, had substituted for florid descriptions, unnatural paragons and sententious, cold morality, heartfelt language, strong passions, interesting situations and an endlessly varied spectacle. The success of the work justified my maxims, and the universal approbation of so enlightened a city has made it clearly evident that simplicity, truth and naturalness are the great principles of beauty in all artistic manifestations. For all that, in spite of repeated urgings on the part of some most eminent persons to decide upon the publication of this opera of mine in print, I was well aware of all the risk run in combating such firmly and profoundly rooted prejudices, and I thus felt the necessity of fortifying myself with the most powerful patronage of YOUR ROYAL HIGHNESS, whose August Name I beg you may have the grace to prefix to this my opera, a name which with so much justice enjoys the suffrages of an enlightened Europe. The great protector of the fine arts, who reigns over a nation that had the glory of making them arise again from universal oppression and which itself has produced the greatest models, in a city that was always the first to shake off the yoke of vulgar prejudices in order to clear a path for perfection, may alone undertake the reform of that noble spectacle in which all the fine arts take so great a share. If this should succeed, the glory of having moved the first stone will remain for me, and in this public testimonial of Your Highness's furtherance of the same, I have the honour to subscribe myself, with the most humble respect,

Your Royal Highness's

Most humble, most devoted and most obliged servant,

CHRISTOFORO GLUCK.

PRECURSORS OF THE MANIFESTO

This was the open declaration of war against the *conventions* of opera, to which all operatic composers other than Gluck paid more or less homage, and had done so in the past. Let it not be believed that the declaration came like a thunderbolt out of the blue. Criticism of opera is nearly as old as opera itself. The species had, at the very beginning, found an ideal aim for itself in the imaginary conception of the antique drama to which it looked up. The more it departed from that conception, the more violent became the assaults of criticism, which took the most manifold forms: parody, satire, aesthetic reasoning and so on. The most fruitful of these forms was the parody, from whose womb the *opera buffa* and the *opéra comique* sprang; and it is difficult to resist the thought that Gluck perhaps became the reformer of the Italian *opera seria* for the very reason that he had lacked the 'safety valve' of a gift to express himself freely, to discharge himself, as it were, in the domain of the Italian *opera buffa*. That is how he was destined to exercise a truly creative criticism on the *opera seria* and to become a critical creator.

The most amusing form criticism of the degenerate opera took was that of the satire. There is no occasion to discuss the satire that assumed the shape of dramatic parody, for that would lead us too far into the history of the *opera buffa*. Literary satire began early in Italy, with the painter-poet-musician Salvatore Rosa (*La musica, La poesia,* between 1640 and 1649), a satire that is, curiously enough, not aesthetic but moral, directing its shafts against the demoralizing influence of music. With the same topic Lodovico Adimari (1644-1708) too is still occupied; but his target is not opera so much as the prima donna with all her irritability, her inconsiderateness and —already in those days—her dread of having babies. Aesthetic satire culminated in Benedetto Marcello's *Teatro alla moda* (*c.* 1721), where, in the form of ironical advice to librettists, composers, singers and so on down to the call-boy, all the absurdities, abuses and conventions are scoffed at which the operatic spate of a century had accumulated like a rubbish-heap, and all of which Marcello himself respected—as an opera composer. The pamphlet, intended only as an ephemeron, had a tremendous success and contributed perhaps more to the reform of the *opera seria* than all the learned treatises together.

Of such treatises there was no lack. Italy and France vied with each other in critical reflections. The first and most radical censor of opera in Italy, a veritable Cato with his *ceterum censeo,* is the famous librarian of Modena, Lodovico Muratori. He endeavoured early to secure the approbation of Apostolo Zeno for the blow he planned to deal the opera, and he actually received a reply from the courteous poet [1] which fully summarized the librettist's woes:

That this use of the dramatic poet's art [the opera] should not gain your approval is by no means surprising. I myself—to tell you the truth frankly —am the first to condemn it, although I have written many librettos of my own. Experience has taught me that it is necessary in many respects to submit to abuses, if the chief aim of such productions, which is sensuous pleasure, is not to be sacrificed. The more one wishes to be a *poet,* the more one displeases, and if the book earns the praise of some, nobody goes to the opera.

This is largely the fault of music, which kills the best scenes thanks to

---

[1] August 1701. *Lettere di Apostolo Zeno,* vol. i, p. 55. (Venice, 1752.)

the composers' small understanding; and a great part of the blame lies with the singers also, who show as little comprehension of interpretation.

Zeno had no inkling of how vehemently Muratori was to hit out. The latter came to condemn utterly not only opera, but all the music of his time, which, he said, had degenerated into boundless effeminacy, unnerving the hearer instead of purging and elevating him. He saw nothing but a monster in the modern opera, an agglomeration of a thousand absurdities, and he hoped for a wiser time that would help music to a reform as well.[1]

A proof of how near Marcello's satire and Muratori's criticism came to the truth is the unconditional surrender to convention to which a poet like Carlo Goldoni was obliged to stoop. Goldoni, the most appealing and most 'natural' of all Italian poets, went to Milan in 1732 with a finished libretto for an opera, *Amalasonta,* which he read to a patron, Count Prata, and to the singer Caffarelli. The malicious and narrow-minded old *castrato* openly made fun of the greenhorn, and the idealistic young poet was soon to learn from the benevolent count that neither the *Poetics* of Aristotle nor the *Epistles* of Horace were of the least use in the making of a libretto, which was subject to very special rules and regulations—in other words conventions.

Goldoni, on hearing this, threw his *Amalasonta* into the fire and never again attempted to break down the despotism of eunuchs, prima donnas and composers. In 1756 he wrote a preface for his libretto of *Statira*—dedicated to the 'nobilissime dame veneziane'—in which he expresses the not unreasonable thought that a libretto meant nothing as a poetical work and had better never be printed, lest the author should lay himself open to an unjust judgment:

When I write for music, the last person I consider is myself. I think of the singers, I think very much of the composer, I think of the pleasure of the audience; and if my dramas were only represented and not read, I should dare to hope for more justice of judgment.

What must Calzabigi have thought when he read that? He probably felt that Goldoni was giving vent to very apt thoughts in

[1] *Della perfetta poesia italiana.* (Modena, 1706.)

order to defend some exceedingly vapid librettos. Calzabigi too
thought of the composer, but without imperilling the dignity of his
subjects. To think of the singers was not his affair. For Goldoni
an opera was nothing more than, as Arnaud says, 'un concert dont
le drame est le prétexte.'

The most powerful urge to reform, to revolt against the opera, was
the quarrel about the relative merits of the Italian and the French
operatic type. 'Revolt' indeed! People are so prejudiced as never
to notice that there is no question of a true 'revolution' and to ignore
those who were the real operatic revolutionaries, if any: the composers of *opera buffa*. The different species and the national types
are so strictly separated from each other that the masters of the *tragédie
musicale* and the *opera seria* quite fail to see what is happening near
them. Voltaire certainly sees nothing. His definition of opera,
which Arteaga prefixed as motto to his history of Italian opera, is
written to the precise measure of Rameau's *tragédie lyrique*:

> Il faut se rendre à ce palais magique,
> Où les beaux vers, la danse, la musique,
> L'art de tromper les yeux par les couleurs,
> L'art plus heureux de séduire les cœurs
> De cent plaisirs font un plaisir unique.

Rousseau sees it, though. In 1752 he attacked French music as
such. In August of that year Italian *buffo* artists came to Paris and
made a powerful party for themselves and for him. The Encyclopaedists seconded him. Grimm scoffed at the tradition of French
opera. Diderot did not conceal his dislike of Rameau's operatic
ideal. They undermined French opera and prepared Gluck's success.

The immediate forerunner of the dedication of *Alceste,* however, is
the *Saggio sopra l'opera* by Count Francesco Algarotti (1712–64),
published in 1755. Algarotti, a friend of Frederick the Great,
represented the tasteful dilettantism of the time. His book, thanks
to the clarity and sensibleness of the ideas it contained and thanks to
its author's unassailable position, became a kind of aesthetic bible.
Opera was for him a unified work of art that had to subdue conventions: the conventions of the singers' despotism, of monotonous
'symphonies,' of mythological and historical subjects; it was to

restore dignity to the recitative by a more general use of the *accompagnato,* and to the aria by judicious changes of expression; chorus and dance were to be regarded as essential elements of an opera. Many of Algarotti's demands are almost literally identical with turns of phrase in the dedication of *Alceste.* Algarotti was the artistic adviser of the ducal theatre at Parma, at which Tommaso Traetta was active, and which was influenced by French operatic practices. He wrote, apart from an *Eneo in Troia,* an *Iphigénie en Aulide* in French prose, thus dealing with a subject which Diderot, who knew Racine's version, had pointed out as suitable for a grand opera as early as 1757.

A year after Algarotti's *Saggio* appeared, anonymously, a *Lettre sur le mécanisme de l'opéra italien,* which must quite certainly have come under Calzabigi's notice, for it takes his dissertation on Meta-stasio for its point of departure. Its author was a Tuscan minister of finance, M. de Villeneuve. He discusses the theatres and theatrical customs of Florence and has no wish to take part in the quarrels over the relative merits of Italian and French opera; his device is 'Ni Guelfe, ni Gibelin; ni Wigh, ni Thory' [*sic*]. He praises the Italian passion for opera, but deplores the unworthiness of Italian opera. He commends the art of the singers, but deprecates their supremacy as destructive of the meaning of a work of art. He regrets the monotony of the 'exit aria' and the sensuality of the spirit of opera: 'The construction of Italian opera is such that eyes and ears alone are required for it, . . . mind and heart are left in utter abeyance.' And what could a work of art that did not captivate mind and emotion mean to the age of Rousseau? It is clear that the time for *Alceste* had arrived.

What are we to say to these aesthetic controversies, seeing them as we do from a vantage-point almost two centuries distant? We say that they never touched the vital point of the matter. The abolition of the male soprano, the avoidance of inopportune *fioriture* and cadenzas, the destruction of the conventional aria form—all these are mere superficialities. A striving after simplicity, truth and naturalness may be questionable and ambiguous, for might not some new aesthetic Pilate ask: what *is* truth in opera? Is Handel as an opera composer not simple and natural too? In the last resort it is a question of the eternal and for ever undecided *fundamental* conflict between opera and drama. As a great and penetrating critic of Shakespeare has said, opera is the natural enemy of the drama.

That is the heart of the matter. What Gluck did was simply this: he once again shifted the balance between opera and drama, more or less as, before him, the Venetian musicians after Monteverdi had moved the operatic centre of gravity in the direction of music, or as later Hugo Wolf, after Schubert and Schumann, moved the centre of gravity in song towards declamation and the accompaniment. Gluck forced music back in favour of drama; but it was only a question of finding the *balance* between music and drama, a stroke of fortune that has occurred rarely in the history of opera—three or four times at the most. He wrote operas *different* from those of his more ingenuous Italian contemporaries; but it nevertheless remains an open question whether his are better than theirs.

Opera is the drama's natural enemy; but it is also something essentially different from the drama and cannot be said to have merely swallowed it whole, as the wolf swallowed Red-Riding-Hood. The excellence of an opera does not depend on the degree to which it submits to 'reform.' That an opera cannot do without dramatic content and must not be a bare succession of beautiful musical numbers is certain. But does not the proportion of music and drama often fluctuate within one and the same opera? Is not everything that happens in the second act of *Don Giovanni*, up to the churchyard scene, so much trifling, dramatically speaking? Yet Mozart bridges this dramatic gap by music, music that is doubly enchanting. Does not in the second act of *Tristan* the outward action stand still until the appearance of the king? And yet this colloquy in song is perhaps the peak, or at any rate the deepest, most abysmal depth in Wagnerian music-drama. On the other hand, it is equally certain that opera is incapable of expressing dramatic significance with too small a modicum of music. Gluck once declared he forgot that he was a musician when he composed an opera, a pronouncement which, like the pronouncements of all 'reformers,' had better be accepted *cum grano salis*. The truth is that he never forgot it and that he merely intended to make it understood, as politely as possible, that the common or garden operatic musicians of his time too often forgot that they were *dramatists*. Gluck did not defeat Piccinni by his principles (if indeed he defeated him at all), but by his personality.

'ALCESTE'

Alceste has not the youthfulness and the undying theatrical charm of *Orfeo,* but it was destined to remain Gluck's and Calzabigi's chief work and masterpiece. Let Calzabigi himself relate the plot:

Admetus, king of Pherae in Thessaly, husband of Alcestis, finding himself about to lose his life, Apollo, who had been received by him on being exiled from heaven, induces the Fates to spare his life on condition that one be found to die in his stead. Alcestis agrees to the exchange and dies; but Hercules, the friend of Admetus, who had come to Pherae at this juncture, recovers Alcestis from Thanatos and restores her to her husband.

Such is the content of the famous tragedy of Euripides entitled *Alcestis*; but in the place of Hercules I have introduced Apollo beholden to Admetus, to work this miracle out of gratitude.[1]

This independence of Euripides on Calzabigi's part proves his dramatic sense. The *Alcestis* of Euripides is not a glorification of conjugal devotion, but of hospitality. Hercules comes by chance into the house of mourning, whence the body of Alcestis is about to be removed; but Admetus, not to offend against the laws of hospitality, tells him that a stranger has died under his roof. Intemperate Hercules eats, drinks and blusters in his quarters until a servant

[1] 'Admeto Rè di Fera in Tessaglia Sposo di Alceste, trovandosi sul punto di perder la vita, Apollo che esiliato dal Cielo era stato accolto da lui, ottiene delle Parche, che non morrà, purchè si trovi che muoja in vece sua. Alceste accetta il cambio, e muore; ma Ercole amico d'Admeto che giunge in Fera in tal circostanza, ritoglie Alceste alla Morte, e la rende al suo Sposo.

Tale è il piano della celebre Tragedia d'Euripide intitolata Alceste: ma io in luogo d'Ercole ho introdotto Apollo beneficato da Admeto, ad operar per gratitudine questo prodigio.

indignantly reproves and enlightens him. Whereupon Hercules lies in wait for Thanatos (Death) at the funeral monument and leads the veiled Alcestis back to her husband.

Only where drama was a cult could such a solution be admitted; only in the Athenian amphitheatre was this Hercules possible. Unfortunately, in the Paris *Alceste* of 1776—if one may anticipate—the reviser, Guillard, reintroduced Hercules, and it is probable that the aria for that character, 'C'est en vain que l'Enfer,' is not by Gluck at all, but by Gossec, who furbished it up from an old aria from Gluck's *Ezio* ('Ecco alle mie catene'). Hercules enters the sacred grove while Admetus and Alcestis are still engaged in the noble contest for the sacrifice. He scares the divinities of death away with his club, and Apollo appears, promising the athlete immortality and admittance to the assembly of the gods. Alcestis never carries out her sacrifice, so that the unravelling approaches that of the old *festa teatrale*. But again, exactly as in the case of *Orfeo ed Euridice,* we cannot simply decide in favour either of the Italian or the French version of *Alceste.* Gluck made more radical changes in this work for Paris than in any other opera of his, and this cost him more labour than the writing of a new work would have done; his representation of the inward conflict of Alcestis, the wife and mother held to life by so many tender bonds, is much more affecting; he made a broader scene of the incident where the crowd gives vent to joy at the restoration of its ruler; he made the scenes between husband and wife more profound. Thus the ideal form of *Alceste* for present-day use would again be a compromise between two versions.

The earlier *Alceste,* too, has its dramatic faults. Two Metastasian confidants are still retained in it, a relapse on the poet's part to which relapses on Gluck's correspond, such as an occasional use of *recitativo secco* that is hard to explain. Apollo's gratitude for the kindly treatment he received in the disguise of a servant is no *visible,* plastic motive, so that he remains to some extent in the character of a *deus ex machina.* On the other hand the apparition of the spirits in the death scene is perhaps too theatrical, for Hades should not become as palpable here as in *Orfeo.* The greatest weakness lies in the character and the position of Admetus. He should unquestionably grow into the

chief figure next to Alcestis, as in *Parsifal* Amfortas is the chief
figure next to the hero. A sacrifice such as he accepts should not
be acceptable even to the hallowed person of a king whose duty it
is to preserve himself for his people. But the conflict in Admetus's
soul is but languid, and even during the flattering chorus of the
conclusion he remains too much in the background and too inactive.
Here none but Beethoven could have given Gluck the lesson he
needed, *i.e.* with the finale of *Fidelio,* that cantata-like glorification
of the heroine, and Admetus should have taken a share similar
to that of Florestan. That, however, would have meant an abandonment to music of which Gluck, the dramatist and anti-musician,
was not capable, nor desired to be capable.

Still, what a great artistic feat is here, taken all round, and what an
abundance of incidental beauty! The realistic proclamation of the
oracle by the herald (*banditore*), the people's great scene of lamentation
before the palace, with the solos of Ismene and Evander, the mourning
dumb-show, the orchestral interjections, Alcestis's resolve to sacrifice
herself, her adjuration of the spirits of Hades to whom she offers
herself, her farewell from Admetus and her last request to him,
weighed down as she is with the heaviness of death. Beauty enters
with the overture, called an *intrada* by Gluck, presumably because
it leads without a break into the scene. It is the first truly tragic
introduction to an opera:

The *tutti* is darkly coloured by the trio of trombones, the form not in the least sonata-like and 'dramatic,' but heavily charged, neutral, purely a prologue to a gloomy action, and especially disconsolate where it becomes gentle and supplicating:

But fate is inexorable, like the sustained A in the basses. This piece in D minor is the ancestor of an illustrious line, from the overture to *Don Giovanni* to the *Tragic Overture* of Brahms.

The concentration of the 'symphony' is set off by the amplitude of the mourning scene, resolved by the herald's announcement. Contemporaries were hardly fit to appreciate this breadth, and it is this, one must suppose, which provoked the unfair designation of 'the dismal *Alceste*.' But see how mightily Gluck gathered up the whole in the choral refrain:

which persists even at the appearance of Alcestis. This appearance—the words of which Mozart also composed—takes shape in a majestic recitative and an aria embracing all the feelings of Alcestis as queen, mother and wife, an aria without *da capo* which must have struck the hearers as the most audacious breach of convention and yet as pure and convincing form.

This simplicity and persuasive power grows in the temple scene that follows: a procession to the altar with a 'march' in G major for strings and flutes; a short address from the high priest, supported by swelling chords of bassoons, horns and trombones, and his urging, almost importunate antiphonal song with chorus, repeated by the latter after Alcestis's touching entreaty of Apollo; the priest's growing agitation which gravely prepares the solemn oracle:

the crowd benumbed with horror, with the male chorus aghast behind the scene; the general dispersal; Alcestis alone on the stage with her children—for mankind is alone in misfortune; the thought of self-sacrifice flashing through her; her heroic resolution culminating in her glorious invocation of the nether world in an *aria eroica*—yes, still an *aria eroica*, but one already raised above all conventions. Thus when the two agitated messengers, Evander and Ismene, rush in to announce the imminent death of the king, and when the chorus concludes the act by showing a despondent and too complaisant resignation, we are already aware that the king is not to die.

At the beginning of the second act Gluck and Calzabigi make a concession to the exigencies of the 'parti secondarie.' Ismene, the confidante who accompanies Alcestis to the grove dedicated to the divinities of the underworld, is given her share in the dialogue and her aria, which, although apt and sincerely felt in itself, retards the action and remains a set number for all that it is once interrupted by Alcestis. But soon Alcestis is left alone, and now the recitative begins a description of the terrifying region in which she finds herself that can only be called a lofty counterpart to the description of Elysium in *Orfeo,* and one scarcely less great. One of the finest traits is the 'lonely' entry of the oboe, descending from B to B flat as it paints the dread silence of the night in which brood the spirits of Hades. Gluck has his own system of key relationships in recitative: turns towards flat keys symbolize depression and those towards sharp keys excitement, and he had already handled this most sensitively in *Orfeo.* This oboe passage is, so to say, a concentration and symbol of this system in the smallest possible form.

The following aria is no less magnificent. Acheron becomes vocally audible, an awful sound that makes Alcestis shudder to the marrow and takes away her breath so that she can express herself but haltingly, until, listening to those monotonous calls, she becomes accustomed to them and finds courage to attempt another appeal, which only induces the spirits to make their welcome all too urgent. This dialogue between the mortal woman and the powers of darkness is a weakening; but how else was it to be made plausible that Alcestis should ask to return once more to the house of the living in order to take leave of them? The E flat major aria of Alcestis that follows, with its accompaniment of muted strings and English horns, has the softness and 'tenderness' of the age of sensibility, a softness which again, as in *Orfeo,* appeases the infernal spirits: with a 'roundelay' they accompany Alcestis out of their realm, as it were, and to the threshold of life.

In the next scene, inside the palace, the unexpected recovery of the king is first of all brightly and festively celebrated with choral dance and song, and in a short dialogue with Evander Admetus learns, half startled and half touched, that a stranger has died for him. He ardently hails Alcestis, until he is taken aback by her half concealed sigh, plies her with questions in an *andante appassionato,* to which she replies hesitantly, and at last tears the secret from her. His anguish is expressed more profoundly and convincingly in the recitative than in the A minor aria ('No crudel, non posso vivere') that follows, in spite of the tempestuous *allegro* of the middle section. As an aria it is somewhat out of place here.

Admetus rushes away. The great mourning ceremony with which Alcestis prepares for her own death, with childlike piety invokes the blessing of the gods upon her children's heads and for the last time greets the sacred marriage-bed, is crowned by this glorious *lento:*

with its agitated conclusion. Each lyrical expansion is framed and held together by the people's choral lamentations.

The opening of the third act is given up to an outline of Admetus's state of mind, with violent recitative and a long—too long—aria in C minor: the fruitless raving and fruitless grief of a man who must obey the decrees of the gods. Alcestis approaches to bid him farewell and to implore him not to give the children a stepmother. Here again the recitative is more expressive than the succeeding duet between the couple and the outpouring of Admetus. The nether world announces itself—unfortunately much too palpably and too disputatiously—and carries off Alcestis. Admetus follows. A *lento* with a terrifying sustained horn note, mounting plaints of flutes and oboes, and stifled chords in the strings depicts the stunned feelings of those left behind. A choral threnody comes next, then Admetus's attempt at suicide, and the apparition of Apollo, who had been the guest of Admetus and now restores Alcestis to life. A short final chorus brings the work to its close, an abrupt, chilling close, for our memory returns again and again to the second act and to all the tragic scenes.

The outward success of *Alceste* was great. Calzabigi, in a letter to Montefani, speaks of sixty performances in Vienna, and in his *Riposta* even of seventy in two series, of which the second began in 1778. In Italy the work was a complete failure only in Bologna (1778), which ever since 1763 had been unfavourably disposed towards Gluck. In Padua (1777), Naples (1785) and Florence (1786), on the other hand, it was afforded at least respectful attention, although we may be sure that the representations nowhere did justice to Gluck's demands. Calzabigi pointed out that, with the exception of *Orfeo*, which Gluck was able to produce personally at Parma in 1769, none of his works was seen in Italy in the light it required for its effect:

They are pieces for the *theatre* and not for the chamber, rather like the Athena of Pheidias, which at first sight in the studio looked raw, rude and carelessly hewn out; but afterwards, seen on the noble site for which it was predestined, had an effect of the most surprising beauty. . . . The Italian public has as yet little idea of these theatrical optics.

Gluck

Gluck was certainly dissatisfied. In the dedication of *Paride ed Elena* he (or rather Calzabigi as his spokesman) makes use of the same image:

The only reason that induced me to issue my music of *Alceste* in print was the hope of finding followers who, by way of the paths already opened up and stimulated by the ample suffrages of an enlightened public, would be quickened into abolishing the abuses that have insinuated themselves into the Italian spectacles, and to bring them to the highest possible degree of perfection. I am grieved to say that I have so far tried this in vain. Dilettanti and smatterers, of whom there is an infinite crowd, and who are the greatest of obstacles to the progress of the fine arts, have set themselves against a method which, once it gained a foothold, would destroy at one blow their pretensions to any power of decision and any capacity for action. It has been thought that *Alceste* may be judged after having been rehearsed at haphazard, badly conducted and worse performed; that it is possible to calculate in a chamber the effect it is capable of making in a theatre, which is as wise as it would have been, in a city of Greece in the old days, to attempt to judge at the distance of a few feet the statues intended to be set upon the highest columns.

How right Gluck was to complain about the lack of successors and a want of comprehension is proved by the fact that a few years after the creation of *Alceste* Christoph Martin Wieland wrote another libretto of that title, which was composed by Anton Schweitzer and performed at Weimar in 1773 and 1774. It cannot be called an attack on Gluck, whom Wieland revered. Indeed Wieland was a virtuoso of aesthetic assimilation, of second-hand sensibility, and much too cultivated a man not at least to suspect the significance of Gluck, just as he was the first in Germany to understand at any rate part of the poetic greatness of Shakespeare—the fantastic and lovable side of the Shakespeare of *The Tempest* and *A Midsummer Night's Dream*—while Lessing had become merely theoretically conscious of the English poet's genius.

Wieland wrote his *Alceste* in the first place for patriotic reasons. He had been annoyed by Burney, who had seemed to him to deal too contemptuously with German vocal music, and wished to prove that German could be at least as sonorous an operatic language as French. But he also had practical reasons. He wanted to create an opera capable of being performed in the most modest setting, an opera for such pocket-size courts as Weimar or Gotha and for free cities of the realm like Augsburg or Nuremberg, to which Gluck in his magnificence had never given so much as a thought. Wieland therefore reduced the mighty subject to familiar and sentimental terms, and he does not improve matters by giving Admetus an important dramatic function next to Alcestis: the whole is once again a Meta-stasiad, as far removed from the spirit of antiquity as eighteenth-century Weimar was from the old Hellenic Pherae. For his mawkishness Wieland received a well-deserved corrective in a serio-comic vein from Goethe (which he never resented), and with that the matter was settled, Schweitzer's music not having exceeded pocket-size either. But it must have been a sad experience for Gluck to learn that one of the shrewdest and most receptive minds of the time had shown so little understanding of Gluckian pro-portions.

The year 1768 in Gluck's life is again plunged in some darkness. It was certainly not a year of great creative activity; we know only of the remodelling of the *Innocenza giustificata* into *La Vestale*. But 1769 finds him as composer at the court where his ideas of reforms had been so effectively prepared: the court of Parma. For the marriage of the Infante Don Ferdinando to one of Maria Theresa's daughters, Maria Amalia, he performed his *Orfeo* as a one-act opera, i.e. without an interval, preceding it with an *Atto di Bauci e Filemone* and an *Atto d'Aristeo,* and these again were prefaced by a prologue, *Le feste d'Apollo.* The books of the three pieces that came before *Orfeo* were written by the court poet of Parma, Carlo Innocenzio Frugoni. The singers were of the highest eminence, among them the eunuch Giuseppe Millico, who became the friend of Gluck (and of Calza-bigi), and Lucrezia Agujari, of whose fabulous compass and skill in florid singing the young Mozart gives us so striking a sample in a letter of 1770. For this singular undertaking Gluck borrowed more than a dozen numbers—about half of the complete score—from earlier works, for which he can hardly be blamed. In the prologue the aid of Apollo is invoked for the marriage festivities with song, dance and three solemn arias; in *Bauci e Filemone* the hoary pair

Philemon and Baucis are transformed into a shepherd and shepherdess by Jupiter, who promises them immortality, not without
giving a sample of his power in the part of thunderer; the *Atto
d'Aristeo,* too, introduces pastoral demigods and closes with the
voci di giubilo appropriate to a wedding. The only remarkable
feature is the modish Graecization of these accustomed *feste teatrali.*

'PARIDE ED ELENA'

The year 1770 ripened the last fruit of Gluck's collaboration with
Calzabigi, *Paride ed Elena,* performed on 30th November and published in Vienna before the end of the year. Millico sang Paris,
Mlle Katharina Schindler Helen, Mme Theresia Kurz Cupid,
and Noverre directed the dancing. The work is judged by posterity
in relation to *Orfeo* and *Alceste* much as the last common production
of Mozart and da Ponte, *Così fan tutte,* had for a long time been judged
in relation to *Figaro* and *Don Giovanni.* The two earlier operas were
praised, but the last was dropped or at least objected to for various
reasons. Actually *Paride ed Elena* is a very curious and daring work.
Calzabigi made a wholly unheroic transformation of the abduction
of Helen that was to unchain the Trojan war. True, Helen is
Queen of Sparta, but only the betrothed of Menelaus, so that the
contemporaries and ourselves are spared a tale of adultery. Paris
lands with his companions on the Peloponnesian coast to claim the
fairest woman in Greece as reward for his judgment in favour of
Venus. But the venture is not attended by immediate success, for
Helen is a strict Spartan, brought up on Lycurgan principles before
the time of Lycurgus, and not inclined to fall into the arms of the
voluptuous Phrygian, radiant though he be, without more ado.
The guest is honoured with a great Spartan martial ballet, but received
coolly rather than ardently by Helen; and he makes his first decided
advances with an aria in four strophes, which is so rudely rejected
that he has a fainting fit. He repeats his attack, first in person, then
by letter—both times in vain. The result is a stern order to depart.
Great preparations are feigned and the coffers are packed. But the
farewell at last draws a confession of love from Helen. Vainly does

Pallas appear in the clouds and prophesy the fatal issue of an elopement. The pair take comfort in the thought that Cupid, who had
all the time eagerly played match-maker for Paris under the name
of Erasto, would continue to favour them with his patronage.

It has exercised many minds how Calzabigi could have arrived
at so odd a formation and transformation of the subject; but he
himself solved the riddle in the motto of the printed score, taken from
the *Heroides* of Ovid ('Bella gerant fortes; tu, Pari, semper ama'),
and in his *Risposta* of 1790 (p. 73): 'Paris and Helen are culled and
imitated from the two famous *Heroides* of Ovid.' This, then, is
where the declaration of love by letter comes from. The dramatiza-
tion of the two erotic epistles of Ovid (or of one of his imitators)
follows the classical model sometimes word for word; every motive
that prompted writing and replying is adopted and developed. (In
this explicit reverence for the classics too, by the way, is a sting for
Metastasio, who, as Burney tells us, thought too little of the ancients.)

Helen finds herself in precisely the same situation as Isolde in the
first act of *Tristan,* where she conceals her love behind an appearance
of harshness and hardly admits it even to herself. The central
interest of the Ovidian pair of elegies and of Calzabigi's drama,
however, lies in the contrast between the chaste, stern Spartan woman
and the wanton son of Asia, in a contest of the sexes sharpened by
differences of character and morals. Calzabigi confessed to have
been hampered in his task of writing *Paride ed Elena,* which he was
expected to turn into a work of a festive nature. He was thus
unable, he said, to bring into play either fear or pity, which alone
were capable of moving the hearer deeply. Still, this drama of a
fateful passion that tears down all barriers is in a certain sense a
forerunner of *Tristan and Isolde.* There is a secret tragedy behind all
its scenes.

The defects of the work are palpable. The very fact that we are
spared the tragedy of adultery robs the action of dramatic weight and
Helen's inner conflict of tension. Paris himself learns only at the
beginning of the fourth act that Helen is betrothed, so that until
then he can regard her resistance only as the wilful game of a prude,
the more so because Cupid had assured him already in the first act,

on welcoming him on Spartan territory, that he was to win Helen.
And all this shilly-shallying is prolonged over five acts! And then
this rather harmless abduction becomes the cause of the sack of
Troy! Pallas Athena can hardly wonder if her warnings, her very
conventional aria and the threats of her accompanying chorus are
set at naught.

Gluck nevertheless composed all this with conviction. The contrast between Europe and Asia, between the Greek and the Phrygian,
stimulated him; indeed, it would seem that he had something like
the ancients' characterization of the modes in view when he composed the 'Aeolian' middle section of the 'symphony' and the
'Dorian' chorus of the Spartans. This is what he says in his
dedication of the score to Don Giovanni, Duke of Braganza:

The drama of Paris did not require from the composer's fancy those
strong passions, those majestic images and those tragic situations which
in *Alceste* shook the spectators, nor did it occasion so many grandiose
harmonic effects. Thus the same forceful and energetic music will surely
not be expected. . . . There is here no question of a wife about to lose
her husband, who, in order to save him, has the courage to evoke the
infernal gods in a dread forest wrapt in the blackest shades of night; who
in the extreme agonies of death still trembles for the destiny of her sons,
and has to tear herself from a husband she adores. It is here the case of a
young lover presented in contrast with the waywardness of a lovely and
honest woman, who at last triumphs by all the wiles of a designing passion.
I was obliged to exert myself in order to find some variety of colour, seeking
it in the different characters of the two nations, Phrygia and Sparta, by
contrasting the rude and savage nature of the one with all that is delicate
and soft in the other. I believed, seeing that song in an opera is nothing
else than a substitute for declamation, that I ought to imitate in Helen the
native ruggedness of her country, and I thought that my having preserved
that character in the music would not earn me any reproach for having
sometimes stooped so low as to become trivial. . . .

This 'triviality' is to be felt at once in the opening chorus, where
the companions of Paris offer a sacrifice to Venus on the Spartan
coast, with much the same kind of music that Neapolitan fishermen
might still sing to-day in a light 3-8 time, with solos and with a
swelling dominant held above the orchestral accompaniment; or

where, immediately afterwards, Paris himself sings his famous aria with oboe *obbligato*:

O del mio dolce ardor bramato oggetto,

which is nothing else than a cavatina in a minor key in the later Neapolitan operatic style. 'Trivial' in an entirely different sense is the principal number of the first act: the duet between Paris and Cupid. It is a conversational, dialogue-like duet resembling, let us say, the trio, 'Soll ich dich, Teurer, nicht mehr sehn,' in *The Magic Flute* (see page 119).

But some scenes of the second act are the reverse of trivial, as when Cupid describes the attractions of Paris to the coy princess, with a wheedling, almost lubric *ostinato* sextolet figure in the strings; when the lovers outdo each other in recitative at their first meeting; when Helen in a trio ironically advises Paris to allow himself some respite and to think of some possible forsaken mistresses who might be languishing for him—and the expression of irony was surely something new in the history of opera. The duet in which, after an initial indecision, Helen rejects the pleading Paris, demands the greatest contrast of feelings (see page 121). And this almost *buffo*-like art of concerted writing is pushed even farther in the trio of the fourth act, where Helen becomes suspicious of Cupid-Erasto, who secretly makes merry over her fruitless resistance, and Paris learns with pain the contents of her letter. In striking contrast with such intimate traits are Helen's two great arias: that which concludes the fourth act with an expression of apparent firmness

PARIDE ED ELENA 1770

Elena

ta - ci, par - ti, pre - ten - di in- va - no ch'a un fin·to amore o in·sa - no tut-ti i tri - on - fi t'a - mo, t'a - do - ro, t'a - do ro su - oi ce - da la mia vir - tù.

Paride

of disposition yielding to the wildest lashings of passion, and the heroic one, made more heroic still by its accompaniment of horns, trumpets and drums:

> Donzelle semplici
> No, non credete
> A quelle lagrime
> Che voi vedete
> Sugli occhi spargersi
> Del traditor.

> (Simple maidens, ne'er believe
> In the tears that you see welling
> From the eyes, false anguish telling,
> Of the traitors who deceive.)

It is a *stretto* not unlike that of Manrico, a counterpart to the Duke of Mantua's 'La donna è mobile.' Even more startlingly different is the shallow conclusion, in which the lovers vow their everlasting troth and, after the appeasement of a storm provoked by Pallas, are invited to embark by the full chorus. Gluck has scarcely written a more incongruous work, but precisely because of this incongruity this opera is perhaps his most curious.

INTERMEZZO

Paride ed Elena was a failure, at any rate in comparison with *Orfeo* and *Alceste*. The work reached only twenty performances in Vienna and was at first in demand on no other stage. Only in 1777 was it performed again, in Naples, and with an obviously 'pedagogic' purpose. A number of aristocratic dilettanti, under the guidance of the Marchese di Corleto, desired to stage it as an example whereby the decadence of the Neapolitan opera might be demonstrated. Calza-bigi himself confirmed its 'minore incontro' and readily took the blame for it upon himself. He declared that he did not care to write for the stage thereafter and himself appointed his successor, Marco Coltellini. Whether that is true need not be inquired. His connection with Gluck was not wholly severed, or at any rate it was renewed later; but an estrangement certainly occurred. In any case Gluck never set another line by Calzabigi to music, nor did he engage in collaboration with Coltellini.

Calzabigi's career during the years 1771–4 is obscure. He dis-appeared from the Viennese court, where he never emerged again, and although he retained his title and pension, no occupation was ever offered him again. Pèra's biographical dictionary informs us that he drew the empress's displeasure upon his head by some erotic adventures with goddesses of the stage, which sounds extremely credible, since loose morals were the greatest of crimes in the Vienna of Maria Theresa. In 1778 we find him at Pisa in unaccustomed retirement. But he had attained to his goal in Vienna: the downfall of Metastasio as 'theatre poet.'

After these three dramas [i.e. *Orfeo, Alceste* and *Paride*] Metastasio no longer showed himself upon the stage. For comparison the *Olimpiade* was chosen with music by Gassmann and sumptuously given on a festive occasion at court. It had only three performances. From that moment (Calzabigi being unwilling to write anything more) the management thought of procuring a poet who should write in his manner. He was himself charged with finding such a man; he himself engaged Coltellini at a splendid salary.

Whether the 'able writer' whom Gluck urged to make a dramatic version of Dryden's ode for St. Cecilia's day was Calzabigi is doubtful. We are informed of this by Dr. Charles Burney, who had visited Vienna in 1772:

The chevalier Gluck . . . has lately suggested to an able writer, a plan for a new ode on St. Cecilia's Day, which discovers both genius and discernment. Lord Cowper had, some time since, Dryden's Ode per-formed to Handel's music at Florence; but set to a literal Italian translation given *totidem syllabis,* in order to preserve the music as entire as possible. But this tenderness for the musician, was so much at the expense of the poet, that Dryden's divine Ode, became not only unpractical, but unin-telligible in this wretched version. The music has since been performed at Vienna to the same words, and many parts of it were very much liked, in despite of the nonsense through which it was conveyed to the ears of the audience.

Gluck was exceedingly struck with the thoughts of our great poet, and wished to have an ode on the same subject, but written on a different plan, which would preserve as many of them as possible. His idea was this; a poem of so great a length, could never be sung to modern music by *one person.* Now, as Dryden's Ode is all *narrative*; there seems no pro-priety in distributing it among different persons, in the performance. He wished therefore, to have it thrown into a dramatic form, in which the interlocutors might speak what passion suggests; and this has been done in the following manner: it begins with a feast of Bacchus, at which Alexander and Thais preside. They agree to call in Timotheus to sing to them; but before his arrival, the hero and his mistress differ in opinion concerning his merit; the one supposes him to be inferior to what has been reported of him; and the other, superior. This contention enlivens the dialogue, and interests the audience till the arrival of the bard, who begins to sing of the Trojan war, which animates Alexander so much, that he breaks out into the complaints attributed to him by the old story of having no Homer, like Achilles, to record his actions.

Gluck

Gluck as Handel's rival, forsooth! Gluck as composer of a dramatic oratorio that looks devilishly like a Metastasian *festa teatrale*! He certainly did not compose it, and it is characteristic that the years after *Paride ed Elena* and after the breach with Calzabigi were years of groping during which Gluck regarded one era of his dramatic creation as closed before he had found the opening for another. They are the years of his acquaintance with Klopstock, the poet of the *Messiade,* who after the decline of the rationalistic baroque poetry introduced the age of the German poets of sensibility.

Gluck, curiously enough, came into contact not only with Friedrich Gottlieb Klopstock (1724–1803), the susceptible writer of odes, but also with Klopstock the 'bard,' who, according to Gerstenberg, the author of *Das Gedicht eines Skalden,* had taken fire from northern mythology during his sojourn in Denmark (1764–7). Vienna, too, possessed an eminent representative of this bardic poetry, the Jesuit Denis ('Sined'), one of whose odes Mozart once tried to compose, only to set it aside as 'too bombastic for his fine ears.' Gluck kept to the purest and richest source—Klopstock himself; but it is quite possibly that his attention was drawn to Klopstock by Denis, whom the former had told as early as 1767 that he had been working at his 'Hermanns-Schlacht, a tragedy with bardic songs,' which he intended to have printed before long, and that the acquaintance was brought about by the Austrian ambassador, Count Wellsperg.

The *Hermanns-Schlacht* had appeared in 1769 with a dedication to Joseph II. Klopstock, who turned his eyes eagerly towards Vienna, had pinned extravagant hopes of a professional and personal nature to this dedication, hopes that were nursed by Viennese friends, but were not destined to be fulfilled. Under their spell Klopstock sought to win Gluck as an associate and to persuade him to set the bardic songs in the *Hermanns-Schlacht* to music. (Of a composition of the drama itself or an operatic version of it Gluck never thought, nor could he have done so; and those who state anything of the kind merely prove that they cannot have read the *Hermanns-Schlacht* any more than they, or anybody else, have read the *Messiade.*)

Let us at once pursue the history of this music for the *Hermanns-Schlacht* to the end. On 14th August 1773 Gluck apologized to Klopstock, who was then living at Göttingen, for not having as yet sent him the verses already composed. The reasons he gives are curious and truly Gluckian: from them transpires the instinctive antipathy which the South German continues to feel for the 'Prussian' to this day.[1] He fears that his music is not to everybody's taste, least of all to that of the inhabitants of Berlin, where his *Alceste* had been denigrated. (Nevertheless, Hiller, the cantor of St. Thomas's in Leipzig, had published an admiring notice of this very *Alceste* in the *Wöchentliche Nachrichten* of 24th October 1768.)

A kind of music that requires enthusiasm seems to be as yet quite strange to your neighbourhood, as I saw clearly in the criticisms of my *Alceste* published in Berlin. [But] I am so great an admirer of yourself [Klopstock] that I promise you (unless you should be thinking of coming to Vienna) to make a journey to Hamburg next year in order to make your personal acquaintance, in which case I will engage to sing you, not only many things from the *Hermanns-Schlacht,* but also some of your sublime odes, thus enabling you to judge how near I may have come to your greatness or how much I may have obscured it by my music.

This 'personal acquaintance' materialized in the spring of 1774, at Carlsruhe, when Gluck was on the way to Paris with his wife and his niece (or adopted child). Gluck sang and played some

[1] The strongest proof of 'Prussian' lack of understanding is the letter written by Princess Amalie, the stern and elderly sister of Frederick the Great, to Kirnberger, who had submitted the score of *Iphigénie en Aulide* to her: 'Herr Gluck, in my opinion, will never be able to pass as an adroit man in composition. He has (1) no invention at all, (2) a poor, wretched gift of melody, and (3) no accent, no expression—it all sounds alike. . . . Lastly and chiefly, the whole opera is thoroughly miserable; but this is the new taste, and it has very many adherents.' As Frederick the Great himself judged similarly, if not worse, it is not difficult to understand that Gluck would never have attained to the rank of 'generalissimus' in Berlin. It is the more amusing to note that, thanks to the exertions of Reichardt and later of Spontini, Berlin became, under Frederick's successors, the leading centre for the cultivation of Gluck in Germany, indeed almost the only centre.

portions of the *Hermanns-Schlacht* to the poet and made Marianne, his tenderly loved adopted daughter, perform several of the odes. It was only when Klopstock desired to hear his *Sommernacht* ('Wenn der Schimmer von dem Monde nun herab'), that Gluck said: 'That she cannot sing yet,' and himself sang the three verses, with a raucous voice but with much expression. Marianne was the daughter of Gluck's sister, who had married Claudius Hedler, a riding-master of the hussars. About 1769, when she was some ten years of age, the childless Gluck couple took her into their house and adopted her. The eunuch Millico gave her singing lessons, which had been begun by Gluck himself, but given up in a fit of temper. She must have been a being of rare charm, and up to her premature death (22nd April 1776) she played a part in the house of Gluck similar to that played by Marianne Martinez at Metastasio's. A gentleman of Carlsruhe has left us an attractive description of this first meeting between Gluck and Klopstock:

During his [Klopstock's] presence here appeared one fine morning the Chevalier Gluck with his wife and niece. . . . On two evenings in succession they regaled the court, where nobody was admitted but a few gentlemen, Klopstock and myself, with their divine music. The old man sang and played right *con amore* many a portion of the *Messiade* [read *Hermanns-Schlacht*] set to music by him, his wife accompanied him in a few other pieces, and the amiable niece several times sang the song 'Ich bin ein deutsches Mädchen' most enchantingly.

The visit to the court of Baden was repeated on their return from Paris in the autumn of 1774, and Klopstock received the Glucks again at the beginning of 1775, that time at Strasburg and Rastatt, where Marianne sang 'Che farò' and fragments from *Alceste* for the poet. The evening gave rise to a banteringly gallant engagement, in which Marianne's share was a promise to send these pieces to the poet from Vienna marked with precise directions for their interpretation, in order that he again might convey them to his own niece in Hamburg. On 24th June, however, in a letter which, among other things, deals with the temporary failure of Gluck's 'diplomatic action' on behalf of Klopstock, he confesses that these directions could not be set down on paper:

. . . I believe that it would appear to you just as difficult, if you were asked to instruct anybody by letter, how and with what expression he should declaim your Messiah; all this is a matter of feeling, and cannot well be explained. . . .

With the *Hermanns-Schlacht,* too, Gluck left the poet and posterity in the lurch. He carried the melodies about with him in his head without ever arriving at the decision to write them down. When in 1783 Johann Friedrich Reichardt, the *Capellmeister* of Frederick the Great and at that time still the friend of Goethe and Schiller, who was an enthusiastic partisan of Gluck's, visited him in Vienna, Klopstock was one of the topics of conversation after the midday meal. Gluck promised to let Reichardt hear some of the music from the *Hermanns-Schlacht* as well as a few of the odes. His wife anxiously warned him not to exert and excite himself, for Gluck had already suffered from a stroke and was wont to take fire unawares at the clavier. After coffee and a walk, however, he sang several of these pieces to an accompaniment of a few chords with a weak, rough voice and a heavy tongue, and Reichardt, who was quite carried away, obtained permission to write down one of the odes from memory. 'Between the songs from the *Hermanns-Schlacht,*' he said, 'Gluck several times imitated the sound of horns and the cries of the fighters behind their shields. He even wished to invent a special instrument.'

It was to be his last work. 'Although the *Hermanns-Schlacht* is now to be my last work, I nevertheless believe, that it will not be the least significant of my productions, since I gathered together the chief material for it before the time old age began to enfeeble my powers of thought,' he wrote in his last letter to Klopstock. He became young again whenever he delivered something from the work. Hot tears coursed down his cheeks when he came to the final chorus of the bards:

> Wodan! unbeleidigt von uns,
> Fielen sie bey deinen Altären uns an!
> Wodan! unbeleidigt von uns,
> Erhoben sie ihr Beil gegen dein freyes Volk!

(Woden! unoffended by us
Did they close to thy altars attack us!
Woden! unoffended by us,
Raised they their axes 'gainst thy free people!)

He tried to dictate the music to his pupil, Salieri, but he could no longer contrive it. Not a note of the work is preserved.

It is otherwise with the odes of Klopstock which Gluck set to music. In the last days of 1785 Artaria in Vienna brought out a slender engraved book of *Klopstock's Oden und Lieder beym Clavier zu singen*. It contained but seven numbers, viz.:

(1) *Vaterlandslied* ('Ich bin ein deutsches Mädchen').
(2) *Wir und Sie* ('Was tat dir, Thor').
(3) *Schlachtgesang* ('Wie erscholl der Gesang').
(4) *Der Jüngling* ('Schweigend sahe der May').
(5) *Die Sommernacht* ('Wenn der Schimmer').
(6) *Die frühen Gräber* (1773) ('Willkommen, o silberner Mond').
(7) *Die Neigung* ('Nein, ich widerstrebe nicht mehr').[1]

Gluck composed *Die Sommernacht* a second time: this later version is to be found in Voss's *Musen-Almanach auf das Jahr* 1785 (p. 78). Two of the seven songs published by Artaria (Nos. 4 and 6) had already appeared (No. 4 inan earlier form) in the *Göttinger Musen-almanach* for 1775. An eighth setting of an ode by Klopstock, *Der Tod* ('O, Anblick der Glanznacht, Sternheere'), Reichardt had printed after Gluck's death (1792) in *Der musikalische Blumenstrauss*. It was a trophy of the visit to Vienna in 1783 already mentioned. It is a recitative with figured bass, like a thing cast in bronze, and an inexorable unison between voice and bass makes a full stop to it.

What do these settings of odes stand for? Goethe gives us a clue. He writes on 23rd January 1786 to Philipp Christoph Kayser, then his domestic composer (whom in 1781 he wished to become a pupil of Gluck, but who had to be refused by the latter for reasons of health), when he was looking for new metres for his musical plays, 'differing from the eternal iambics, trochees and dactyls':

[1] The words of this seventh song are not by Klopstock.

It was more especially Gluck's manner of composition which drew me to this . . . and moreover I found his settings of poems by Klopstock, which he had conjured into a musical rhythm, remarkable.

Most of the odes in Artaria's set, in fact, show a syllabic treatment and a scheme of declamation such as we find later in the archaized odes of August von Platen. Goethe felt Gluck's singularity, the

DIE FRÜHEN GRÄBER
Affettuoso

1. Will —
2. Des
3. Ihr

kom - men, o sil - ber-ner Mond,   schö - ner,
Mai - es Er - wa - chen ist nur   schö - ner
Ed - le - ren, ach, es be - wächst   eu - re

stil - ler Ge - fährt der Nacht!   du ent -
noch wie die Som - mer - nacht,   wenn ihm
Ma - le schon ern - stes Moos!   O wie

fliehst?   Ei - le nicht,
Tau,   hell wie Licht,
war   glück - lich ich,

originality and force of his rhythm and his inborn and deliberate striving after simplicity. Burney characterized this very amusingly in his journal:

The chevalier Gluck is simplifying music; and with unbounded invention and powers for creating capricious difficulties, and decking his melodies with meretricious ornaments, he tries all he can to keep his music chaste and sober. . . .

Gluck's songs, like the rest of his works, are intentionally pro-grammatical: they are a plan of procedure and a protest, a protest against the aria, the *arioso,* the subjection of language and of poetry to music. He chose the most susceptible of the poets—not Goethe, whom he knew and admired, but Klopstock—and turned him into sounds of the simplest and most pithy kind. 'Chaste and sober,' indeed (see pages 129-30).

The audacity of this lies in the unity of song and accompaniment. There is no *ritornello* for the singer to return to; the voice itself deter-mines the stream of emotion that is to suffuse the instrumental open-ing; the interludes establish the connection between the separate verses. See how well Mozart marked this:

Mozart, DIE ZAUBERFLÖTE 1791

Dies Bild - nis ist be · zaubernd schön!

No less daring is the radical change of rhythm ('Sehet er bleibt'), which the instrumentally engendered, aria-like song before Gluck would never have permitted itself. When Gluck makes use of the *da capo* in a song, as in *Die Neigung,* it is logically justified: the maiden who offers her lover (whose name unfortunately is Selmar) 'the pledges of troth—oath and handclasp, tears and kisses,' shows anxiety in the middle section lest the adored one should misuse her unreserved devotion, but returns unfalteringly (*risoluto*) to her confession.

For all their simplicity, these songs vary greatly in form. *Schlacht-gesang* and *Der Jüngling,* in spite of their rhythmically, though not melodically, quite identical strophes, can hardly be called anything else than scenes or lyric monodies. Mozart must have known them when he composed his *Abendempfindung*; but it was on Reichardt and his successors that they made their deepest impression, and without Gluck neither Reichardt nor Zumsteeg could ever have done justice to Goethe's formal variety. They could never have clothed songs with music without damaging the poems. Schubert, it is true, was to become the antithesis of Gluck with his melodic abundance.

In the year 1773 we meet Gluck as 'reviser' of another's work. A very mediocre Viennese poet, Tobias von Gebler (1726–86), councillor of state and vice-chancellor of the imperial and royal Bohemian court chancellery, had written a heroic drama entitled *Thamos, König in Aegypten,* for the performance of which he required two choruses and some incidental music. The composer he entrusted with this, Johann Tobias Sattler by name, was evidently a dilettante, for Gebler begged Gluck to 'look over the music throughout,' in other words, to check it. Which Gluck accordingly did; but in the end the poet changed his mind and asked young Mozart to replace Sattler's piece of work by entirely new music, which turned out to be one of Mozart's most magnificent works (K. 345). Gebler's drama reached the Berlin stage in 1786, probably with Sattler's music as revised by Gluck rather than with the much more exacting score by Mozart.

CHAPTER III

THE PARIS OPERAS

CONNECTIONS AND PREPARATIONS

FOR a man like Gluck, who had the disposition of a conqueror and whose 'powers of thought' were so strongly developed, the years after *Paride ed Elena* must have been years of deliberation. He must have been conscious that he had anything but captured the world with his three 'reformed' operas. They had become no international operatic event, but merely a matter of internal, Italian politics, so to speak. Indeed, hardly even an Italian concern, but only a local Viennese one, although Gluck at once tried to carry it into the Italian territory that was both hostile and ready for conquest. (To this Italian territory belonged also the King's Theatre in London, where in 1773 *Orfeo* was performed with Millico, Signora Girelli-Aguilar and Signora Sirmen in the cast). He had to admit to himself that his attempt had failed. Even a penetrating connoisseur like Burney, who admired Gluck, but who loved Hasse, would not let himself become a partisan:

Metastasio and Hasse, may be said, to be at the head of one of the principal sects; and Calsabigi and Gluck of another. The first, regarding all innovations as quackery, adhere to the ancient form of the musical drama, in which the poet and musician claim equal attention from an audience; the bard in the recitatives and narrative parts; and the composer in the airs, duos, and chorusses. The second party depend more on theatrical effects, propriety of character, simplicity of diction, and of musical execution, than on, what *they* style, flowery descriptions, superfluous similes, sententious and cold morality, on one side, with tiresome symphonies, and long divisions, on the other.

This was published in 1772, when the supposed decisive battles had long been fought! Gluck recognized that he would have to betake himself to a new field of action. He sought it, and found it, in Paris.

It has been asserted that Marie Antoinette, who was still dauphine at that time, was instrumental in bringing Gluck to Paris; but it is quite clear that the idea emanated from himself. She ordered the imperial ambassador in Paris, Count Florimond Claude de Mercy-Argenteau, to whom we are indebted for so many intimate details of her marriage, to tie the connecting threads and keep them from breaking; but Gluck's immediate correspondent was one of the ambassador's three secretaries, Franz Kruthoffer, forty-five of Gluck's letters to whom, dating from 1775 to 1783, are still preserved. Whether Gluck was known in Paris is doubtful. We only know that in 1765 some arias of his were interpolated, with a French text, into the comic opera of *Isabelle et Gertrude* by Blaise, and that on 2nd February 1768 was sung at the Concert Spirituel a 'Motet à voix seule de M. le chevalier Gluck, célèbre et savant musicien de S.M. Impériale.'

But—and this is the decisive factor—not only had Gluck become ripe for Paris, but Paris for Gluck. Paris was by no means the most important musical city in Europe at that time, but it was the capital of European culture and felt that this disparity should be remedied. In musical matters, and more especially in operatic matters, it had remained a long way behind Italy, behind the England of Handel and behind Germany, thanks to that curious, almost Chinese traditionalism which is a trait of the French character side by side with all that is revolutionary. Thus it came about that the French capital was positively caught napping by the appearance of the Italian *buffo* artists in 1752. It was of no avail that they were driven out again: they won an advocate in Jean-Jacques Rousseau and captured the Opéra-Comique unawares by their example. At the same time the Encyclopaedists—d'Alembert, Diderot, Grimm—undermined the foundations of the French *tragédie lyrique*. They demanded what Gluck demanded: a renovation of the operatic libretto, a renovation of the torpid dramatic music, a renovation of the manner of performance.

Rameau's opera had long been dead when Gluck arrived in Paris. Moreover, the great success which Bohemian, Viennese and German *instrumental* musicians made in Paris, both personally and with their works, had prepared the soil for the appearance of a great man of the opera who came from Vienna, for if Paris was prejudiced in matters appertaining to national opera, it was unprejudiced in those of all other musical questions. Gluck and Paris were bound to find each other, as iron is found by a magnet when the experimentalist's hand brings them close enough together. A further inducement to look for a new arena for his activities may have been of a financial nature. At the end of the sixties Gluck appears to have taken a share as contractor in the Burgtheater and thus, as he informed Prince Kaunitz in 1769, 'frittered away' his and his wife's fortune. And he was not the man to accept material losses with resignation.

The intermediary on the Viennese side was the attaché to the French embassy in Vienna, du Roullet, or, as his full name ran, François Louis Gaud Le Bland du Roullet, a nobleman from Normandy. He was some two years younger than Gluck, a Knight of Malta and holder of the grand cross of that order (hence 'M. Bailly du Roullet'). Earlier in his life, about 1750, he had been an intimate in the house of the greatest musical Maecenas in Paris, the farmer-general of taxes de la Poupelinière, and Rousseau's attack on the French language is said to have drawn a reply from him which either was never written or has been lost in the flood of pamphlets published at that time. Diderot's and Algarotti's indication of Racine's *Iphigénie en Aulide* as an ideal opera subject bore fruit in him. He shaped Racine's tragedy into an opera—we shall see how —in order to prove the musical nature and adaptability to music of the French tongue: a new 'programmatic' text Gluck tackled about 1772, after having met du Roullet socially, probably at the residence of the English ambassador to Vienna, Lord Stormont.

The moves by which Gluck and du Roullet set to work on the conquest of Paris were diplomatic in the highest degree. Their action was difficult, for although it was calculated to heighten the fame of the French nation, it was at the same time directed against J.-J. Rousseau, who himself wielded an influential pen as partisan of the Italians and had a powerful following behind him. While Gluck was finishing his composition, du Roullet wrote to one of the directors of the Paris Opéra, the Chevalier Antoine d'Auvergne, an open letter (1st August 1772) concerning 'M. Glouch,' a letter that appeared in the *Mercure de France* on 1st October. M. Glouch, du Roullet wrote, was indignant at the insolent assertions of some of our (French) famous authors, who denied that the French language was fit to be set to music. . . . M. Glouch wished to assert the weight of his favourable opinion of the French language by a practical proof, when by chance the libretto of *Iphigénie en Aulide* fell into his hands. He had recognized that *this* was the work for which he had been looking.

To disarm Rousseau and his adherents Gluck then wrote his famous letter to the editor of the *Mercure de France,* published on 1st February 1773:

I might justly be reproached, and I should most gravely reproach myself, if, after having read the letter written from here to one of the directors of the Académie Royale de Musique, which you inserted into the *Mercure de France* of last October and of which the opera of *Iphigénie* is the purport; if, I say, after having shown my gratitude to the author of this letter for the praise it his pleased him to lavish upon me, I did not hasten to declare that his friendship and too favourable a prepossession doubtless carried him away, and that I am far from flattering myself that I deserve the eulogies he gives me. . . .

Gluck then sings the praises of Calzabigi as the first to have enabled him to reveal the sources of his art; he himself had merely striven to impart the greatest expression to his music and to reinforce the declamation of the poetry. And then comes a kind of betrayal of the Italian language with a compliment for the French:

This is the reason why I do not make use of the shakes and florid passages, nor of the cadenzas, with which the Italians are so lavish. Their language, which lends itself to all this [so] easily, is thus of no advantage to me in this respect; it has without doubt many others: but, born in Germany, what studies soever I may have been able to make of the Italian language, as well as of the French tongue, I do not think that it would be possible for me to appreciate the delicate distinctions which may make the one preferable to the other, and I think that every foreigner should refrain from judging between them; but what I believe I may be permitted to say, is that the one which will always suit me best, will be the one in which the poet will offer me the most varied means of expressing the passions: this is the advantage which I thought to have found in the words of the opera of *Iphigénie,* the poetry of which seemed to me to have all the energy needed to inspire me with good music. . . .

And although he never had any need, he continues, to offer one of his works to a theatre, he could not be angry with du Roullet for having proposed his *Iphigénie* to an opera director. To conclude, we have this *captatio benevolentiae* for Jean-Jacques:

I confess that I should have produced it in Paris with pleasure, because by its own effect and with the aid of the famous M. Rousseau of Geneva, whom I proposed to consult, we might have succeeded together, by searching for noble, sensitive and natural melody and with a careful declamation suited to the prosody of each language and the character of each people, in hitting upon the means I have in view to produce a music fit for all the nations, and to let the ridiculous distinctions of national music disappear. . . .

An opera that was to be neither Italian nor French, but super-national and human! It will be admitted that Gluck's letter lacked neither diplomacy nor audacity.

The result was, at least, that d'Auvergne had the score of the first act of *Iphigénie* sent to him. Perhaps he intended to deter Gluck, who was by this time a man of nearly sixty, in a polite way when he wrote to du Roullet, after looking through this act, that he would be the first to advocate the acceptance of the opera, provided that the Chevalier Gluck engaged to supply the Académie with six operas of the kind, but that without this guarantee he could not do so, as such a work would be sure to drive all the French operas off the stage. But Gluck was not to be discouraged.

For all that, this acceptance by the Parisian opera director would have remained what so many acceptances by people of his kind are apt to remain, had Gluck not brought the dauphine, his former singing-pupil Marie Antoinette, into action. He completed his work, and on 19th April 1774 the first performance took place, prepared with the utmost tenacity by Gluck himself and looked forward to in great suspense. Marie Antoinette wrote a week later to her sister Maria Christine Josepha:

. . . a great triumph, my dear Christine! On the 19th we had the first performance of *Iphigénie*: I was carried away by it, and people can no longer talk of anything else. All heads are fermenting as a result of this event, as much as could possibly be imagined—it is incredible, there are dissensions and quarrels, as though it were a matter of some religious dispute; at court, although I publicly expressed myself in favour of this inspired work, there are partisanships and debates of a particular liveliness; and in town it seems to be worse still. . . .

Gluck experienced what only Paris had to offer at that time: a 'sensation,' and he had a 'world success,' if one may be allowed to apply to the eighteenth century two of the most revolting expressions of the nineteenth and twentieth. And the world success already brought with it the consequences it still brings: 'publicity.' Gluck could not make the slightest movement without seeing it recorded, and if press photographers had existed in those days, we should have as many snapshots of him as we have of Richard Strauss or Igor Stravinsky. He granted interviews, his rehearsals became public, his clever sayings provoked still cleverer answers, and it must unhappily be admitted that he profited by this new publicity as quickly and adroitly as any astute celebrity of the twentieth century.

'IPHIGÉNIE EN AULIDE'

Did *Iphigénie en Aulide* really become a 'super-national' opera such as Gluck set up as his ideal in his open letter? Or had he merely projected this ideal picture on the horizon to disarm the partisans of the old French operatic tradition? For disarmed they would have been even if the new work had been neither 'Italian' nor 'French' —and *tertium non dabatur*. The truth is that the work was at once a blow to French opera and a renewal of it. That it was a blow at Lulli and Rameau was still felt by such timid, tradition-ridden minds as Claude Debussy's, who saw in Rameau the height of French opera and in Gluck only a naturalistic barbarian.

That it was a renewal the development of French opera itself teaches us, be it through Cherubini's *Médée* and Lesueur's classicist operas or through the development from Spontini to Meyerbeer and Berlioz. An opera like *Iphigénie,* which laid so much stress on French prosody, could not be 'super-national,' and again, an opera that borrowed such an overwhelming amount of music from earlier works was so saturated with the spirit of Italian opera that within the framework of the French operatic tradition it could not fail to have a new, strange and revolutionary effect. As Gluck's bibliographer, Alfred Wotquenne, had noticed before, the works written for Paris 'contain a far larger number of borrowings from earlier operas than any of his Italian operas.' To which Gevaert adds that from the time of *Iphigénie* onwards Gluck no longer regarded the works of his youth as anything but sketches or studio pieces, to be used up arbitrarily as fancy dictated. True, he had by this time become an old man for whom the stream of creative invention had ceased to flow as rapidly as it had done of old, although as a personality he had grown even more tense and energetic, not to say more brutal and autocratic, well knowing that his fame supported him and surrounded him like an aura.

Du Roullet followed the tragedy of Racine in his libretto; but it must be admitted that he very much improved the court poet's work of 1674 or 1675, or as much as the spirit of the time would allow. He was by no means endowed with the courage and the radicalism that was Calzabigi's, at any rate in theory. Among his most praiseworthy notions is that of discarding Racine's Ulysses, whose only function is to remind Agamemnon of the cruel will of the gods and to give news of the catastrophe and its solution. Instead du Roullet introduces the people, the Greek army, clamouring wildly for departure and for the sacrifice of Iphigeneia, always ready behind the scenes, so to speak, to break out as a threatening and driving power. It is almost impossible to dismiss a comparison with the *turbae,* the choruses of Jews in Bach's Passions, from one's mind. No less laudable, in fact more so, is the elimination of Eriphyle, who haunts Racine's play as a black intriguer and Iphigeneia's rival, only to turn out to be the secreted daughter of Helen and Theseus with the

true and proper name of Iphigeneia—that is, Iphigeneia No. II—
who is sacrificed most revoltingly in place of Agamemnon's daughter
(for is is only another form of sacrifice when she stabs herself at the
altar), so that there is no longer any obstacle to the marriage of
Iphigeneia No. I to Achilles and to the setting sail of the Greeks.
But most commendable of all is du Roullet's introduction of the
high priest Calchas, whom Racine does not allow to appear in
person, as a visible representative of the exacting, angry and
finally placated goddess.

The faults of the libretto are clear as daylight. They are not only
of a dramaturgic nature, but show signs of a defective dramatic
attitude of mind. How truly in the vein of French classicism is that
intrigue of Agamemnon to blacken Achilles to Clytemnestra and
Iphigeneia as faithless, which furnishes the plot for the rest of the
first act! This act closes, like the worthiest *opera seria* or *tragédie
lyrique,* with a duet of reconciliation and love for Achilles and
Iphigeneia, which needless to say has been preceded by the regula-
tion clearing-up of misunderstandings. The second act, which ends
with Gluck's magnificent realization of Agamemnon's inner conflict,
begins as an episode compounded of a feast, a ballet and courtly
ceremonies. The way in which Achilles introduces his friend
Patroclus (whom du Roullet brings in in order to gain a bass voice
for a quartet) borders on the comic.

What is most offensive to all who know the *Iliad* is the unravelling
of the catastrophe. Agamemnon and Achilles, Greeks and Myr-
midons, clash in the utmost excitement; Clytemnestra in the fore-
ground wrestles with all the emotions of Tartarus, while in the
background the sacramental chants of the sacrificial procession are
already heard. Suddenly Calchas proclaims that the goddess Diana
has been appeased by the heroic conduct of all concerned—Agamemnon and Clytemnestra, Iphigeneia and Achilles—and that the
Trojan war may now begin without let or hindrance. And so
Iphigénie en Aulide ends with a grand ballet into which an aria for
soprano is sandwiched and where solo voices and chorus too take their
share. It is this last feature which shows a musical advance beyond
Orfeo; but the conciliatory ending of that work in the manner of

a *festa teatrale* is much less reprehensible than this connivance at and obeisance before the *genius loci* of the Paris opera ballet. Nietzsche once asked scornfully how Parsifal came to be the father of Lohengrin. One might as well have asked Gluck how Iphigeneia, the wife of Achilles, managed to get to Tauris as high priestess.

In this opera Gluck nevertheless expressed things of a dramatic power, a greatness, a delicacy and a penetration into the human soul such as are not to be found even in *Alceste*. This is true at once of the overture, a programme overture that exposes the forces of the drama without developing them: the state in which Agamemnon finds himself as lord of a people but bond-slave of the gods and as an agonized father; the army's threatening unison; the tenderly plaintive voice of Iphigeneia prepared for the sacrifice. Gluck's opera *lives* by the delineation of states of mind set in sharp opposition. It culminates in Agamemnon's vision of the sacrificial scene. That lamentation of the oboe, which cuts Agamemnon to the soul, is not only an innovation in opera, but in the whole dramatic art. For the first time opera demonstrates its superiority over the spoken drama; for the first time the orchestra recognizes its function of saying things and evoking conceptions not to be expressed in words and stirring only in the subconsciousness of the soul. To the inward expression of this monologue corresponds the freedom and inevitability of its form. The *da capo* aria may be recognized in it from afar, for Agamemnon at the end returns again to the beginning: 'Je n'obéirai point à cet ordre inhumain'; but this return is psychologically justified in the most splendid and compelling way: form has been loosened and at the same time newly shaped. For the first time in operatic history one of those rare cases occurs where the tempo of the drama and the tempo of the music become one.

Corresponding to this vision of Agamemnon's is that of Clytemnestra in the third and last act. She is more passionate and violent, being wrought up by the action behind the scene. When Iphigeneia hears of the supposed faithlessness of Achilles her scene alternates between recitative, gentle plaint and wild accusation. A flowing and merging between recitative and *arioso*, between loose and strict forms, is characteristic of this opera. Excitement and repose are contrasted; the introductions preceding the appearances of Iphigeneia and Clytemnestra are shaped like Greek distichs that have become melody. It is easy to understand the upheaval and the raptures called forth by such a work.

The nineteenth century knew *Iphigénie en Aulide* chiefly in the arrangement of Wagner, who in his Dresden period rather patron/izingly devoted his 'great attention and care' to the work. He had it newly translated and 'was in the end determined to undertake a more thorough/going revision of the score itself.'

The poem itself I sought to bring as far as possible into accord with Euripides's play of the same name by removing everything which, according to French taste, was apt to mark the relations of Achilles to Iphigeneia as a sugary love/affair, but more especially by a complete alteration of the conclusion [1] with its inevitable marriage. The generally quite discon/nected arias and choruses I endeavoured, for the sake of dramatic animation, to connect by transitions, postludes and preludes, being particularly careful to make the intrusion of another musician as inconspicuous as possible by making use of Gluck's own themes. Only in the third act was I com/pelled to give Iphigeneia, as well as the Artemis I had myself introduced, melodic recitatives of my own composition. Moreover, I revised the whole of the scoring more or less thoroughly, although always with the sole object of giving due effect to what was already there. . . .

Wagner went on to say how unusually favourably the contemporary critics treated him on that occasion. Our own judgment of to/day, grown historically more sensitive, can no longer share this bene/volence. What Wagner made of *Iphigénie* is no longer Gluck. He produced an overpainting which obscures the true colours and contours to the point of falsifying the original intention. The height of violation occurs probably at Iphigeneia's resolve to die, where the music is not far from the most luxuriant *Lohengrin* romanticism. What attracts us nowadays is only the question what it was that drew Wagner precisely to *Iphigénie en Aulide*. The secret reason was perhaps that it is in a sense devised on a basis of *Leitmotiv,* and it would not be hard to imagine a 'hermeneutically' disposed scholar who might be tempted to elucidate all the relationships between the

[1] Gluck himself had attempted something of the kind in 1775.

separate characteristic numbers and the overture. He would have no great difficulty in discovering an astonishingly determined intention to achieve musical unity.

REVIVALS

On 2nd August 1774 a wish of Gluck's was fulfilled towards the realization of which he seems vainly to have taken steps ten years earlier. It will be remembered that in March 1764, shortly before the performance of *Orfeo* during the coronation festivities at Frank- fort, he had gone to Paris for a few days to supervise the final corrections in the engraved score of the work and to sound the Opéra, or the Comédie-Italienne, about a performance. But he found little response, as may be judged from Count Durazzo's correspondence with Favart: no more than half a dozen copies of the score were sold in the course of ten years.

Now, however, the success of *Iphigénie* paved the way for a produc- tion of *Orfeo*: a very thorough French adaptation was staged under the title of *Orphée et Eurydice*, with Le Gros (the Achilles of *Iphigénie*) as Orpheus, Sophie Arnould (the Iphigeneia) as Eurydice and Mlle Rosalie (the Greek girl) as Cupid. Gluck's assistant in this labour was Pierre-Louis Moline, the librettist of *L'Arbre enchanté,* who had already furnished a prose translation of the text when the score was engraved in 1764, under the title of 'Orphée et Eurydice, Tragédie- Opéra, par M. Calzabigi. Traduite de l'Italien par Mr. M— avec des réflexions sur cette pièce,' published by Bauche on the Quai des Augustins. These 'reflections' on the tendencies of the new opera libretto were in turn merely the reprint of an essay in the *Journal des Dames*. Moline (1739–1820), who came from Montpellier, was a lawyer and *bel esprit,* and after this 'Orpheus' he wrote, among countless other literary products, some sixteen librettos, only five of which, however, found a composer. About 1778 he must either have joined the opponents of Gluck, for he turned out a parody of *Armide* under the name of *Madame Terrible,* or else he did this simply because he was a scamp and a poor devil, like dozens of others who went about Paris. Gluck did not make the adaptation of *Orfeo* easy for him, or for himself, for apart from the addition of arias, dances, extensions and touchings-up of colour, which have already been referred to, *Orphée et Eurydice* shows a thoroughgoing adjustment to the spirit of the French language.

After the production of *Orphée*, in the autumn of 1774, Gluck returned to Vienna. By a decree dated 18th October he was now formally appointed to the post his right to which had been disputed in Durazzo's time: Maria Theresa acknowledged him as imperial court composer with a salary of two thousand florins per annum, 'in consideration of his thorough knowledge of music and his proven especial skill, as also an ability practised in various compositions.' He hardly needed either the title or the emolument any longer.

A few months later, accompanied by his wife and niece, he again took the road to Paris, another visit to Klopstock being paid at Strasburg and Rastatt. This time the purpose was only the glorifica- tion of an event at court: on 27th February Monsieur, the king's brother, held a reception at Versailles in honour of the Archduke Maximilian, the king's brother-in-law, which culminated in an adaptation of *L'Arbre enchanté,* performed by the *Comédiens Italiens.* The score, designated as 'Œuvre IV,' is accordingly dedicated to Monsieur. The event took place among the surroundings of a fair held on a race-course. Gluck added but a single number to his Vienna score, an arietta for Lubin that forms an introduction to the one-act opera after the overture.

A much more ambitious new version is that of *La Cythère assiégée* of 1759, which the Académie Royale performed on 1st August 1775, in the absence of Gluck, who was kept in Vienna by a severe illness. He was even unable to complete the score himself, for when he was forced to return to Vienna before the appointed time, evidently on account of the threatening illness, Pierre-Montan Berton, one of the conductors of the Opéra, undertook to complete the ballet music for the final scene of the work. Favart's one-act *opéra comique* thus became a lavish opera-ballet in three acts, the engraved score of which ran to 216 pages and cost as much as *Iphigénie* or *Alceste*. It contained a great many numbers borrowed from early and more recent works, especially from *Paride ed Elena*. It is difficult to imagine

anything much more absurd than this combat between the nymphs
of Venus and the wild Scythians Barbarin and Brontes, who of
course are signally defeated in the end. What is and remains
remarkable is the kind of antiphonal chorus in which this combat is
symbolized by decorative music. Not even a great man escapes
punishment for letting himself go and relying on the weight of his
unchallenged successes. *La Cythère assiégée* was a fiasco, which
did not fail to depress Gluck mightily. It reached only twenty-one
repeat performances and the judgment of the connoisseurs is summarized in the well-known *bon mot* of the Abbé Arnaud: 'Hercule
était plus habile à manier la massue que les fuseaux.'

He intended to repair the damage later on:

I hear that M. Noverre has been engaged by the Opéra, and if that is
so, I shall produce *Le Siège de Cythère* again next year, if God keep me alive,
as this opera, with dances made on purpose for it, will take on a very
different air, and I cannot doubt but that it will be successful,

he wrote on 29th August 1776 to Kruthoffer. The following year
he still indulged the same hopes; but the plan never materialized.
The hopes would have been vain, in any case.

Meanwhile, having got over the grave illness of the summer of
1775, Gluck prepared to deliver a new blow with his 'club': the
French version of *Alceste*. On New Year's Eve of that year he sent
Kruthoffer the first two acts for transmission to the publisher (Peters)
and the engraver; at the beginning of March he himself took the
third act with him to Paris, where he went this time without his wife,
who remained behind to nurse the sick Marianne. (At the end of
April he was to receive news of the death of this tenderly loved
adopted daughter, who had succumbed to smallpox on the 22nd.)

He was deeply hurt by the fact that *Alceste* too was a failure,
despite the affectionate labour he had devoted to the remodelling of
the work together with du Roullet. It has been said that a cabal
of his opponents was to blame; that Sophie Arnould, the interpreter
of Iphigeneia and Eurydice, had mobilized Gluck's enemies in her
anger with him for having given the part of Alceste to Mlle Rosalie
(the Cupid in *Orphée*), who had by this time grown into Mlle
Levasseur, and that Gluck himself had done his best to prejudice

the Parisian public against him when his 'armour-plated' letter to du Roullet concerning the rivalry of Piccinni was published in the *Année littéraire*. The second reason, at least, is not valid, for this famous letter—to which we shall return later—cannot have been written before the autumn of 1776, nor published before February 1777. In short, we know as little about the causes of the Parisians' dislike of *Alceste* as we do about those of a similar antipathy provoked by *The Barber of Seville* or *Carmen* at their first performances. After his first consternation, Gluck pulled himself together once more. He prophesied a gradual success for the work, and he was right. Indeed, he was able to observe this slow-mounting success in person, for he apparently remained in Paris with his wife, who had joined him after the death of Marianne, until the beginning of June.[1] Then he returned home in order to devote himself to the composition of *Roland* and *Armide*.

Roland was never finished. The reasons for this were indicated by Gluck himself in that famous letter, which may here be translated in full, seeing that it mirrors Gluck whole and undistorted, being one of the few of his letters that have escaped literary polishing:

I have just received, my friend, your letter of 15th January, whereby you exhort me to continue my work upon the words of the Opera of *Roland*; this is no longer feasible, for when I heard that the Management of the Opéra, not unaware that I was doing *Roland,* had given this same work to M. Piccini to do, I burnt as much of it as I had already done, which perhaps was not worth much, and in that case the Public must owe an obligation to M. Marmontel for having prevented them from listening to bad Music. Moreover, I am no longer the man to enter into competition, and M. Piccini would have too great an advantage of me, since, his personal merit apart, which is assuredly very great, he would have that of novelty, I having already given Paris four Works, good or bad—no matter; this uses up one's fancy, and then I have paved the way for him, and he need but follow it. The protection he enjoys I will not mention to you. I am sure that a certain Politician of my acquaintance will offer dinner and

---

[1] But already at the end of May 1776 the management of the Opéra replaced *Alceste* by a ballet three years old by Étienne-Joseph Floquet, *L'union de l'Amour et des Arts.*

supper to three-quarters of Paris in order to win him proselytes, and that Marmontel, who knows so well how to tell Stories, will tell the whole Kingdom of the exclusive merits of the sieur Piccini. I am in truth sorry for M. Hébert for having fallen into the clutches of such people, the one an exclusive Lover of Italian Music, the other a Dramatic Author of would-be Comic Operas. They will make him see the Moon at midday. I am really vexed about it; for he is a gentleman, this M. Hébert, and that is the reason why I shall not refrain from giving him my *Armide,* although on the conditions that I have indicated to you in my preceding Letter, and of which the essentials are, I repeat, that I shall be given at least two months, after my arrival in Paris, to shape my Actors and Actresses; that I shall be at liberty to hold as many rehearsals as I shall judge to be necessary; that no Part shall be allowed to be doubled, and that another Opera be kept in perfect readiness, in case some Actor or Actress should be indisposed. Such are my conditions, without which I shall keep *Armide* for my own pleasure. I made the Music for it in such a manner that it will not soon age.

You tell me in your Letter, my dear friend, that nothing will ever be as good as *Alceste;* but I shall not yet subscribe to your prophecy. *Alceste* is a complete Tragedy, and I confess to you that I think very little is wanting to make it perfect; but you cannot imagine of how many different shades and ways Music is capable; *Armide* as a whole is so different from *Alceste,* that you will not believe them to be by the same Composer. I have thus employed what little sap remained to me to complete *Armide;* I endeavoured there to be more Painter and Poet than Musician; in short, you will judge of this, if it is to be heard. I confess to you that I should like to close my career with this Opera. It is true that where the Public is concerned, it will require as much time to understand this as it took to understand *Alceste.* There is a kind of delicacy in *Armide* which is not in *Alceste*: for I have found a means to make the characters speak in such a way that you will know at once from their manner of expressing themselves whether it is Armida who speaks, or an attendant, etc. I must conclude, else you will believe that I have become a madman or a Quack. Nothing has so ill an effect as self-praise, that was proper only for the great Corneille; but when Marmontel or I extol ourselves, we earn but scorn, and people laugh in our faces. By the way, you are quite right to say that the French Composers have been too much neglected; for, or I am much mistaken, I believe that Gossec and Philidor, who understand the cut of French Opera, will serve the Public infinitely better than the best Italian Authors, if only people did not grow so enthusiastic over everything that has the air

of novelty. You tell me furthermore, my friend, that *Orphée* loses in comparison with *Alceste*. Dear me! how are these two works to be compared,
since they are not comparable? The one may please more than the other;
but have *Alceste* performed with bad Actors and any Actress other than
Mlle Le Vasseur, and *Orphée* with the best you have, and you will see
that *Orphée* will turn the scale: the best-made things, badly performed,
become all the more insufferable. No comparison can be upheld between
two works of different nature. Yes indeed, if for example Piccini and I
should each on his own account write the Opera of *Roland,* then it would
be possible to judge which of the two had done better; but different Poems
must necessarily produce different Music, which may be, in various styles,
all that is most sublimely invented to match the expression of the words;
but then every comparison *claudicat.* I almost tremble at the thought that
Armide may be compared with *Alceste,* two such different poems, one of
which must call forth tears and the other produce a voluptuous sensation;
if that should come about, I shall have no other expedient than to have
prayers offered to God that he may restore its good sense to the good city
of Paris.

Farewell, my dear friend, I embrace you, etc.[1]

What had happened? It was a case of one of those indiscretions
or thoughtless disloyalties which characterize the conduct of the
young dauphine and queen, Marie Antoinette, and which so greatly
troubled Count Mercy-Argenteau and her imperial mother. The
Marchese Domenico Caraccioli, the Neapolitan ambassador to the
French court, had tried ever since the beginning of 1774 to persuade
Marie Antoinette to invite the Neapolitan composer Niccolò Piccinni
to Paris, as she had invited Gluck earlier. The suspicious Mercy-
Argenteau in September 1775 informed Vienna of the evidently
decisive interview between the Marchese and Marie Antoinette. A
dash of comedy is added to this questionable transaction by the fact
that the Dubarry as well as the dauphine had a share in the intrigue.
Piccinni left Naples on 6th November 1776 and arrived in Paris on
the last day of the year. News of his arrival echoed as far as Germany, and Forkel, Gluck's most virulent German opponent,
spitefully announced from Paris:

[1] For the original text see Appendix E.

Piccinni Called to Paris

The famous *Capellmeister* Nicolo Piccinni has arrived here, and has become director of a singing-school for three years, with an annual salary of 2,000 *Reichsthaler*. . . . He and the chevalier Gluck will soon provoke a theatrical squabble here. . . .[1]

In order to make this squabble as enjoyable as possible for the frequenters of the Opéra, Gluck and Piccinni had been handed the same libretto, Quinault's *Roland* revised by Marmontel. But Gluck would not lend himself to this contest, which on the one hand makes one think of the rivalries between composers of older schools, who perhaps compared their powers with the aid of one and the same libretto by Metastasio, and on the other of modern fights between prize boxers or prize wrestlers. Not that we need believe every word of his assertion that he burnt everything he had so far composed for *Roland*. But he must have asked himself, as we ask ourselves to-day, why it should have been precisely Piccinni who was set up as his rival.

PICCINNI

It seems that the Abbé Galiani had a hand in the game, the clever Neapolitan correspondent of Madame d'Épinay and—needless to say—of the Marchese Caraccioli. One would have thought that Tommaso Traetta, the one serious opponent of Gluck in tragic opera, would have done better, or perhaps Giovanni Paisiello. But Traetta had returned to Italy from Russia and England in 1775, a tired and ailing man, and Paisiello's star, the most radiant in the Italian operatic firmament during the second half of the eighteenth century, was only just rising. Niccolò Piccinni belonged to the same generation as Gluck, being only a little younger—fourteen years, to be exact—and he was at the height of his fame. His reputation, it is true, was based to a larger extent on his *opere buffe,* especially those written in the Neapolitan dialect, which were as difficult to export as those little sweet, red berries that grow on the cacti in the neighbourhood of Naples. With one *opera buffa,* however, composed to a book by Carlo Goldoni, Piccinni had had a

[1] *Musikalisch-kritische Bibliothek,* vol. i, p. 313. (1777)

149

success that would be called a 'world success' in the journalistic and theatrical jargon of to-day. This was *La buona figliuola,* produced two years before *Orfeo* (1760). It marks an epoch in the history of *opera buffa.* Goldoni had one day transformed the contents, or the approximate contents, of *Pamela,* Richardson's half virtuous and half concupiscent novel, into a sentimental comedy; and later he turned this comedy into an *opera buffa* for Piccinni, with the place of action moved to Italy and all the characters and situations more or less altered. Pamela became 'Mariandel,' the lost daughter of an Austrian officer; but her pitiable situation and her gentle character remained, Piccinni gave her the tenderest, most tear-laden melodies, and the contemporarias were thus given in a specimen of *opera buffa* the kind of mixture they craved: 'sensibility' and sentimentality blended with the grotesque and the scurrilous.

The direct occasion of Piccinni's call to Paris, however, was an unexpected success in the domain of the *opera seria.* It was the *Alessandro nelle Indie*—the same libretto of Metastasio's which Gluck had once composed under the title of *Poro*—performed at Naples in the carnival of 1774 in Piccinni's new, second version. Galiani, who in 1773 had already been inclined to throw Piccinni on the scrap-heap ('. . . we have had only excellent comic operas, that is to say, two by Piccinni and two by Paisiello. Those by the latter were even superior to the other's, who is beginning to age. . . .'), wrote to Madame d'Épinay on 15th February 1774:

Piccinni has just given an opera in our grand theatre which surpassed everything in the way of good music heard so far. The *Orphée* of Gluck, which was given at court at the same time, has been furiously eclipsed by it. As I know that Prince Pignatelli will have the complete copy of Piccinni's opera, I am convinced that you will hear it; hear it, however, with all the accompaniments.

The news of this pretended failure of *Orfeo* was an untruth. It had, in fact, had a considerable success. But the lie worked. And it is quite true that Piccinni's *Alessandro nelle Indie* contains here and there passionate and highly-strung music with which Gluck's statuesque stiffness and musical parsimony compares as a classical marble statue does with Bernini's St. Teresa or a quasi-antique picture by Poussin with a painting by Albani. Gluck is infinitely greater than Piccinni, but Piccinni is infinitely more gifted with sensuousness. As a personality he was much inferior.

Grétry has an amusing description of how, as a young stipendiary in Rome, he adulated Piccinni for an hour on end without his idol allowing himself to be disturbed in his work. Burney, who looked him up at Naples in 1770, characterized him as an agreeable man of forty-four or forty-five, very serious for a Neapolitan (but Piccinni was an Apulian, having been born at Bari). Galiani thought his conversation not up to much, and not as good as his pieces, but he was an excellent man. ('Sa conversation ne vaut pas ses pièces; mais c'est un très-honnête homme. . . .'). And as such he always behaved towards Gluck. He was clearly never quite aware that the Parisians regarded him only as a pawn in their game against Gluck, and his situation in Paris became before long as pitiable as that of his 'buona figliuola,' nay, even worse, for he was snubbed, cheated and led by the nose, defenceless against all these proceedings, which he did not even understand. His collision with Gluck was like the encounter of a sponge with an agate. It was easy for Gluck to show magnanimity to so weak an opponent.

Berton, the Opéra conductor, soon arranged a personal meeting of the rivals at dinner, at which Gluck (and the Naples-bred Piccinni too) was always in good humour. They embraced, chatted together, and Gluck remarked cynically: 'Believe me, in this country you must think only of earning money,' to which Piccinni is said to have courteously replied that Gluck 'proved by his example that one may concern oneself with one's glory at the same time as with one's fortune.' Which is wholly characteristic, for Gluck, in fact, died rolling in wealth and Piccinni in poverty and bitterness. Here again Gluck was the more fortunate of the two: he died before the Revolution, which his robust stomach would have enabled him to digest as well as anything else; Piccinni was fated to live through it.

Piccinni dedicated the score of *Roland* to the queen, as Gluck's pupil Salieri later did his *Danaïdes,* and alludes in his preface to his many trials: 'Transplanted, isolated, in a country where all was new to me, intimidated in my work by a thousand difficulties, I needed all my courage, and my courage forsook me.' The score of *Roland* shows that this is literally true. Piccinni had the misfortune in Paris of being always on the wrong side: Marmontel, in spite of the inspiration which made him reduce the five acts of *Roland* to three, stands far below du Roullet in the matter of dramatic adroitness. No greater piece of bungling can be imagined than this story of the love of Princess Angélique, who is constantly accompanied by her lady-in-waiting, Thémire, for the shepherd Médor, and of the craziness of the betrayed bass Roland, to whom the fairy Logistille restores what little reason he ever had immediately after his mad scene and whom the chorus directs towards the path of glory.

It is hard to believe that Gluck can have occupied himself seriously with the composition of Quinault's libretto in this form. Before Piccinni set to work on it, he was evidently handed the score of a work by Rameau. He anxiously did his best to be as French as possible, and he is, in fact, much more so than Gluck, so that naïve relapses into the Italian manner, like the aria of Médor that concludes the second act with a degeneration into coloratura, look doubly incongruous among all those choruses, ballets, *ritornelli* and declamations heavily laden with orchestral accompaniment. It is clear that Piccinni had no notion of Gluck's real intentions, nor, in spite of greater repose and stylistic certainty, did he become aware of them in his later French operas: the *Atys* of 1780, the *Iphigénie en Tauride* of 1781 and the *Didon* of 1783. The rivalry between the two composers could have led to a decisive contest only if Piccinni had been allowed to display himself as an *Italian* composer, and if he had been capable of turning out a masterpiece of Italian *opera seria*. Such a masterpiece alone could have proved that the *opera seria* had not been dethroned by Gluck's reforms. But the struggle between the two principles — between 'dramatic' opera and 'musical' opera — was never fought out. It has, indeed, remained undecided to the present day. The Italian opera, with its absolute supremacy of music over drama, with its eunuch singers and all its absurdities, is the more irrational drama, yet stands far above all the 'reasonableness' of the *tragédie lyrique*—and Gluck too had rationalized the opera. It is at this that Nietzsche aims when he leaves it an open question whether

Piccinni was not in the right rather than Gluck after all. What is certain, all the same, is that historically considered Piccinni was not the superior of Gluck and never will be regarded as his superior.

'ARMIDE'

Gluck was nevertheless disquieted at first. 'I beg you,' he wrote to Kruthoffer on 15th January 1777, 'to give me reliable information as to why, at whose call and for what purpose Piccinni has been called to Paris and what salary he receives'; and on the 31st: 'Do write much news to me, for theatrical affairs must be teeming at this time. . . .' In May he once more set out for Paris, in the company of his wife—for the fourth time. He arrived on the 29th and 'sa demeure est rue des Fossoyeurs,' as the *Journal de Paris* piquantly announced, all Paris being aware that this was the domicile of Mlle Levasseur, who had in the meantime become the mistress of Count Mercy-Argenteau. Early in July the rehearsals began, and on 23rd September the first performance of *Armide* took place. Piccinni's *Roland* followed only on 27th January 1778, and it is but too easy to understand why it could no longer make a great impression.

Both *Armide* and *Roland* were attempts at winning two great Italian composers—for Gluck too was an Italian composer for Paris—over to the French operatic ideal, or at least at getting them both to try their strength in that field. But Piccinni was enticed away by Metastasio, and Gluck, no longer open to that influence, by Calzabigi. It is possible that Calzabigi might have half approved of *Iphigénie en Aulide,* but never of *Armide,* where Gluck once again showed that he was not a man of principles and by no means sworn for ever to mythological opera, since he pretty well composed Philippe Quinault's old libretto, skin, bone and all, in five acts, while Marmontel had wisely condensed Quinault's *Roland* into three acts for Piccinni.

Years ago, in 1686, this *Armide* had been written by Quinault for Jean-Baptiste Lulli, and so the Chevalier Gluck's *drame héroïque* was now issuing out of Lulli's *tragédie.* This meant a return to the baroque, 'romantic' choice of subjects of the seventeenth century, which Zeno and Metastasio had so anxiously avoided. *Roland* was taken from Ariosto's *Orlando furioso* and *Armide* from the *Gerusalemme liberata* of Torquato Tasso. The Christian hero, like Parsifal, untried by love and the great sorceress, the 'maga furiosa,' who disdains love and marriage, come together and become inflamed with passion for each other: Kundry's magic garden blossoms and withers a century before Bayreuth. A ballet at Armida's court and a ghostly dance before Rinaldo's companions are important features; but most important of all are the changes of Armida herself, who intends to stab the sleeping Rinaldo, but is captivated by the sight of him; who conjures up the Fury of Hate to 'rescue her heart from the peril of love,' but sends the enraged messenger of the nether world home again; who, abandoned by the hero turned virtuous once more, destroys her magic garden and palace. These spheres were not quite unfamiliar to Gluck: he had already depicted both Hades and Elysium, although not yet an Elysium of love that was but a phantom of Hades.

Armide is nevertheless an entirely dualistic work. Dualistic in style, to begin with, for it is neither wholly French nor wholly Italian, whereas Lulli's *Armide,* although the work of a Florentine, is French to the marrow, so to speak. Thus there are still critics to-day who for that reason prefer it greatly to Gluck's *Armide,* and not without reason. (If Gluck, as we are told, expressed his admiration for Lulli and his intention to form the true lyric tragedy after his model, that may safely be regarded as pure diplomacy once again.) The duality lies not only in an outward mixture of opera-ballet and tragic opera; it goes deeper. The Fury of Hate is not to be compared with the Erinyes and the spirits of the underworld; she is only a decorative demon, almost an allegory; like the rest of the action, she is suited to the seventeenth century, but no longer to the eighteenth. Armida deprecates the homage brought her by her ladies, Phenice and Sidonie, having foreseen her destiny with Rinaldo in a dream; she sets aside the exhortations of her fatherly friend Hidraot, who can only be described as an uncle, although Gluck endeavoured to disguise his avuncular character by a kind of energy in his arias, 'Je vois de près la mort qui me menace' and 'Pour vous, quand il vous plaît.' This Hidraot has no other function than that of adding a male voice to the chorus of revenge that closes the first act; after the second act he disappears, never to be seen again. The climax of this first act does not lie in the adulatory choruses and ballets, nor in the excited recitatives unchained by Aronte's evil tidings of Rinaldo's new misdeeds, but in that short movement in which Armida expresses her resolve to safeguard her freedom from the inroads of love:

ARMIDE 1777
Andante

La chaî_ ne de l'Hy-men   m'é

-ton_____ ne,   je

It will be seen that this is an instrumentally conceived movement into which the vocal part has been subsequently fitted—but how sensitively fitted! The 'sweet shackles' of Cupid are suggested by the declamation as well as by the orchestra, and Armida herself appears in the whole magic of her form. Among all Gluck's female characters she is the most feminine and attractive. There are many borrowed numbers in *Armide,* but it is just this one which does not seem to have come from an earlier opera.

The second act begins with a dialogue between Rinaldo and a liberated knight, a dialogue that becomes enhanced into a duet: the knight, that is, simply takes the middle section of a heroic aria to himself. Armida and Hidraot then join in an invocation of the nether world, and in their duet 'we meet for the fifth time with a theme used already in 1744 (in *Sofonisba*),' according to Wotquenne, which may at any rate be taken for a proof of the unity of Gluck's work, if this grandiloquent piece could still do duty here. Revenge has been prepared; Armida has reserved it for herself. The victim, Rinaldo, approaches, and this time gives vent to bucolic feelings:

> Plus j'observe ces lieux, et plus je les admire!

With this he falls asleep. Now follows, with dances, solo voices and female choir, that pre-*Parsifal* flower-maidens' scene, only not as visionary as yet, unfortunately, as it was to become with Nietzsche's 'old sorcerer,' but wholly in the vein of realistic French operatic art. Next comes Armida's great scene, where she begins as a goddess of revenge and ends with an aria expressive of shame:

> la pitié me surmonte:
> Cachez ma faiblesse et ma honte
> Dans les plus reculés déserts!

It is a grandiose conclusion, and the conflict of emotions in Armida's bosom grows fiercer still in the third act. She feels that Rinaldo succumbs only to her magic, whereas she, for all her pride, is subdued by love itself. So she calls up the Fury of Hate from Hades in her famous scene: invocation, exhibitionist aria of the demon, chorus of spirits, dance of Furies. It does not detract from the theatrical effect of this scenic array that it consists wholly of older ideas strung together piecemeal. For compensation it culminates in a climax that is new even for Gluck: the clash of opposed feelings in a concerted piece. The demon sings in harsh accents:

> Sors! sors du sein d'Armide, Amour!

into which Armida declaims:

> Arrête, arrête! affreuse haine.

All this is accompanied by a hammering orchestral tumult with an inexorably onward-pacing bass. It is a magnificent notion, save that Gluck was not capable of infusing into the part of Armida the songfulness required for its true expression and for the suggestion of a sensuous contrast. The more ingenious is the conclusion of the act, where Armida, shattered by the reproaches of the demons, remains behind alone, a prey to gnawing pangs of conscience and premonitions of evil:

It says as much for Gluck's dramatic instinct as for his human tact that this conclusion is his own invention. It is not to be found in Quinault.

The fourth act might almost be passed over. Ubaldo and the Danish knight appear with their shield of truth, which is to release Rinaldo from his spell. They have first of all to submit to an attack from various monsters, with *tremolo*, rapping chords and wild scales, and afterwards to the seductions of Armida's ladies, who appear to them in the shape of their loved ones—very foolishly one after the other, so that one knight is always able to warn and save the other. This repetitive scene, not without its comic side, is positively the height of dramatic clumsiness. When the two heroes withdraw to the sound of fanfares, they are accompanied also by indulgent smiles on our part. Gluck himself was unable to be much more than conventional here.

The fifth act is his compensation. The love duet between Armida and Rinaldo truly has an infinity of simple melody. The ballet which Armida's court performs for the hero during the absence of his beloved fascinates not Rinaldo alone. It opens with a chaconne in B flat major, the most magnificent piece Gluck ever wrote next to the ballet of Furies in the second version of *Orfeo*. The minor shading towards the end is a stroke of genius: that drop of worm-wood which at once embitters and deepens every delight, that sub-consciousness beneath the conscious. How deeply Gluck still felt at sixty-three! This chaconne merges into a chorus of blessed spirits in which imitation—almost a canon—makes what is a very rare appearance in Gluck. Here is enchantment by sheer *sound* of a kind not met again until we come to the chorus of fairies in Weber's *Oberon*.

The ending of this great scene is short and abrupt. Fanfares disenchant Rinaldo, in a musical sense as well: his words of farewell to Armida are poor and mean, compared with the mounting pain of her entreaties. Her scene is the summit of what operatic conven-tion used to call the *recitativo accompagnato,* and in fact it outsoared that summit. Those two paragons of virtue, the knights, soon drag Rinaldo away; Armida, left alone, panting for breath and no longer able to utter a word:

ARMIDE 1777
Moderato

(a motive that already takes us far into the operatic region of the nineteenth century), lets her emotions rise from plaints to self-reproaches, to contemplation of revenge and finally to self-destruction. The effect of this close—the collapse of all the glories of her palace, as at the end of the second act of *Parsifal*—is, in much the same way as in that work, scenic, not intrinsic, but no less effective.

'IPHIGÉNIE EN TAURIDE'

On 1st March 1778 Gluck returned home to Vienna. 'Yesterday afternoon,' he wrote to Kruthoffer on the 2nd, 'we arrived here safely, after having endured much hardship on this journey, with the diligence and wheels broken, stuck in the snow, and sampled all manner of other mischief. . . .' The homeward journey was broken at Ferney, where a visit was paid to the aged Voltaire shortly before his death (30th May). Gluck, the man of the world, thus did not think of Voltaire as young Mozart did, who, quite in the spirit of his father, commented as follows on Voltaire's death: '. . . You may already know that the godless arch-rogue Voltaire has perished so to speak like a dog or cattle—that is the reward!'

Gluck seems to have regretted his return to Vienna a little: '. . . for the rest, I arrived here at the wrong time, for everybody is preparing for war, which will hardly prove avoidable.' He was right. The war over the Bavarian succession between Frederick the Great (whom Gluck, as a good patriot, wished every calamity) and the emperor broke out. Not that this prevented him from working at two new operas for Paris. He asked Kruthoffer for frequent news: '. . . you refresh my head, which is at present quite heated with my two operas, *Iphigénie* and *Narcisse*, which are already stuck fast in it,' he writes on 28th June.

They were *Iphigénie en Tauride* and *Écho et Narcisse*, Gluck's last operas, for which he set two librettists to work at once, Nicolas-François Guillard for the former and Baron Ludwig Theodor von Tschudi for the latter. With both these men we shall become more closely acquainted before long. By the middle of June Gluck had arrived at the end of the third act of *Iphigénie en Tauride*. There his work stagnated, as he had to discuss the shaping of the librettos with Guillard and Tschudi: '. . . I shall not be able to finish my two operas in Vienna; I must come into touch with the poets, for we do not understand each other well at a distance,' he wrote to the Abbé Arnaud on 15th July. At first he hesitated to take his departure, for M. de Vismes, the new director-general of the Paris Opéra, who had been appointed in September 1777, let him wait for news too long and treated him in the matter of fees and reimbursement of expenses 'like a Parisian loafer' ('comme un homme qui vit sur le pavé de Paris'). Gluck had asked twenty thousand livres for *Écho et Narcisse* alone, but in the end he declared himself satisfied with half that amount. The journey he wished to postpone until the spring of 1779; but on 1st November he was obliged to announce that 'the empress let me know that I could travel to Paris, since this might contribute to the amusement of the queen, particularly if a dauphin were to come into the world.' (What did come into the world, however, on 19th December, was only a princess, Marie-Thérèse-Charlotte.) This amounted to a command: 'I thus have no longer any excuse for procrastination.' Towards the end of November—it is uncertain whether on the 19th or the 28th—he arrived in Paris. This was his fifth and last visit. He did not stay at Mlle Levasseur's this time, but quartered himself at the Hôtel de Valois in the Rue de Richelieu. On 18th May 1779 the first performance of *Iphigénie en Tauride* took place; on 24th September that of *Écho et Narcisse*. Gluck was sixty-five years of age when he closed his career with these two operas.

Guillard, the author of *Iphigénie en Tauride,* was a young Parisian poet. If we may believe the memoirs of the Girondist Brissot, Guillard wrote his libretto out of enthusiasm for Gluck's *Iphigénie en Aulide* and sent it to du Roullet, who so warmly recommended it to Gluck that the musician, full of ardent admiration, composed the whole of the first act without interruption. But the plan for *Iphigénie en Tauride* certainly goes back to discussions between Gluck and du Roullet himself at the time of the Paris *Alceste,* and Guillard merely gave the libretto its final shape.

It is the best opera book that ever came into Gluck's hands. The merit lies neither with du Roullet nor with Guillard, but with their model, the *Iphigeneia in Tauris* of Euripides. But then they must be given credit for having followed the example of the Greek poet more faithfully than the treatment of the same subject by a French play-wright, Guymond de la Touche. The work of the Greek tragedian, who was already so remote from mythology and therefore had to endure such violent attacks from Aristophanes, the political reac-tionary and greatest master of comedy, is the crown of his whole achievement. 'A sharp penetration of motives does not let a single thread escape in this drama. It may be regarded as an hour of dramatic verisimilitude in the knotting and untying of a peripeteia of recognition. . . .'

What characters there are in this opera! Iphigeneia, what a feminine figure: the victim of her father, so full of woe, but so full too of nobility and humanity that she is able to lift the curse that weighs down her dynasty! When Diana appears at the end of the drama, she is no longer a *dea ex machina*: the heavenly messenger only confirms with her divine authority the sentence already pro-nounced *de jure* by her priestess. There is Orestes, avenger of his father and murderer of his mother, hunted and scourged by the Furies, who at the moment he thinks to have found the death he craves beholds the blessed light of expiation. Then there is Pylades, his friend, who appears to succumb in a contest of friendship and is thereby destined to save Orestes. And there is Thoas, the Scythian, the barbarous king devoured by superstitious fear of death, inexorable in his blind cruelty, neither reasons nor pleadings being capable of moving a barbarian. (This figure reminds one of Flaubert's saying: 'Nothing so complex as a barbarian.') Situations press onward, drawing from all concerned the most immediate and most acute emotions. Mythology was no longer needed here: the whole action is humanized and such humanity exceeds all that is mythical.

Iphigénie en Tauride, we have seen, was first performed in Paris on 18th May 1779. Exactly six weeks before, on 6th April, at a small Thuringian court, the first version, in prose, of Goethe's *Iphigenie auf Tauris* had been given. Gluck knew as little of Goethe as Goethe knew of Gluck. It would be useless and fruitless to compare these two works and to measure them with each other; but it is almost unavoidable to examine the attitude of Gluck and Goethe, not towards Euripides, but towards the Grecian ideal of their time. Both sought 'the land of the Greeks with their soul,' out of the spirit of the eighteenth century, or, as Goethe has it in his first version, they both 'longed for the fair land of the Greeks.' What did this mean for Goethe? One of the noblest documents of the century's humanity, of the German classicism that centred at Weimar; one of the most glorious transfigurations of the Goethe circle: Frau von Stein (Iphigeneia) and Goethe himself (Orestes); a work as foreign as possible to true Graecism; an intimate modern drama clad in classical drapery. The transfigured, forgiving Thoas is a ruler of the Josephine era, almost a descendant of the magnanimous tyrants of Metastasio. The inmost sense of Goethe's *Iphigenie* is a clarification, the clarification of the last scions of a race accursed by the gods, the exorcism of the curse of necessity, of the ἀνάγκη, to which every human life is subject; the self-clarification of Goethe, in brief.

An opera required more robust and visible situations and contrasts. It neither could nor would make the action deeper and more intimately personal, and it could thus keep closer to its classical model. But Gluck's *Iphigénie en Tauride* is not classical either; only classicist. As Goethe's work wears the fundamental colour of Weimar, so Gluck's wears that of French art. This Parisian colour comes through everywhere and only too often grows discernible. The overture, which paints the calm and the raging storm ('le calme et la tempête'), is for all its magnificence still descriptive in the French manner; the noble contest between Orestes and Pylades for the privilege of being allowed to die is pure French heroic drama; the ceremony with which Orestes is dedicated to the sacrifice is nothing if not heroic opera. The French colouring is at once to be recognized on comparing *Iphigénie en Tauride* with *Alceste,* which is much weaker as a dramatic work of art, but in its character of Italian opera much more purely Hellenic.

However, this was the given framework within which grand opera was alone possible in the Paris of 1779, and what is enacted within that framework is as grandiose as Gluck alone could make it about that time. Where else in opera was there a *recitativo accompagnato* comparable to Iphigeneia's dread narration of her dream in the first act, interrupted by the subdued chorus of the priestesses and coming to a head in the aria with the lovely oboe solo, a prayer to Diana such as a younger sister might trustingly address to an elder one? The characterization of the barbarian Thoas and his people is incomparable. In his first aria already, 'De noirs pressentiments,' Gluck makes use of his finest and most elemental artistic means: a counter-pull (not counterpoint) of rhythms. Horns provide the basic sound (the tonal functions of the separate instruments are still quite different in Gluck from those of our own time, established by classicism and romanticism); the string parts, for all their hardness, remain somewhat aloof; but in the basses a close *tremolo* hammers away, which presently encroaches on the upper strings:

> Je ne sais quelle voix crie au fond de mon cœur:
> Tremble, ton supplice s'apprête!

The dance and chorus of the Scythians, who drag in Orestes and Pylades for the sacrifice, conjures up in its sound (side-drum and cymbals), its rhythms, its unisons and its horrifying joyousness the wildest fancies that the adventures of explorers among African cannibals might awaken. The ballet that follows is a series of murderous dances such as could hardly be invented more realistically. When the first act closes with the chorus, 'Il nous fallait du sang,' the strangers' fate seems to be sealed.

The second act finds them in the custody of the priestesses, and one of the most unexpected features is the passage of a few notes and bars which depicts this kind of dungeon solitude long before the immortal prelude to the second act of *Fidelio*:

IPHIGÉNIE EN TAURIDE 1779

A wild, 'unbridled' aria for Orestes and an affectionate one for Pylades (*andante grazioso*) rise high above the merely typical, although they plainly originate in it. In that of Pylades, it should be noted, the murderous stroke of the priestess plays its part in the orchestra:

IPHIGÉNIE EN TAURIDE 1779

But this act reaches its climax only when the two friends are torn apart and Orestes remains behind alone, a prey to his lacerated feelings and his terrible visions. Anguish prostrates him, and now, after the last words of his recitative:

> Où suis-je? A l'horreur qui m'obsède,
> Quelle tranquillité succède?

is heard that aria in which the accompaniment gives the lie to his words (see page 165).

Orestes has slain his mother; the memory of it bores and hammers unceasingly and pitilessly in his heart. He falls asleep, but before him, and before us, appear the Eumenides in the fearsome, slow tread of a dance and to a horrifying chorus, with a scale of trombones in unison cutting across its measured beats (see pages 166–8). It is a passage of which Gluck had had a presentiment in his *Telemacco*, where Telemachus approaches the magic grove ('Quai tristi gemiti').

The dark torment of this scene is heightened by Orestes's cry of pain and the dumb apparition of Clytemnestra's blood-stained shade, and we cannot believe that we can be still further affected, both theatrically and emotionally, when the gates open and, at the head of the priestesses, Iphigeneia, the daughter and younger likeness of the murdered mother, stands before the awakened Orestes. The dialogue between brother and sister could not have been more magnificently and effectively introduced; the act could not have been more gloriously concluded than with the plaintive song of Iphigeneia and the female choir, a funereal ceremony in a twilight of C minor and C major, clearing in the last eight bars into a consolatory major close.

IPHIGÉNIE EN TAURIDE 1779

Gluck

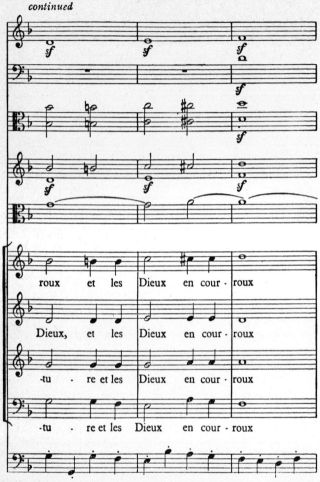

continued

roux   et   les   Dieux   en cour - roux

Dieux,   et   les   Dieux   en cour - roux

-tu - re et les   Dieux   en cour - roux

-tu - re et les   Dieux   en cour - roux

The climax of this act was not to be outdone. The third act reveals, by a rather tame aria, how Iphigeneia wavers between fear and hope. The deliberations follow between her and the pair of victims, one of whom she can and will save in order to send him as messenger to her home. Obeying an inner voice, she inclines to the choice of her brother, and now the magnanimous struggle between the two friends ensues in a duet divided between wild and gentle expressions, a new 'pathological' *recitativo accompagnato* for Orestes, an aria-like dialogue, the victory of Orestes, which—a great scenic notion, this—takes place in the presence of Iphigeneia, and a grand heroic aria for Pylades, who intends to make use of his unexpected freedom to liberate his friend—a somewhat superficial, tenorish curtain, though dramatically quite justified.

The last act opens with a short recitative for Iphigeneia, in which she expresses her resolution never to perform the sacrifice, and with that aria where—strangest of all musical relationships—Gluck made free use of the jig in Bach's B flat major Partita. It is a splendid but somewhat too magniloquent number, a piece for a prima donna And indeed, in the *Telemacco* of 1765, it had actually been given to a prima donna, the sorceress Circe ('Se estinguer non bastate'). Then comes the solemn ceremony of the sacrifice, with its suave choruses of priestesses, a few wonderful bars expressive of Orestes's resolution, the recognition of the brother at the moment the knife is raised, and the expiation announced by the candid notes of joy from the sister and priestess. A wild agglomeration of catastrophe follows: the news of the approach of the irate Scythian king, the excited altercation by means of solo, dialogue and chorus, the intervention of Pylades, the death of Thoas, the fight between Scythians and Greeks—until Diana's majestic recitative makes the happy and rather too festive conclusion possible. It is unfortunately the most 'French' feature of this wonderful opera, which so often lifts itself out of its Gallicism to the azure skies, the timelessness of pure humanity.

The Parisians this time grasped the magnitude of the event. There was no difference of opinion among the public, no polemic among the arbiters, hardly a 'critical' pronouncement. This was Gluck's greatest victory, inwardly and outwardly.

'ÉCHO ET NARCISSE'

Just as in the view of music-lovers of to-day the thought of Mozart's last dramatic works conjures up only *Die Zauberflöte,* while *La clemenza di Tito* is forgotten (not wholly, perhaps, but nevertheless unjustly), so do we regard the *Iphigénie en Tauride* as Gluck's last work. But it was followed four months later by *Écho et Narcisse*, produced on 24th September 1779 (not on the 21st, as the libretto has it). For his libretto Gluck engaged the services of a new literary collaborator, Jean Baptiste Louis Théodore Baron de Tschoudi (Tschudi), a diplomat like du Roullet, a botanist, agronomist and occasional poet. Du Roullet was once again involved in the origin of the libretto. Tschudi was a newcomer to Paris. He was born in 1734 at Metz, but his name points to a Swiss origin in the canton of Glarus. He did, in fact, at first serve in a Swiss regiment, became bailiff and royal councillor at Metz in 1760, in 1774 minister to the Prince-Bishop of Liége, and had not come to Paris until 1777. Only here, in that literary atmosphere, does he appear to have discovered his talent as a poet. *Écho et Narcisse* was certainly his first dramatic essay.

It was not a happy one, this 'drame lyrique en trois actes.' A prologue was added to it on the occasion of the revival, on 8th August 1780, and it is in this revised version, not in the original one, that the work is printed and preserved. We can only judge this effort, or non-effort, of Tschudi's, and the reasons that induced Gluck to compose the libretto, from a knowledge of what the poet made of his theme. The fable of Echo and Narcissus is found in the third book of Ovid's *Metamorphoses,* and it is one of the most mysterious and profound of the ancient myths. The nymph Echo loves the beautiful shepherd Narcissus; but her love is not returned, for Narcissus is enamoured only of his own beauty. From sheer grief Echo dissolves into nothing but a voice, which awakens only on being called upon by human sounds, when she is able to answer the caller from the hollows and caverns of mountains and groves. Narcissus is made aware of his selfishness by the death of the nymph and delivered from his remorse and despair by being transformed into a flower:

The water Nymphes his sisters wept and wayled for him sore,
And on his bodie strowde their haire clipt off and shorne therefore.
The woodnymphes also did lament. And *Echo* did rebound
To every sorrowfull noyse of theirs with like lamenting sound.

The fire was made to burne the corse, and waxen Tapers light.
A Herce to lay the bodie on with solemne pompe was dight.
But as for bodie none remain: In stead thereof they found
A yellow floure with milke white leaves now sprong upon the ground.[1]

Tschudi's version goes as far as the death of Echo, but reaches only the attempted suicide of Narcissus, and not his metamorphosis. It is uncommonly easy to put one's finger on all the faults and clumsinesses of his libretto: its destruction of the tender melancholy that pervades the ancient fable; the utterly unnecessary dramatic presupposition that Apollo once pursued Echo with his amorous suits and visits the lover with his wrath because he was rejected by her; the introduction of the god Cupid, who patronizes the pair in defiance of Apollo, fills a prologue with *ariosi,* sets chorus and ballet into much too long-winded an action there, and appears at the end as *deus ex machina*; the use of the shepherd Cynire as a pastoral Pylades for the Orestes of the play, Narcissus, and of not less than two nymphs, Eglé and Aglaé, for its gentle Armida, Echo; not to mention a dozen other ineptitudes.

Still, the libretto must have had qualities to attract Gluck, who was at the end of his career, knew what he wanted, and was not the man to accept a libretto as a child does an apple. What were these qualities? They lay in the fundamentally tragic content presented in a pastoral framework. Gluck took *Écho et Narcisse* very seriously, no less so than *Orfeo ed Euridice.* The work is like a return to his reformatory beginnings, as though it were meant as a counterpart to *Orfeo.* The resemblances are obvious and become even more so if the original version of the work is considered and the purely decorative prologue disregarded. After the first scene, a chorus and ballet of nymphs and fauns who are strictly separated choreographically and characterized musically by tender wind colours and stamping rhythms respectively, Echo appears, her soul filled with premonitions of her loss, and sends the noisy crowd off the stage:

> Nymphes, éloignez-vous un moment de ce lieu . . .

and they accordingly withdraw, suddenly turned serious and troubled,

[1] Arthur Golding's translation, 1567.

171

in dumb-show accompanied in C minor. What follows is not the expected solitary lament, but a plaintive dialogue with the sympathetic friend Cynire. Echo's recitatives, with their frequent string *tremoli,* have a wholly tragic and Gluckian accent. Narcissus is no languishing shepherd, but one blinded by madness, like Orestes. He is as one possessed and imagines that he sees in his own reflection a goddess so dazzling that the gentle nymph Echo cannot but yield to her. He is an out-and-out pathological figure. Note the 'hidden' melodic line with which he invokes his own image in the water:

and note, too, the beginning of the *ritornello* in this scene, where in growing agitation he implores the surface of the water to open (see pages 173-4).

This is nothing else than Paris's aria, 'Le belle immagini,' but infinitely heightened, a psychological or pathological snapshot not inferior to the famous one of Orestes, except that Narcissus is far from being an Orestes. And the score contains one of the most glorious and heart-seizing arias Gluck ever wrote: the plaint of Narcissus:

> Beaux lieux, témoins de mon ardeur,

in which his dead beloved suddenly answers the invocation of a remorseful lover. His agitation, his rapture, his emotional upheaval:

> Au bord du Styx peux-tu l'aimer encore?

mark one of the summits of Gluck's penetration into the human soul.

What Gluck may not have succeeded in doing in *Orfeo* with the persuasion of Hades and the loss of Eurydice he triumphantly did

here by the sheer power of music.   Was it really possible to believe
that he could furnish an indifferent or even a weak work after
Iphigénie en Tauride and treat himself to one of those 'relapses' of his
earlier and middle periods?   This work is full of great, tragic ideas,
and from their own point of view Gluck's contemporaries judged
by no means wrongly when they preferred the concluding 'Hymne

ÉCHO ET NARCISSE 1779

à l'Amour,' which is certainly charming, to this aria, of whose
beauty they clearly had no inkling. Gluck was never more lavish
in the instrumentation either—how full and tender the pastoral overture
with its double orchestra sounds!—though never more unequal, for
this work of his advanced age wavers in style between an eclogue and
a tragedy, between psychological drama and *festa teatrale,* between
old-fashioned, almost Lullian declamation and truly Gluckian
downrightness of diction, and it repeats scenes such as had already
made greater and deeper impressions with a finer dramatic logic and
a stronger coherence in *Orfeo, Alceste* and *Iphigénie en Tauride.*

CHAPTER IV

CLOSE OF LIFE AND INFLUENCE

WITHDRAWAL TO VIENNA

'ÉCHO ET NARCISSE' was a failure. The work reached but twelve performances, only nine after its revival, and the takings fell from evening to evening. Only at the third attempt, when after the fire at the Opéra (8th June 1781) it was given again on the rapidly erected provisional stage at the Porte Saint-Martin, was its reception more friendly. The 'Hymne à l'Amour' that closes the opera was praised, as we have seen, but it was considered that the music suffered from a paltry subject and a poor poem. In the *Mémoires secrets* of 30th September 1779 we read:

> . . . it is true that it would be impossible to set eyes on worse words. The stilted, precious, ludicrous style of this poet goes to unexampled lengths, and his very scheme, which is entirely contrary to the fable, is the most ridiculous thing imaginable.

Gluck took the Parisians' judgment in bad part. It is possible that his disappointment and anger were aggravated by those first strokes from which he suffered during the rehearsals and soon after the production, unless it was the other way about, and the annoyance caused him by the stage gossip before the performance and by the ungrateful public of Paris contributed to these seizures. Be that as it may, Gluck left Paris in the middle of October, resolved never to return to that city, in which he had so shortly before declared that he meant to end his life. At the end of October he was in Vienna once more, after 'the most beautiful journey in the world.' He wished to put *Écho et Narcisse* on the stage in Vienna. The reasons why it never came to that are not known.

He was implacable at first. A poet, Gersin, who had published

a *Traité du Mélodrame ou Réflexions sur la Musique dramatique* in 1771,
offered him a new libretto at the end of 1779; but he refused it:

> I shall not write another opera hereafter . . . my career is finished,
> my age, and the disgust I had to endure lately in Paris in connection with
> my opera of *Narcissus* have for ever put me out of conceit to write still
> others. . . .

In spite of all his bitterness towards Paris, however, he was by no
means disinclined some time later to 'adjust' the revision and revival
of the work, eagerly urged by Tschudi, and to take an active part in
it. He took as much interest as ever in all the theatrical news from
Paris, though he speaks with contempt of the 'Marmontellian gang,'
and he wished Piccinni's *Atys,* produced on 22nd February 1780,
a 'good success,' in order that he may himself remain 'unmolested.'
Not that he took it all very seriously, not even when he wrote on
31st March 1780:

> But as to my going to Paris again, nothing will come of it, so long as
> the words 'Piccinnist' and 'Gluckist' remain current, for I am, thank
> God, in good health at present, and have no wish to spit bile again
> in Paris. . . . I shall hardly allow myself to be persuaded again to become
> the object of the criticism or the praise of the French nation, for they are
> as changeable as red cockerels—if it were to be, it would have to be made
> very comfortable, since idling is now my only pleasure. . . . I could
> wish that someone might come one day to take my place, and to please
> the public with his music, so that I might be left in peace, for I am still
> unable to forget the tittle-tattle to which friends and foes made me listen
> concerning *Narcissus,* and the pills I have had to swallow, for Messieurs
> the Frenchmen cannot yet see any difference between a musical eclogue
> and a 'poème épique' . . .

True, during the time the revival of *Écho et Narcisse* was being
prepared his mood grew more amenable again.

> If the stupid reasonings were to grow out of fashion, which arise there
> out of music and spectacles, I might perhaps resolve once more to go there,
> and to whistle something more to them; howbeit, I no longer trust them;
> the burnt child fears the fire,

he wrote on 30th June 1780, forgetting that it was he who had
created the fashion of 'reasoning' with the preface to *Alceste.*

But when the 'new arrangement' of the opera proved a new failure on 8th August (it survived only nine or ten performances), he declared bluntly, angrily and conclusively (30th September): '*Nothing will come of my return to Paris.*'

'LES DANAÏDES'

Meanwhile Gluck had entered into negotiations in quite another direction—that of Naples. At the end of October 1780 he wrote to Kruthoffer of secret news he hoped to be able to tell in a couple of months, which would be very agreeable to him. On 29th November he announced: 'I am to go to Naples, to write four operas there; I wished to conceal it from you until I knew whether my conditions would be accepted or not.' But on 3rd January 1781 he was obliged to announce: 'The death of the empress [Maria Theresa, 29th November 1780] has frustrated my journey to Naples.'

There is no doubt that for these new relations with Naples Gluck's former collaborator, Calzabigi, was responsible, who had moved from Pisa to Naples early in 1780, and that one of the four projected operas was to have been composed to a new libretto of his: *Ipermestra* or *Le Danaidi*. What happened? Calzabigi himself tells us in his famous letter to the editor of the *Mercure de France* of 21st August 1784:

It was in 1778, and after the great success of my Orpheus and my Alceste upon your stage, that M. Gluck desired *iterum antiquo me includere ludo.* He induced me, with great promises, to write a new drama for him. I wrote a Semiramis, which I sent to him. I do not know its fate. . . . M. Gluck greatly approved of it at first; but he perceived afterwards that it did not suit the actors who shone at that time on the lyric stage. I had once spoken to him about a Hypermnestra; he urged me so earnestly to write it, that I decided to comply; he received that poor Hypermnestra in Paris, where he was, in the month of November of the same year; he was enthusiastic about it; he sent word that he would have it translated in order to give it to the stage; and that was all he let me know about it.

It is certain that Gluck occupied himself with *Le Danaidi* and seriously undertook its composition, presumably, as was his custom, without at first writing down a note of it. It was a subject that must have appealed to him, a subject not without its secret or open elements of aggression, for it was once again a blow at the Metastasian operatic ideal. For Metastasio himself had written an *Ipermestra* that had been often composed, in which the strong and fierce dramatic motives are, as usual, converted into amorous entanglements and episodes exhibiting generous actions. In his *Risposta* of 1790 Calzabigi took particularly deadly aim at this *Ipermestra* of Metastasio's, and he was entitled to do so. As the author of *Le Danaidi* he restored its whole force to the subject. Danaus is a barbarian like Thoas, who for revenge orders the death of the husbands of his fifty daughters; Hypermnestra is not a puppet put together from the constituents of magnanimity and love, and stuffed with straw, but a loving woman who curses her cruel father. We are at once plunged *in medias res* of the preparations for the sanguinary wedding; the work opens with dances and closes with the sight of Danaus's hapless daughters in Hades, 'agitate da diverso tormento, e disperazione in diverse figure, gruppi e attitudini,' not unlike the situation in Claudio Monteverdi's *Ballo delle ingrate* of long ago. On the other hand, there are long dialogues in that awkward arrangement in five acts, superfluous choruses, dances and arias: Calzabigi was too educated an aesthetician and too much imbued with all sorts of classical reminiscences to supply a poem that was as such quite pure and free from dross.

The letters to Kruthoffer tell us that it must have been the frustration of the Naples plans alone which made Gluck abandon *Le Danaidi*; but what the composer committed on that occasion was a piece of inconsiderateness that offended even against such notions of 'author's rights' as the eighteenth century could conceive. Without consulting him, he handed Calzabigi's manuscript to Messrs. du Roullet and Tschudi, and without the author's least knowledge of what was going on, it was translated, adapted and composed. In the autumn of 1783 Bachaumont announced *Le Danaidi* in his *Mémoires secrets* [1] among the works prepared for performance at the Opéra, under the title of *Hypermestre,* by Baron Schudy and the Chevalier Gluck, and on 26th April 1784 [2] appeared at the Théâtre

[1] Vol. xxi, 10th September 1783.

[2] The title-page of the score, engraved by Des Lauriers and dedicated to Marie Antoinette, says 19th April.

de l'Académie Royale de Musique a 'tragédie-lyrique en cinq actes, *Les Danaïdes,*' the libretto of which informs us that 'La Musique est de MM. le chevalier Gluck et Salieri.' The librettists bashfully withheld their names. One of them, Tschudi, died from the consequences of erysipelas while the work was being rehearsed; the survivor, du Roullet, unabashedly inserted the following notice in the libretto:

A manuscript by M. de Calzabigi, author of the Italian Orpheus and Alcestis, has been handed to us, to which we have helped ourselves liberally. We have borrowed from the ballet of the Danaides by the celebrated M. Noverre, that modern rival of Bathyllus and Pylades; to these we have joined our own material, and out of this whole we formed our scheme.

One of our friends, whose family has forbidden us to name him, was good enough, in order to accelerate our work, to turn part of our composition into verse, and this will certainly not be that of which the style will be thought the most careless. Death has just removed from us this excellent man, known by several works in prose and in verse, both equally esteemed.

The mention of Gluck on the libretto as part-composer was a stratagem calculated to impress the Parisian public favourably by the weight of his powerful name, or at any rate to make it cautious. When the success of the work seemed assured after the twelfth performance, Gluck came forward with a declaration that Salieri should be taken as the only creator of the music and that his own collaboration was confined to his having offered a few hints and counsels to his former pupil. Salieri in his turn says of the work in his dedication to the queen:

I wrote it under the eye and under the direction of the famous Chevalier Gluck, that sublime genius, the creator of dramatic music, which he has carried to the highest degree of perfection it is capable of attaining. I hope, with the advice of this great man, to succeed in composing some other work, more worthy of the enlightened taste of Your Majesty. . . .

Friendly as Gluck's attitude towards Salieri was, that towards Calzabigi is indefensible. In the twentieth century Calzabigi might have prosecuted Gluck and du Roullet for a grave breach of his author's rights, and would have obtained from any judge an incontrovertible and irrevocable verdict in his favour. In the eighteenth century he had no other redress than that of protesting publicly in that letter to the *Mercure de France* against the injustice he had suffered. He had a few scenes of his *Ipermestra* composed by Millico, Gluck's Orpheus at Parma and former housemate, and he had the satisfaction of having them performed in the presence of the emperor, who was then the guest of the Neapolitan court. He had them printed in their original form in February 1784. He showed that the criticism levelled against the French libretto could not be applied to his own book. He declared that the composer of the French version, who-ever he might be, could not possibly have conformed to his inten-tions, which rested on the only true and correct declamation of his verses, and that therefore 'the music written for my Danaides by M. Millico must needs be infinitely superior to that given in Paris with the copy of my drama.'

There he was unjust to Salieri, much as he was unjust, not to the inequitable procedure, but to the dramaturgic insight of du Roullet and Tschudi. The two adapters gave their libretto the most concise form without departing from Calzabigi's plan. They attenuated neither the character of the drama nor the fate of the forty-nine daughters who are so pitiless in their obedience: we hear the death cries of the murdered husbands and see the torments of the Danaides and their progenitor in hell; we are spared nothing. The scenes between Danaus and Hypermnestra, between Hypermnestra and Lynceus, have their full dramatic weight. The wedding choruses and dances are anything but interpolations. And the manner in which Salieri composed this libretto cannot in truth be characterized otherwise than as 'mock-Gluck.' The Paris audiences of the first twelve performances, still constrained to guess at the shares taken in the score by Gluck and Salieri, may have ascribed the almost Nea-politan wedding choruses and dances and some of the more 'tender' arias of the lovers Lynceus and Hypermnestra to the latter; but to his contemporaries, who were unaware of the situation, Gluck must have unquestionably seemed to be the creator of the strongest scenes, and certainly the inspirer of the terseness of these progressive and never static five acts. It may well have been overlooked that all this was more richly and at the same time more conventionally orchestrated than a 'real Gluck,' and had a thicker coating of theatricality, although we can no longer overlook it to-day.

The 'Auteur du Poème des Danaïdes,' du Roullet, needless to say, addressed a 'Réponse' to Calzabigi,[1] weakly defending his weak position, mainly by hiding behind the broad back of Gluck.

OLD AGE AND DEATH

Gluck himself never replied to Calzabigi's open letter, and indeed it would be difficult to tell what he could have replied. He was by this time an invalid, too, and illness is apt to make a man indifferent to the world's events. On 28th March 1781 he wrote that he was 'not well, the March weather upsets me, I suffer much from melancholy,' and on 1st May: 'I must needs have patience until good weather arrives, when I hope to recover my health in my garden.' But a few weeks later he had a serious apoplectic seizure, which wholly paralysed his right side, so that he could no longer write. 'I have been ill for several months as the result of an apoplectic stroke that afflicted me last year,' he dictated on 17th April 1782 in a letter to the conductor Valentin at Aiguillon; 'my head is enfeebled and my right arm useless, and I am incapable of doing any work that involves a continuous occupation; it is forbidden me. . . .' A cure at Baden brought about a gradual improvement after the summer of 1781, when he had

once more escaped from the jaws of death, without having first recovered from my earlier illness. Pneumonia, accompanied by a fever, robbed me entirely of the little strength that had remained, and I am once again a weak convalescent.

In March 1783 he spoke once more of a plan for a visit to Paris, and in August even of an invitation to London, 'to produce my Italian opera that is already done'; but the intention was not realized.

The increasing performances of his Paris operas in Vienna somewhat brightened his days. 'The Iphigeneia in Tauris, which is soon to be represented, will set me in motion again and stir my blood,' he wrote on 1st May 1781, and this event took place on

[1] *Mercure de France,* 9th October 1784.

23rd October, with scenery by the Paris painter Moreau, with Antonia Bernasconi in the title part, and 'with great success.' What was more, the performance was given in a German translation. Mozart was not present at the crowded first performance, but 'I was at nearly all the rehearsals,' he says. With the German translation Gluck himself took great pains, together with the young Viennese poet Johann Baptist von Alxinger (whom Mozart, too, would have liked to engage to translate and adapt his *Idomeneo*). *Iphigénie* was followed on 3rd December by the Italian *Alceste* and on 31st December by *Orfeo*. At repeat performances of *Alceste* and *Iphigénie* Gluck had as an admiring hearer and spectator the Grand Duke Paul Petrovitch, afterwards Tsar Paul I, who, together with Prince Ludwig of Württemberg, paid him a visit with half Vienna looking on in the streets, heaping compliments upon him ('he said he had already heard much music, but none so far that had gone so near his heart as mine') and praising especially the aria, 'Ah per questo già stanco mio core,' with which Alcestis takes leave of her children.

Reichardt, in the summer of 1783, found Gluck apparently in full possession of his powers again. But in 1784 the man of seventy had yet another severe stroke. That was the end. Yet he seems to have thought of a German opera during this last span of life as well as formed operatic plans for Naples. On 10th February 1780 he had written to the Duke Carl August of Weimar, Goethe's friend and Maecenas, the letter already quoted from:

I have now grown very old, and have squandered the best powers of my mind upon the French nation, regardless of which I feel an inward impulse to write something for my own nation yet.

Whether Klopstock's *Hermanns-Schlacht* was meant to be, or could have been, this 'something' remains questionable; but a German chronicler was right when he wrote in 1775 that 'as yet no court has had a theatre built in which it could be represented.' German opera was not to be helped out with an exceptional work, a 'tragedy with music,' but only with a true opera. One may well ask whether Gluck noticed that the creator of German opera was already active side by side with him; whether he suspected that the beginnings of this German opera were present in a modest German *Singspiel* and not in any German *opera seria*; whether he knew that the future was not dedicated to German imitations of his work, the endeavours to bring forth a 'national song-spectacle,' like Ignaz Holzbauer's *Günther von Schwarzburg* or Anton Schweitzer's *Alceste,* but to the works descended from *Die Zauberflöte,* which appeared four years after his death.

His relations with Mozart were friendly, but reserved owing to the mere fact that he patronized Mozart's natural opponent, Salieri. The Mozarts, father and son, had mistrusted Gluck ever since their first visit to Vienna in 1768. When Mozart went to Paris in 1778, his father peremptorily instructed him to avoid Gluck. During the Viennese period Mozart was once Gluck's guest at dinner, and the elder master went to *Die Entführung,* which delighted him. He also went to the younger's concerts, and the latter honoured him by a set of variations on a Gluckian theme. But no sincere friendship ensued, and it is easy to feel that Gluck's 'grand politics' were not looked on sympathetically by Mozart.

What were Gluck's secret feelings when he heard *Die Entführung?* He cannot have helped noticing what a wealth of *music,* what invention and spirit, what a gift of divine ease too, there was in this work, whose subject so closely resembled his own *Rencontre imprévue.* Neither could it escape him that there was in the characterization of Osmin a truth that went far beyond his own rationalism, and an adroitness and psychological insight in the final quartet of the second act such as could be attained only in *opera buffa.* What, on the other hand, did Mozart think of *Iphigeneia* in German, of which he missed hardly a rehearsal? Technically he had nothing to learn from Gluck. He, the greatest instrumental composer of his time, who was just about to conquer the realm of 'learned' music for himself, can only have smiled at all the stiffnesses and awkwardnesses of Gluck. But without his visits to those rehearsals at the end of 1781 the Commandant in *Don Giovanni,* nay, perhaps the whole of *Don Giovanni,* that *dramma giocoso* illuminated by tragic lights, that underworld which embodies a moral principle, would not have come into existence.

To the last years of Gluck's life belongs a piece of so-called church music, a *De profundis* for four-part chorus with a curious, dark-coloured accompaniment of lower strings (violas, cellos and basses only), bassoon, horn and a trio of trombones. The oboe alone adds a lighter colouring. It is a moving invocation of the godhead, *adagio espressivo,* rising from D minor into the regions of brighter tonalities and sinking back again into a questioning half-close that seems to leave everything unsolved. It is antique rather than ecclesiastical, subjective rather than 'catholic,' a sombre counterpart to Mozart's *Ave, verum corpus.* One would think that Gluck wrote this pessimistic work, which might also be brought into biographical and artistic comparison with the *Vier ernste Gesänge* of another Viennese master, on the day on which he 'suffered much from melancholy'; but one must suppose that he composed it for the Concert Spirituel in Paris. Even dejection does not find a tired and resigned expression in Gluck, for although there is no lack of such turns in this musical reflection of a whole state of mind, especially in the interludes, its tone is in the main urgent, tense and manly (see pages 185-9).

The passage must be reproduced in full score if the high lights of the oboe, the *sforzato* of the solitary horn notes and the doublings of the high violoncello parts that cut across the texture are not to be lost to the eye. Here again Gluck proves himself the greatest master of psychological orchestration. Here, too, he shows himself as a universal genius—and we do not know how many works he may have written in other branches beside his operatic output, for we do not possess his personal heritage, which after the death of his widow in 1800 went to his nephew Carl von Gluck and was destroyed by fire or plunder in Gluck's country house at Kalksburg during the French occupation of Vienna in 1809. And it is significant that he, who was so eager, not to say ruthless a usufructuary of his own music, should have written a work like this *De profundis,* created, as it were, for himself alone and hardly 'communicable.'

Gluck died of a forbidden pleasure of the table. It is like the vengeance of fate for an act of wantonness: he once—about 1778— had his and his wife's portrait painted as they sit at dessert, he looking exultantly at the spectator over his shoulder, glass in hand, she about

DE PROFUNDIS

De Profundis

187

Gluck

to fill it from a bottle. On 15th November 1787 he entertained two friends from Paris at luncheon; they were at the stage of coffee and liqueur—the latter strictly forbidden him. His wife left the room to order the carriage for their daily drive, and when her back was turned Gluck encouraged his two guests to drain their glasses of the fatal beverage. When one of the friends declined, he tossed off his glass himself in feigned anger and with a request not to give him away to his wife. In the carriage he had another apoplectic seizure, and a few hours later he was dead. He was buried on 17th November at the cemetery of Matzleinsdorf. His tombstone bears the usual impressive untruths and half-truths: what we may be certain to accept as true is only the epithet:

OF THE SUBLIME ART OF SOUND THE GREAT MASTER.

THE SUCCESSION

About the succession of Gluck, Christoph Martin Wieland, the poet of Schweitzer's *Alceste,* said some tolerably prophetic words in his *Versuch über das deutsche Singspiel* of 1775, when Gluck was still alive. He concludes his essay as follows:

At last we have lived to see an epoch at which the mighty genius of a Gluck has undertaken this great work, which—if it was ever to materialize —had needs to be awakened by a fiery spirit like his own. The great success of his Orpheus and Eurydice, his Alcestis, his Iphigeneia, would induce the utmost hopes, were it not that his enterprise is opposed by invincible moral causes in the very capitals of Europe where the fine arts have their noblest temples!—arts which the masses are accustomed to regard only as means to sensual enjoyments and which must be reinstated in their original dignity, with Nature upheld on a throne so long usurped by the arbitrary power of fashion, of luxury and of the most exuberant sensuality—a great and audacious undertaking! but too like the great enterprise of Alexander and Caesar to create a new world out of the ruins of the old not to share its fate. A whole succession of Glucks would be needed for this (as for the project of a universal monarchy a whole succes- sion of Alexanders and Caesars) to ensure the reign and the continuance upon the lyric scene of this suzerainty of unspoilt Nature over music, of this simple song capable, like Mercury's caduceus, of awakening and lulling passion and conducting souls to Elysium or Tartarus, of this banishment of all sirens' arts, of this harmonious assent of all the parts in a single unity of the whole. Gluck himself—for all his enthusiasm— knows mankind and the course of things below the moon too well to hope for anything of the kind! It is enough that he should have shown us what music might achieve, if in these our days there were an Athens anywhere in Europe, and in that Athens appeared a Pericles, to do for opera what he did for the tragedies of Sophocles and Euripides.

Let us not go into details of this extract, which anticipates Schiller's conception of the theatre as a moral institution—a conception Gluck was as far as possible from sharing. Wieland was doubtless right to resign himself to the fact that the succession of Glucks necessary to the regeneration of the operatic domain would never appear. He could not suspect that this regeneration of opera would be effected in quite a different field from that enclosed within the boundaries of *opera seria,* of the classicist opera to which Gluck's work belongs. It came about in the realms of the *opera buffa* and the *opéra comique.* The *dramma giocoso* of *Don Giovanni* belongs far more closely to the spiritual descendants of *Alceste* than *Idomeneo* or *La clemenza di Tito,* and not the *Brenno* of Reichardt, the *Démophon* of Cherubini or his *Medée* (1797), which is a vast hybrid work, nor yet any other classicist operas by North German or Parisian Gluck enthusiasts continue the history of the post-Gluckian music-drama, but the *Zauberflöte,* a coarse piece for the display of stage machinery at a Viennese suburban theatre, and *Fidelio,* a simple *Singspiel.*

In Paris Gluck's example was imitated only by average or small French, German and Italian musicians; but his spirit, as Romain Rolland acutely observes, was revived only in passing through the songs of the Revolution: 'Some portions from his operas (among others the chorus, "Poursuivons jusqu'au trépas" from *Armide)* were "republicanized" and frequently performed at revolutionary festivities.' During the Napoleonic era Gluck was thrust into the background; the cultivation of his work passed from Paris to classicist Berlin. The one successor of Gluck who rose above mediocrity and carried his operatic ideal on into the nineteenth century is Gasparo Spontini. His development shows curious analogies with that of Gluck, for his work too classifies itself into an Italian, a French and a German phase, of which the German shows the weakest impulse. But in Spontini everything remained more obviously conditioned by external considerations, more mask-like, more rhetorical and more tied up in theatrical 'grandezza.' All the same, without Spontini there would have been no *Rienzi*, which does not point to Meyerbeer so much as to impressions of *La Vestale* and *Fernando Cortez*. The nineteenth century's true adorer of Gluck, however, is Berlioz.

Berlioz, not Wagner. At the time Wagner sought for recognition from Germany and the rest of the world it was a favourite theme of his adherents to draw a parallel between him and Gluck, and what they liked better still was to designate him as the 'consummation' of Gluck, the master who had brought to perfection what good old Gluck had striven after. His opponents were no less pleased to prove that Gluck had realized the ideal of opera long before him. The truth is that Gluck and Wagner as musical creators are perfectly incommensurable giants, who have nothing more in common than a few theoretical exigencies, especially those of the dissolving of the 'set' forms in opera, the merging of recitative and aria, and the subordination of music to the drama. 'The confusion of the artistic boundaries in opera consisted in the fact that a means of expression (the music) was made into its purpose and the purpose (the drama) into the means,' was Wagner's dictum. That might already have been thus formulated by Gluck. Both denied the musico-dramatic ideal of their time: Gluck the operatic type of Metastasio, which served a convention of opera in which music was predominant; Wagner the singer's opera of Rossini and the 'grand opera' of Meyerbeer, although he did not renounce the latter's framework, but merely filled it with more genuine and reasoned contents.

But on looking closer we find that these affinities evaporate. Gluck was a child of the rationalist age, Wagner of the romantic century. It may even be said that these periods are most purely and visibly embodied in them. Gluck, too, uses myths in *Orfeo,* in *Alceste* and in *Écho et Narcisse,* but he uses them in order to 'humanize' his figures; while Wagner is fond of letting some very human actions— take *Lohengrin* or *Tristan*—dissolve into mythical mists. Diderot once planned an *Essai sur le tolérantisme musical,* which Gluck would doubtless have welcomed with enthusiasm, for did he not once write to Padre Martini in Bologna about his progress in Paris: 'The obstacles will be great, because national prejudices must be attacked from the front, and reason does not prevail against them'?[1] Wagner was, or at any rate superficially believed that he was and theoretically defended his belief, a nationalist of the purest water, however international his influence may have been for a time.

What is entirely disparate in the two masters is their distribution of the vocal and instrumental parts in opera. Infinitely though Gluck enriches the range of orchestral colours in his work, he never lets the orchestra dominate the voice. He always writes *vocal* opera. In the later Wagner the symphonic principle and symphonic structure reign supreme wherever a decisive effect is intended, and the voice is merely fitted in. One need only point to Isolde's 'love death' or to Wotan's 'farewell.' Gluck was serious about the 'subordination of music to drama,' while Wagner in his own dramas let music in again by the back door—the symphonic back door.

The true Gluckian of the nineteenth century, then, is Hector Berlioz. *Les Troyens* is the last shoot from Gluck's soil, not only in subject, but spiritually and instrumentally, the *Chasse royale* the last descriptive ballet. All that Berlioz contributed to the under-standing of Gluck in his criticisms, his essays and his *Traité d'instru-mentation* is born of love and enthusiasm; he alone succeeded, at a time when Gluck had almost disappeared from the stage again, in awakening new admiration in Paris at least for *Orphée* and *Alceste*. It was he who about 1860 inspired a great and intelligent singer, Pauline Viardot, with a desire to appear as Orpheus, since which time the part of the Thracian singer has remained the possession of the heroic contralto voice, failing eunuch singers in the nineteenth century. It was he, too, who induced a patroness, Mlle Fanny Pelletan, to finance the edition of at any rate Gluck's six 'French' operas.

Gluck's example has remained an object of study and experiment in revival both in Germany and France, and to a smaller extent in Italy and England. Essays and biographies have appeared, material has accumulated and his life, with the exception of the years of his youth, has been elucidated. Wotquenne furnished a thematic catalogue (not quite complete and not quite reliable) that forms a

[1] 26th October 1773.

basis for every work on Gluck. A biography or monograph on a large scale is still lacking. Several works have appeared in new editions. The bi-centenary of his birth seemed to bring about new activity and brought forth 'Gluck Societies,' whose enterprise was paralysed not so much by the tragic times in which we live as by internal weaknesses. Some of the less important works have been reprinted, also a few of the great ones; but we are still without a new edition of the Italian *Alceste* and without *Paride ed Elena* or *L'innocenza giustificata,* while resurrections of all sorts of indifferent works abound. As for stage revivals of his operas, Gluck shares the fate of all the older masters. The farther a dramatic work is removed in time from the present, the more freely may theatrical fancy play with it, and so *Orfeo* in particular becomes the victim of arbitrary operations on the part of ambitious producers and modernistic choreographers. The real Gluck still remains to be discovered by us all. Let us hope that a happier, purer and more reverent age may discover him once and for all.

APPENDICES

APPENDIX A

CALENDAR

(Figures in brackets denote the age reached by the person mentioned during the year in question.)

Year	Age	Life	Contemporary Musicians
1714		Christoph Willibald Gluck, born, July 2, at Erasbach, Upper Palatinate, son of Alexander Johannes Gluck (*c.* 33), a huntsman and forester of German-Bohemian birth.	Bach (C. P. E.) born, March 8; Homilius born, Feb. 2; Jommelli born, Sept. 10. Abaco aged 39; Albinoni 43; Arne 4; Ariosti 48; Bach 29; Bach (W. F.) 4; Benda (F.) 5; Bonno 4; Bononcini 42; Boyce 4; Caldara *c.* 44; Campra 54; Couperin 46; Croft 36; Desmarets 52; Destouches 42; Durante 30; Eccles 46; Fasch (J. F.) 26; Fux 54; Galuppi 8; Geminiani 34; Graun 10; Graupner 27; Handel 29; Hasse 15; Holzbauer 3; Keiser 40; Kuhnau 54; Lalande 57; Leo 20; Locatelli 19; Lotti *c.* 47; Marcello 28; Martini 8; Pergolesi 4; Porpora 28; Rameau 31; Richter (F. X.) 5; Sammartini (G.) *c.* 21; Sammartini (G. B.) 16; Scarlatti (A.) 54; Scarlatti (D.) 29; Steffani 60; Tartini 22; Telemann 33; Veracini 24; Vinci 24; Vivaldi *c.* 40.

Year	Age	Life	Contemporary Musicians
1715	1		Wagenseil born, Jan. 15.
1716	2		
1717	3	Removal of the family to Bohemia, Aug. They settle at Neuschloss near Böhmisch Leipa, where G.'s father (*c.* 36) is appointed ranger to Count Kaunitz.	Nichelmann born, Aug. 13; Stamitz (J. W.) born, June 19.
1718	4		
1719	5		
1720	6		Agricola (J. F.) born, Jan. 4.
1721	7		Kirnberger born, April 24.
1722	8	Removal to Böhmisch Kamnitz, where his father (*c.* 41) becomes forester to Count Kinsky, Chancellor of Bohemia.	Benda (G.) born, June; Kuhnau (62) dies, June 5; Nardini born, April 12; Reinken (99) dies, Nov. 24.
1723	9	As the son of an official, G. receives a good education, including some private instruction and music lessons.	Tartini (31) becomes conductor of Kinsky's band in Prague; Francœur (25), Fux (63), Graun (19), Quantz (26), Rebel (22) and Veracini (33) all visit Prague for the coronation of Charles VI (38).
1724	10	(?) Removal to Reichstadt, where G.'s father (*c.* 43) becomes forester to the Duchess of Tuscany.	Theile (77) dies, June.
1725	11	Return to Böhmisch Kamnitz (?), where his father (*c.* 44) re-enters the service of Count Kinsky.	Bertoni born, Aug. 15; Krieger (J. P.) (75) dies, Feb. 7; Pisari born; Scarlatti (A.) (65) dies, Oct. 24.
1726	12	(?) Is sent to a Jesuit college at Komotau, where, in addition to a general education, he receives lessons in harpsichord and organ playing.	Lalande (68) dies, June 18; Philidor born, Sept. 7; Pistocchi (66) dies, May 13.

Year	Age	Life	Contemporary Musicians
1727	13	(?) Education at Jesuit college continued.	Anfossi born, April 25; Croft (48) dies, Aug. 14; Gasparini (59) dies, March 22; Traetta born, March 30.
1728	14	(?) Makes progress in music at the Jesuit college.	Guglielmi born, Dec. 9; Hiller (J. A.) born, Dec. 25; Marais (72) dies, Aug. 15; Piccinni born, Jan. 16; Steffani (73) dies, Feb. 12.
1729	15	(Approx.) His father (c. 48) becomes head forester to Prince Lobkowitz at Eisenberg.	Gassmann born, May 3; Monsigny born, Oct. 17; Sarti born, Dec. 1.
1730	16		Loeillet (49) dies, July 19; Sacchini born, June 14; Senaillé (43) dies, Oct. 8; Vinci (40) dies, May 27.
1731	17		Cannabich born.
1732	18	(?) Enters Prague University.	Haydn born, March 31/April
1733	19	While at Prague University (?), G. learns the violin and violoncello in addition to the keyboard instruments he already plays. He is also an excellent singer.	1; Böhm (71) dies, May 18; Couperin (64) dies, Sept. 12.
1734	20	Earns some money by playing the organ at various churches, the Tein Church and St. James's, where he learns much from Černohorsky (50).	Gossec born, Jan. 17.
1735	21	Gives singing and violoncello lessons and continues to play at churches.	Bach (J. C.) born, Sept. 5; Eccles (66) dies, Jan. 12; Krieger (J.) (83) dies, July 18.
1736	22	Leaves Prague and goes to Vienna, where, Prince Ferdinand Philipp Lobkowitz (12), who in spite of his youth is already at the head of his house, takes him into his service as chamber musician.	Albrechtsberger born, Feb. 3; Caldara (c. 66) dies, Dec. 28; Fasch (C. F. C.) born, Nov. 18; Pergolesi (26) dies, March 16.

Year	*Age*	*Life*	*Contemporary Musicians*
		He continues his musical studies and hears much Italian opera.	
1737	23	Prince Melzi hears G. and induces him to accompany him to Milan. He becomes chamber musician to Melzi there and pupil of G. B. Sammartini (39).	Haydn (Michael) born, Sept. 14; Montéclair (69) dies, Sept. 27; Mysliveček born, March 9.
1738	24	Studies under Sammartini (40) in Milan continued.	Battishill born, May; Murschhauser (74) dies, Jan. 6.
1739	25	Hears many contemporary operas in Milan and is on very friendly terms with Sammartini (41).	Dittersdorf born, Nov. 2; Keiser (65) dies, Sept. 12; Marcello (52) dies, July 24; Rust born, July 6; Wanhal born, May 12.
1740	26	Is still chamber musician to Prince Melzi and continues his studies with Sammartini (42), with whom he goes into the questions of greater freedom of expression and of a harmonic style as opposed to counterpoint.	Arnold born, Aug. 10; Lotti (c. 73) dies, Jan. 5; Paisiello born, May 8.
1741	27	First opera, *Artaserse,* produced, Dec. 26. The libretto is by Metastasio (43) and the work is dedicated to Count Traun (64), governor of Milan. The rehearsal is severely judged by a select audience, but the first performance is well received by the general public.	Desmarets (79) dies, Sept. 7; Fux (80) dies, Feb. 14; Grétry born, Feb. 11; Jannaconi born; Naumann born, April 17; Vivaldi (c. 67) dies, July.
1742	28	Visit to Venice to hear the singers for whom he is commissioned to write a new opera. Production of *Cleonice* (originally called *Demetrio*) at	Abaco (67) dies, July 12.

Year	Age	Life	Contemporary Musicians

the Teatro San Samuele in Venice, with great success, Ascension Day (May 2). Third opera, *Demofoonte,* produced in Milan, Dec. 26.

1743 29 Opera, *Tigrane,* produced at Crema, Sept. 9, where it was commissioned for the fair. The libretto, by Francesco Silvani, is newly arranged for Venice by Goldoni (41). G. conducts, at the opening of the Milan opera season, Lampugnani's (*c.* 37) *Arsace,* for which he has written additional music.

Boccherini born, Feb. 19; Gazzaniga born, Oct.

1744 30 Opera, *Sofonisba* (or *Siface*) produced in Milan, Jan. 13. Visit to Bologna, where *Demofoonte* is produced, carnival, and to Venice, where he is to produce two new works. Comic opera, *La finta schiava,* produced there, at the Teatro Sant' Angelo, May 13. It is written in collaboration with Lampugnani (*c.* 38) and Maccari, and contains numbers by Vinci (54). Production of the opera, *Ipermestra,* Oct. Metastasio's (46) libretto has shortly before been composed by Hasse (45). Opera, *Poro,* produced at Turin, Dec. 26.

Campra (83) dies, June 29; Leo (50) dies, Oct. 31; Hasse (45) composes the opera, *Ipermestra,* for the marriage of the Archduchess Marianna of Austria to Prince Carl of Lorraine.

1745 31 Production of the opera, *Ippolito,* in Milan, Jan. 31. At the invitation of Lord Middlesex, G. accompanies

Dibdin born, March; Stamitz (C.) born, May 7.

Year	Age	Life	Contemporary Musicians

Prince Lobkowitz (21) to England. Visit to Paris on the way, where G. becomes acquainted with French opera and admires Rameau (62). Arrival in London, autumn. The political situation is unfavourable, but Lord Middlesex obtains permission to reopen the Italian Opera with a work by G., who hastily makes a pasticcio from earlier works to a libretto by the Abbate Vanneschi, *La caduta de' giganti*. G. visits Handel (60), who thinks him a poor contrapuntist, but esteems and befriends him.

1746   32   *La caduta de' giganti* produced in London, Jan. 7. A second pasticcio, *Artamene,* produced, March. Concert at the King's Theatre, in which Handel (61) takes part, March 25. G.'s benefit concert, at which he plays a concerto on the musical glasses, April 23. Meeting and friendship with Arne (36). Six trio Sonatas published by Simpson, Nov. Departure for Hamburg, (?) autumn, where he joins Pietro Mingotti's Italian opera company as conductor.   Cambini born, Feb. 13.

1747   33   Mingotti goes to Leipzig with part of his company, including G., early spring. The company moves on to Dresden,   Bononcini (76) dies, July 9; Rebel (J. F.) (85) dies, Jan. 2; Schulz born, March 31.

Year	Age	Life	Contemporary Musicians
		May, to prepare for the double wedding between the Saxon and Bavarian royal houses. Meeting with Hasse (48). Production of the wedding Serenade, *Le nozze d' Ercole e d' Ebe,* before the Saxon court at Pillnitz, June 29. (?) Visit to Hammer, near Brüx, in Bohemia, where his father (*c.* 66) has just died, Sept. (?) He sells the land he has inherited and goes to Vienna, end of year.	
1748	34	Production of the opera, *Semiramide riconosciuta,* in Vienna, on Maria Theresa's (31) birthday, May 14. G. joins Mingotti's company again as conductor and goes with it to Hamburg, autumn, and to Copenhagen, end of Nov., at invitation of Frederic V (25).	Stadler born, Aug. 7.
1749	35	Appears at Copenhagen as solo instrumentalist on the harpsichord and musical glasses as well as in his capacity of conductor. Dramatic serenade, *La contesa de' numi,* produced at the royal castle of Charlottenborg, April 9, to celebrate the birth of the crown prince (afterwards Christian VII). Return to Vienna, (?) after a visit to Holland with Mingotti's company. He is asked to many noble and wealthy houses, including that of the	Cimarosa born, Dec. 17; Destouches (76) dies, Feb. 3; Vogler born, June 15.

Year	*Age*	*Life*	*Contemporary Musicians*

rich merchant and banker Joseph Pergin, with whose daughter Marianna he falls in love. (?) Pergin withholds his consent to a marriage.

1750	36	Visit to Prague, where the opera, *Ezio,* is produced during the carnival. Death of Pergin and of G.'s mother at Hammer in Bohemia. Marriage to Marianna Pergin, who brings him a considerable fortune, Sept. 15. He settles down in Vienna.	Albinoni (78) dies, Jan. 17; Bach (65) dies, July 28; Salieri born, Aug. 18; Sammartini (G.) (*c.* 57) dies (approx.); Veracini (*c.* 60) dies.
1751	37	*Ezio* brought out in Leipzig.	Bortniansky born.
1752	38	Production of the opera, *Issipile,* in Prague during the carnival. Departure for Naples, summer, having been invited to compose an opera for the Teatro San Carlo, for the name-day of Charles III (36). Production there of *La clemenza di Tito,* Nov. 4, with Caffarelli (49) in the cast. A novel effect in one of the arias leads to a dispute among the Neapolitan composers, who are jealous of G.'s success, but Durante (68), to whom the question is submitted, decides in his favour. Return to Vienna, Dec. Bonno (42) introduces G. to Prince Hildburghausen, whose private band he is engaged to conduct. He meets Dittersdorf (13), who is in the orchestra.	Clementi born, Jan. 23; Kozeluch born, Dec. 9; Reichardt born, Nov. 25; Zingarelli born, April 4.

Year	Age	Life	Contemporary Musicians
1753	39	Aria, *Pace, amor,* from a cantata by Metastasio (55) composed for Hildburghausen's concerts (or possibly the whole work).	Dalayrac born, June 13.
1754	40	Departure for Hildburghausen's summer residence, the palace of Schlosshof, May. Opera, *Le Cinesi,* performed there, Sept. 24, on a visit of Maria Theresa (37) and Francis I (46). The emperor makes arrangements for its production in Vienna and presents G. with a gold snuffbox containing 100 ducats. Return to Vienna, autumn. G. is engaged as musical director to the court by Count Durazzo, director of the imperial theatres.	Clari (76) dies, May 16; Martín y Soler born, May 2; Winter born, Aug.
1755	41	*Le Cinesi* produced at the court opera in Vienna, April 17. Pastoral cantata, *La danza,* performed at Laxenburg, May 5, and repeated in Vienna, May 13. Meeting with Haydn (23) during a visit to Prince Hildburghausen at Mannersdorf. Opera, *L'innocenza giustificata,* produced on the birthday of Francis I (47), Dec. 8; libretto by Durazzo. Psalm, *Domine Dominus noster,* composed (approx.).	Durante (71) dies, Aug. 13; Viotti born, May 12.
1756	42	Visit to Rome, where the opera, *Antigono,* is produced, Feb. 9. G. meets Winckelmann (39) at the residence of	Mozart born, Jan. 27; Perti (94) dies, April 10; Righini born, Jan. 22.

Year	*Age*	*Life*	*Contemporary Musicians*

Cardinal Albani. The latter offers to use his influence to quell a cabal set in motion against G. by some Roman composers, but he prefers to defeat it by his own merits. He is knighted by Pope Benedict XIV (81), receiving the Order of the Golden Spur and the title of Cavaliere (approx.). Return to Vienna. Opera, *Il rè pastore*, produced on Francis I's (48) birthday, Dec. 8.

1757 43

Pleyel born, June 1; Scarlatti (D.) (71) dies, June 23.

1758 44 French comic opera, *L'Isle de Merlin*, produced at Schön-brunn, Oct. 3. A similar work, *La Fausse Esclave,* produced there, (?) carnival.

Dagincourt (74) dies, June 18; Zelter born, Dec. 11.

1759 45 Comic opera, *L'arbre enchanté,* produced at Schönbrunn, Oct. 3; *La Cythère assiégée* produced in Vienna and at the castle of Schwetzingen, before the Elector Carl Theo-dor of the Bavarian Palatinate. The libretto is by Favart (49).

Graun (55) dies, Aug. 8; Handel (74) dies, April 14.

1760 46 Prince Hildburghausen, after being defeated in the battle of Rossbach, dissolves his orchestra and G. is no longer attached to any patron; but thanks to his successes and his wife's wealth, he wel-comes rather than regrets his freedom.

Cherubini born, Sept. 14; Dussek born, Feb. 12; Filtz (*c.* 30) dies; Graupner (77) dies, May 10; Lesueur born, Feb. 15; Zumsteeg born, Jan. 10.

Year	Age	Life	Contemporary Musicians
		Dramatic serenade, *Tetide,* produced at the wedding of the Archduke Joseph (19) to Isabella of Parma, Oct. 8. Comic opera, *L'Ivrogne corrigé,* at Schönbrunn. The conductor of the court opera, Reutter (52), quarrels with the director, Count Durazzo, on account of G.'s conducting works other than his own.	
1761	47	Comic opera, *Le Cadi dupé,* produced at Schönbrunn. Production of the dramatic ballet, *Don Juan,* Oct. 17, at the court theatre and subsequently at the Kärntnertor Theatre.	Gaveaux born.
1762	48	Production of the opera, *Orfeo ed Euridice,* at the court theatre, Oct. 5. The libretto is by Ranieri Calzabigi (48). In spite of its disconcerting novelty, it makes an immense impression before long, and enthusiastic partisans group themselves round G., against the adherents of the school of Metastasio (64), on which he has now turned his back.	Geminiani (82) dies, Sept. 17.
1763	49	Visit to Venice and Bologna in the company of Dittersdorf (24), the singer Chiara Marini and her mother. At Bologna the singers of the newly built theatre give a concert for G., who is to write an opera for	Gyrowetz born, Feb. 19; Mayr born, June 14; Méhul born, June 22.

them. He reverts for this to a libretto by Metastasio (65), *Il trionfo di Clelia,* and the work is produced, May 14. Visits to Farinelli (58) and Martini (57). After a visit to Parma, he is recalled to Vienna by Durazzo, giving up intended visits to Milan and Florence, early summer.

1764	50	Comic opera, *La Rencontre imprévue* (*The Pilgrims to Mecca*), produced, Jan. Count Durazzo retires from the direction of the opera and is succeeded by Count Wenzel Sporck. G. also resigns his appointment, in favour of Gassmann (35), March. Short visit to Paris, where *Orfeo ed Euridice* is published, March. Coronation of the Archduke Joseph (23) as King of the Romans at Frankfort - on - Main, April 3. G. writes an aria to be sung there by Guadagni (later incorporated in Act I of the Paris version of *Orfeo ed Euridice*).	Fioravanti born, Sept. 11; Leclair (67) dies, Oct. 22; Locatelli (68) dies, April 1; Rameau (81) dies, Sept. 12.
1765	51	Dramatic serenade, *Il Parnasso confuso,* produced at Schönbrunn, Jan. 24, to celebrate the second marriage of Joseph II (24), to Maria Josepha of Bavaria. The libretto is specially written by Metastasio (67), the first expressly written by him for G. Ballet-	Attwood born, Nov. 23; Eberl born, June 13; Eybler born, Feb. 8; Himmel born, Nov. 20.

Year	Age	Life	Contemporary Musicians

pantomime, *Semiramide*, produced, Jan. 31.   Opera, *Telemacco*, produced.   The libretto is by C. S. Capeci, revised by M. Coltellini. Metastasio's *La corona* composed for the archduchesses, to be performed by them on the birthday of Francis I (75), summer. Sudden death of the emperor, Aug. 18. *La corona* is never performed.

1766 52 Ballet-pantomime, *L'orfano della China*, produced (approx.).

Porpora (79) dies, Feb.; Süssmayer born; Weigl born, March 28; Wesley (S.) born, Feb. 24.

1767 53 Visit to Florence, where he produces the dramatic cantata, *Il prologo,* to celebrate the reappearance of the Archduchess Maria Luisa after her confinement, Feb. 22. He also conducts Traetta's (40) *Ifigenia in Tauride.* After his return to Vienna he works at a new opera to a libretto by Calzabigi, *Alceste,* modelled on Euripides.   Production of *Alceste,* Dec. 16.

Berton born, Sept. 17; Telemann (86) dies, June 25.

1768 54 G. buys a fine house in the Rennweg. *L'innocenza giustificata* revised and entitled *La Vestale,* summer.

1769 55 G. and his wife adopt his niece, Marianne Hedler (10), who takes their name (approx.).   She shows considerable musical talent.   Score of

Asioli born, Aug. 30.

Year	*Age*	*Life*	*Contemporary Musicians*
		Alceste published with a preface and dedication to the Grand Duke of Tuscany. Visit to Parma for the wedding of the Infante Don Ferdinando (18), at which the dramatic trilogy, *Le feste d' Apollo,* is performed, Aug. 24. It consists of *Orfeo* arranged in one act, an *Atto di Bauci e Filemone* and an *Atto d'Aristeo.* G. takes the singer Giuseppe Millico back to Vienna with him.	
1770	56	Production of the opera, *Paride ed Elena,* Nov. 30. The libretto is by Calzabigi (56), to whose house G. goes to hear Salieri's (20) first opera, the public performance of which he furthers.	Beethoven born, Dec. 16; Tartini (77) dies, Feb. 26.
1771	57	G. for the first time plans a setting of the bardic songs in Klopstock's (47) *Hermanns-Schlacht.* He also sets several of Klopstock's odes to music (approx.). Visit to Bologna, where he conducts *Orfeo ed Euridice.*	Baillot born, Oct. 1; Paer born, June 1.
1772	58	François du Roullet, attaché to the French embassy, writes a French libretto for G., based on Racine's *Iphigénie en Aulide.* Meeting with Burney (46), who visits Vienna, Sept. 2.	Daquin (77) dies, June 15; Reutter (63) dies, March 11.
1773	59	Visit to Paris with his wife and adopted daughter Marianne (14), who attracts much	Catel born, June 10; Quantz (76) dies, July 12.

Year	Age	Life	Contemporary Musicians

attention in musical circles by her singing, beginning of year. G. publishes a letter on the new style in opera in the *Mercure de France,* Feb. 1. The Paris Opéra, not anxious to encourage him, refuses to accept *Iphigénie en Aulide* unless he undertakes to write five other operas. He accepts the proposal.

1774 60 Visit to Klopstock (50) at Carlsruhe on the way to Paris, spring. Marianne (15) sings some of G.'s settings of the poet's odes to him. Production of *Iphigénie en Aulide* at the Paris Opéra (Académie Royale de Musique), April 19. Sophie Arnould (34) sings the title part. The dauphine, Marie Antoinette (19), formerly G.'s pupil in Vienna, is present. Parties for and against G. at once begin to form. Production of *Orphée et Eurydice,* a new French version of *Orfeo ed Euridice* with important musical revisions, Aug. 2. Return to Vienna, after a second visit to Carlsruhe, autumn. He is appointed Imperial Court Composer with 2,000 florins per annum, Oct. 18.

Gassmann (44) dies, Jan. 22; Jommelli (59) dies, Aug. 25; Spontini born, Nov. 14.

1775 61 Visit to Klopstock (51), this time at Strasburg and Rastatt, on the way to Paris. Comic

Baini born, Oct. 21; Boieldieu born, Dec. 16; Crotch born, July 5; Isouard born,

Year	Age	Life	Contemporary Musicians

opera, *L'Arbre enchanté* (second version, see 1759) performed at Versailles, Feb. 27. Duplessis (50) paints G.'s portrait. Return to Vienna, where he is kept by a prolonged illness. (Meanwhile a new version of *La Cythère assiégée* (see 1759) is performed in Paris, Aug. 1.) He makes a new French version of *Alceste* to a translation by du Roullet and also works on two French operas, *Roland* and *Armide,* to librettos by Quinault.

Dec. 6; Rebel (F.) (74) dies, Nov. 7; Sammartini (G. B) (76) dies, Jan. 15.

1776 62 New visit to Paris, early March. First performance of the French version of *Alceste* at the Opéra, April 23. The Piccinnists hiss the work, but at later performances it asserts itself more and more triumphantly. G.'s wife arrives in Paris with the news of the death of their niece and adopted daughter Marianne (17, d. April 22), end of April. G. is deeply affected by the loss. Return to Vienna, *c.* beginning of June.

Cavos born; Seyfried born, Aug. 15. Arrival of Piccinni (48) in Paris, Dec. 31.

1777 63 On hearing that *Roland* has been given to Piccinni (49) as well, G. writes an indignant letter to du Roullet, which is published without his consent in the *Année littéraire.* This begins the war of partisans in Paris. Although Piccinni has

Wagenseil (62) dies, March 1.

Year	Age	Life	Contemporary Musicians

as yet produced no French opera, his Italian works are well enough known in Paris to keep the quarrel between the Gluckists and the Piccinnists alive. Marmontel (54), La Harpe (38) and Ginguené (29) are on the Italian's side, the Abbé Arnaud and Suard (44) on the German's. G. returns to Paris, May. Production of *Armide* at the Opéra, Sept. 23. G. has destroyed the sketches of his setting of Quinault's *Roland* because Piccinni is engaged on a libretto on the same subject by Marmontel. He suspects that the rivalry between them, which has not been sought by either, is to be artificially exploited.

1778 64 The production of Piccinni's (50) *Roland* (Jan. 27), which his partisans thought would at once ruin G.'s cause, only serves to inflame the quarrel between the adherents of the two composers, who still take no part in it, Jan. Visit to Voltaire (84) at Ferney shortly before his death (May 30). Return to Vienna, March 1, where he sets to work on Guillard's libretto of *Iphigénie en Tauride* and on Baron Tschudi's (44) of *Écho et Narcisse*. Houdon's (37) bust of

Arne (67) dies, March 5; Hummel born, Nov. 14.

Year	Age	Life	Contemporary Musicians
		G. is placed next to those of Lulli and Rameau at the Opéra, March 14. Return to Paris, Nov. G. is asked to open the newly built Teatro alla Scala in Milan with a new opera, but refuses.	
1779	65	Production of *Iphigénie en Tauride* at the Opéra, May 18. It has an immediate success. *Écho et Narcisse*, on the other hand, in which he attempted a new style, fails at its first performance, Sept. 24. Unwilling to give up new experiments and to repeat merely what pleases the public, he decides to leave Paris. He has several apoplectic seizures, from which he recovers, and returns to Vienna with his wife, end of Oct. He retires from public life.	Boyce (69) dies, Feb. 7. Traetta (52) dies, April 6.
1780	66	Klopstock (56) writes for news of the operatic setting of his *Hermanns - Schlacht* (see 1771), which G. has been unable to touch during the Paris years. He becomes much occupied with this work again, but does not write down any of his ideas. Naples approaches G. with a request for four operas, including Calzabigi's (66) *Ipermestra* or *Le Danaidi,* but the death of Maria Theresa (63, Nov. 29) frustrates this plan.	Kreutzer (C.) born, Nov. 22.

Year	Age	Life	Contemporary Musicians
1781	67	Again suffers from a stroke, which partly paralyses him, and his wife insists on his abandoning all work on the *Hermanns-Schlacht*. At the command of Joseph II (40) a German version of *Iphigénie en Tauride* is performed, Oct. 23. G. is visited by the Grand Duke Paul of Russia (27) and his wife, Nov. 28. *Alceste* and *Iphigénie en Tauride* are performed in Italian in their honour.	Mysliveček (43) dies, Feb. 4.
1782	68	A special performance of Mozart's (26) *Entführung*, which G. is anxious to hear, is arranged for him, Aug. It highly delights him and he invites Mozart to dinner. Composition of a *De profundis* for chorus and orchestra, the manuscript of which G. gives to Salieri (32) (approx.).	Auber born, Jan. 29; Bach (J. C.) (46) dies, Jan. 1; Field born, July 26.
1783	69	G. goes to Mozart's (27) concert, March 23, and Mozart improvises variations on a theme from *La Rencontre imprévue*. G. is visited by Reichardt (31), to whom he plays some of the music for the *Hermanns-Schlacht*, which is still not written down. Reichardt writes down G.'s composition of Klopstock's (59) ode, *Der Tod*, which he has heard him play.	Hasse (84) dies, Dec. 16; Holzbauer (71) dies, April 7; Kirnberger (62) dies, July 27.
1784	70	Recommends Salieri (34) to	Bach (W. F.) (73) dies, July

Year	*Age*	*Life*	*Contemporary Musicians*

the Paris Opéra as a composer likely to write a grand opera worthy of that house. *Les Danaïdes* produced in Paris, April 26, as the work of G. and Salieri. Calzabigi (70) complains in a letter to the *Mercure de France,* Aug. 21, about his treatment by G. in the matter of the libretto of *Ipermestra,* or *Le Danaidi,* he had promised to compose in 1778.

1; Martini (78) dies, Oct. 4; Onslow born, July 27; Ries born, Nov.; Spohr born, April 5.

1785 71 Lives now in complete retire-ment and in a precarious state of health. Seven Odes of Klopstock for voice and clavier published, end of year.

Galuppi (78) dies, Jan. 3; Homilius (71) dies, June 5.

1786 72

Bishop born, Nov. 18; Rai-mondi born, Dec. 20; Sac-chini (56) dies, Oct. 6; Weber born, Nov. 18.

1787 73 G. is visited by two friends from Paris, Nov. 15. He drinks a glass of liqueur after dinner in the momentary absence of his wife, who has doctor's orders to diet him strictly. The guests are asked to excuse him and his wife for half an hour, while he has his daily ride in the carriage. He is attacked by a stroke on the way and returns home un-conscious.
Gluck dies in Vienna, Nov. 15.

Carafa born, Nov. 17; Fran-cœur (88) dies, Aug. 6. Albrechtsberger aged 51; Anfossi 60; Arnold 47; Attwood 22; Auber 5; Bach (C. P. E.) 73; Baillot 16; Basili 20; Beethoven 17; Benda (G.) 65; Berton 20; Bishop 1; Boccherini 44; Boieldieu 12; Bonno 77; Bortniansky 36; Cannabich 56; Catel 14; Cherubini 27; Cimarosa 38; Clementi 35; Crotch 12; Dalayrac 34; Dibdin 42; Dittersdorf 48; Dussek 27; Eberl 22; Eybler

Year	Age	Life	Contemporary Musicians
			22; Fasch (C. F. C.) 51; Field 5; Fioravanti 23; Gazzaniga 44; Gossec 53; Grétry 46; Guglielmi 59; Gyrowetz 24; Haydn 55; Haydn (M.) 50; Hiller (J. A.) 59; Himmel 22; Hummel 9; Isouard 12; Kozeluch 35; Kreutzer (C.) 7; Lesueur 27; Martín y Soler 33; Mayr 24; Méhul 24; Monsigny 58; Mozart 31; Nardini 65; Naumann 46; Onslow 3; Paer 16; Paisiello 47; Philidor 61; Piccinni 59; Pleyel 30; Raimondi 1; Reichardt 35; Richter (F. X.) 78; Ries 3; Righini 31; Rust 48; Salieri 37; Sarti 58; Schenk 34; Schulz 40; Seyfried 11; Spohr 3; Spontini 13; Stadler 39; Stamitz (C.) 42; Umlauf 41; Viotti 32; Vogler 38; Wanhal 48; Weber 1; Weigl 21; Wesley (S.) 21; Winter 33; Zelter 29; Zingarelli 35; Zumsteeg 27.

APPENDIX B

OPERAS AND FESTE TEATRALI

Alceste, in Italian (Calzabigi), Vienna, 1767 (1, vocal score only).
Alceste, in French (du Roullet), Paris, 1776 (2, 3).
(*Alessandro nelle Indie.*) See *Poro.*
Antigono (Metastasio), Rome, 1756.
(*Aristeo.*) See *Feste d'Apollo.*
Armide (Quinault), Paris, 1777 (3).
Arsace (Salvi, Act I only), Milan, 1743.
Artamene (Vitturi: Vanneschi), London, 1746.
Artaserse (Metastasio), Milan, 1741.
(*Bauci e Filemone.*) See *Feste d'Apollo.*
Caduta de' giganti, La (Vanneschi), London, 1746.
Cinesi, Le (Metastasio), Schlosshof, 1754 (2).
Clemenza di Tito, La (Metastasio), Naples, 1752.
(*Cleonice.*) See *Demetrio.*
Contesa de' numi, La (Metastasio), Charlottenborg (Copenhagen), 1749.
Corona, La (Metastasio), Vienna, 1765. Never performed.
Danza, La (Metastasio), Laxenburg, 1755.
Demetrio (Metastasio), Venice, 1742.
Demofoonte (Metastasio), Milan, 1742.
Écho et Narcisse (Tschudi), Paris, 1779 (2, 3).
Ezio (Metastasio), Prague, 1750.
(*Fedra.*). See *Ippolito.*
Feste d'Apollo, Le: Il prologo; Bauci e Filemone; Aristeo (Frugoni); *Orfeo,*
Parma, 1769.

[1] Modern editions are referred to above by the following numbers: (1)
Breitkopf & Härtel, Leipzig; (2) *Sämtliche Werke* (Bärenreiter, Kassel);
(3) Édition Pelletan (Richault, Paris; Durand, Paris); (4) *Denkmäler der
Tonkunst in Österreich*; (5) Eulenburg Edition, London; (6) Peters, Leipzig;
(7) *Denkmäler der Tonkunst in Bayern*; (8) Callwey, Munich; (9) Senff, Leipzig;
(10) Gluckgesellschaft I (Max Arend); (11) Universal Edition, Vienna; (12)
Oppenheimer, Hamelin; (13) Reinecke, Leipzig; (14) Gluckgesellschaft
II (Breitkopf & Härtel, Leipzig); (15) Joseph Liebeskind (see Bibliography);
(16) Bärenreiter, Kassel; (17) Kallmeyer, Wolfenbüttel; (18) Schott, Mainz.

Appendix B.—Catalogue of Works

Finta schiava, La (Silvani, *pasticcio*), Venice, 1744.
Innocenza giustificata, L' (Durazzo: Metastasio), Vienna, 1755 (4: xliv [82]).
Ipermestra (Metastasio), Venice, 1744.
Iphigénie en Aulide (du Roullet), Paris, 1774 (3).
Iphigénie en Tauride (Guillard), Paris, 1779 (3, 5, 6).
Ippolito (Gioseffo Gorino Corio), Milan, 1745.
Issipile (Metastasio), Prague, 1752.
Nozze d' Ercole e d' Ebe, Le (?), Pillnitz, near Dresden, 1747 (7: xiv, 2).
Orfeo ed Euridice, in Italian (Calzabigi), Vienna, 1762 (2, 4: xxi, 2 [44a]).
   See also *Feste d'Apollo*.
Orphée et Eurydice, in French (Moline), Paris, 1774 (3).
Paride ed Elena (Calzabigi), Vienna, 1770 (2).
Parnasso confuso, Il (Metastasio), Schönbrunn (Vienna), 1765.
Poro (Alessandro nelle Indie) (Metastasio), Turin, 1744.
Prologo, Il (L. O. del Rosso), Florence, 1767 (1).
(Prologo.)   See *Feste d' Apollo*.
Rè pastore, Il (Metastasio), Vienna, 1756.
Semiramide riconosciuta (Metastasio), Vienna, 1748.
(Siface.)   See *Sofonisba*.
Sofonisba (Silvani, with arias by Metastasio), Milan, 1744.
Telemacco (Capece, revised by Coltellini), Vienna, 1765.
Tetide (Migliavacca), Vienna, 1760.
Tigrane (Silvani), Crema, 1743.
Trionfo di Clelia, Il (Metastasio), Bologna, 1763.
(Vestale, La.)   Vienna, 1768.   See *Innocenza giustificata*.

OPÉRAS COMIQUES AND VAUDEVILLES

(Amours champestres, Les), Vienna, 1755.
Arbre enchanté, L' (Moline), Schönbrunn (Vienna), 1759; Versailles, 1775
   (8, vocal score only).
Cadi dupé, Le (Le Monnier), Vienna, 1761 (9, vocal score only).
(Chinois poli en France, Le) (Anseaume), Laxenburg, 1756.
Cythère assiégée, La (Favart), Schwetzingen, 1759.
Cythère assiégée, La, second version (Favart), Paris, 1775.
(Déguisement pastoral, Le) (Favart), Schönbrunn (Vienna), 1756.
Diable à quatre, Le (Sedaine), Laxenburg, 1759.   A few airs only.
Fausse esclave, La (Anseaume and Marcouville), Vienna, 1758.
Isle de Merlin, L' (Le Sage and d'Orneval), Schönbrunn (Vienna), 1758 (2).
Isabelle et Gertrude (Favart), Paris, 1765.   3 airs only.

Gluck

Ivrogne corrigé, L' (Anseaume), Vienna, 1760 (2).
Rencontre imprévue, La (*Les Pèlerins de la Mecque*) (Dancourt), Vienna, 1764 (10).

BALLETS

Alessandro (?), Vienna, 1765.
Don Juan (Angiolini), Vienna, 1761 (4: xxx, 2 [60]).
Orfano della China, L' (?), Vienna, 1766 (?) (8, piano score only).
Semiramide (Calzabigi?), Vienna, 1765 (11, piano score only).

VOCAL WORKS

Ariettes, c. 1780:
Amour en ces lieux.
Quand la beauté lance.
Cantata for solo voice, *I lamenti d'amore* (adapted from Act III of the Italian *Alceste*) (13).
Duet, *Minona lieblich und hold.*
Klopstocks Oden und Lieder, Vienna, 1785 (14):
  1. *Vaterlandslied.*
  2. *Wir und Sie.*
  3. *Schlachtgesang.*
  4. *Der Jüngling* (second version).
  5. *Die Sommernacht* (first version).
  6. *Die frühen Gräber.*
  7. *Die Neigung.*
Motets:
  Almae sedes laeta pacis, for solo voice.
  De profundis, for chorus and orchestra, c. 1786 (12).
  Voces cantate, for solo voice.
Ode an den Tod (Klopstock), 1783 (15).
Odes (Klopstock) (14):
  Der Jüngling (first version), in *Göttinger Musenalmanach,* 1775.
  Die Sommernacht (second version), in Voss's *Musen-Almanach,* Hamburg, 1785.

INSTRUMENTAL WORKS

Six Sonatas for two Violins & a Thorough Bass, London, 1746 (1, 2).
Sonata (*Symphonia*) for 2 violins and bass (No. 7), E major (1, 2).
Sonata for 2 violins and bass (No. 8), F. major (2).
14 Symphonies (or Overtures) (single issues: 11, 16, 17, 18).

APPENDIX C

Abel, Carl Friedrich (1723–87), German *viola da gamba* player and composer, educated in Leipzig and associated with Hasse (q.v.) at Dresden. Went to London in 1759 and settled there, giving concerts and composing.

Agujari, Lucrezia (1743–83), Italian soprano singer, who made her first appearance at Florence in 1764.

Albinoni, Tommaso (1671–1750), Venetian violinist and composer.

Anfossi, Pasquale (1727–97), Italian opera composer, pupil of Piccinni (q.v.) at Naples, where he produced his first comic opera in 1758. Later produced operas in Paris, London, Prague and Berlin. In 1791 he became *maestro di cappella* to the Lateran in Rome.

Arnould, Madeleine Sophie (1740–1802), French actress and soprano singer, made her first stage appearance in 1757 and the last in 1778. She was a great wit and conversationalist.

Bach, Johann (John) Christian (1735–82), youngest son of Johann Sebastian Bach, spent his early years in Italy and settled in London as clavier player and composer in 1762.

Bernasconi, Antonia (1741–1803), Italian soprano singer, made her first appearance in Vienna in 1767, singing the title part in the production of Gluck's *Alceste*.

Berton, Pierre-Montan (1727–80), French composer and conductor, was appointed conductor at the Paris Opéra in 1759.

Bonno, Giuseppe (1710–88), Austrian composer of Italian extraction. Master of the imperial chapel in Vienna.

Bordoni, Faustina (1700–81), Italian mezzo-soprano singer, made her first appearance in Venice in 1716 and went to London ten years later. Married Hasse (q.v.) in 1730 and sang at Dresden.

Burney, Charles (1726–1814), English musical historian, who travelled extensively on the Continent to collect material for his *General History of Music* and so accumulated matter for two journals on the state of music in various countries.

Caccini, Giulio (*c.* 1550–1618), Italian singer, lutenist and composer, one of the group of Florentine artists who initiated opera.

Caffarelli (*Gaetano Majorano*) (1703–83), Italian male soprano singer, made his first stage appearance in Rome in 1724 and first sang in London in 1738.

Caldara, Antonio (*c.* 1670–1736), Italian composer, pupil of Legrenzi in Venice, worked in Rome and Madrid and settled in Vienna in 1716 as vice-Capellmeister under Fux (q.v.).

Carestini, Giovanni (*c.* 1705–*c.* 1759), Italian male soprano singer, afterwards a contralto. Came out in Rome in 1721 and made his first London appearance in 1733.

Černohorský, Bohuslav Matěj (1684–1740), Bohemian composer, theorist and friar, held church appointments at Padua and Assisi, where Tartini was his pupil. From about 1735 he was director of the music at St. James's Church in Prague.

Ciampi, Vincenzo Legrenzio (1719–62), Italian composer, mainly of operas, one of which includes the song, 'Tre giorni son che Nina,' usually ascribed to Pergolesi (q.v.).

Cimarosa, Domenico (1749–1801), Italian opera composer, studied at Naples and produced his first opera there in 1772. Travelled much later and went to the court of Catherine II of Russia in 1787.

Cuzzoni, Francesca (*c.* 1700–70), Italian soprano singer, first appeared at Parma in 1716 and in London in 1723.

Dittersdorf, Carl Ditters von (1739–99), Austrian composer and violinist, friend of Haydn and Mozart. Prolific composer in various branches of music.

Durante, Francesco (1684–1755), Neopolitan composer and theorist, studied at one of the four Conservatori in Naples and later became director successively of two others. Teacher of many famous composers, including Jommelli, Paisiello, Pergolesi, Piccinni, Sacchini, Traetta and Vinci.

Farinelli (*Carlo Broschi*) (1705–82), Italian male soprano singer, pupil of Porpora, made his first appearance as a boy, later had a great success in England, then became attached to the Spanish court and retired to Bologna at an advanced age.

Forkel, Johann Nikolaus (1749–1818), writer on music, organist and musical director at the university of Göttingen. Bach's first biographer and enemy of Gluck.

Appendix C.—Personalia

Fux, Johann Joseph (1660–1741), Austrian composer and theorist, author of the treatise on counterpoint, *Gradus ad Parnassum.*

Galuppi, Baldassare (1706–85), Venetian composer of operas and instrumental music, produced his first opera in Venice in 1722. *Maestro di cappella* at St. Mark's in 1762.

Gassmann, Florian Leopold (1729–74), Bohemian composer settled in Vienna, appointed *Capellmeister* to the court in 1772.

Gossec, François Joseph (1734–1829), Belgian composer, boy chorister at Antwerp Cathedral, settled in Paris in 1751, produced many operas and church music, cultivated instrumental music.

Grassi, Cecilia (born *c.* 1740), Italian soprano singer who came to London in 1766, where she married Johann Christian Bach (q.v.).

Graun, Carl Heinrich (1704–59), German composer, studied at Dresden, entered the service of the Crown Prince Frederick of Prussia at Rheinsberg in 1735 and went to Berlin with him when he became King of Prussia (Frederick the Great) in 1740, being appointed *Capellmeister.* Wrote operas, Italian cantatas and church music. His Passion, *Der Tod Jesu,* is still sung.

Grétry, André Ernest Modeste (1741–1813), Belgian composer of comic operas, began to compose at Liège at the age of seventeen, went to Rome in 1759, studied there and settled in Paris in 1767.

Hasse, Johann Adolf (1699–1783), German composer of Italian operas, singer at Keiser's opera in Hamburg in his early days, travelled much, appointed *Capellmeister* at Dresden in 1731.

Hiller, Johann Adam (1728–1804), German composer known as the founder of the German *Singspiel,* studied at Leipzig University, later had a singing school and gave concerts there; in 1789 became deputy to Doles, the cantor of St. Thomas's School, whom he succeeded in the same year.

Holzbauer, Ignaz (1711–83), Austrian composer, member of the Mannheim school of early symphonists.

Jommelli, Niccolò (1714–74), Italian composer, pupil of Feo, Mancini and Leo in Naples, produced his first opera in 1737, became famous all over Italy and in Vienna, appointed *Capellmeister* to the Duke of Württemberg at Stuttgart in 1753. Returned to Italy fifteen years later.

Kirnberger, Johann Philipp (1721–83), German theorist, violinist and composer, pupil of Bach 1739–41, became violinist to Frederick the Great in Berlin in 1751. Wrote a treatise, *Die Kunst des reinen Satzes.*

Lampugnani, Giovanni Battista (1706–81), Italian opera composer who worked in London as well as in Italy.

Le Gros, Joseph (1730–93), French tenor singer, made his first stage appearance in Paris in 1764.

Leo, Leonardo (1694–1744), Neapolitan composer, first appeared with the production of a sacred drama in 1712 and brought out his first opera in 1714. He wrote a vast number of operas, also oratorios and church music.

Lesueur, Jean François (1760–1837), French composer, who came to Paris in 1779, but never had any systematic instruction. He nevertheless became a distinguished composer of church music, operas and instrumental works and an excellent theorist. He was appointed professor of composition at the Conservatoire in 1818.

Levasseur, Marie Claude Josèphe (*Rosalie*) (1749–1826), French soprano singer, made her first stage appearance in 1766 under the name of Rosalie, taking her own name in 1775.

Majo, Gian Francesco di (1732–70), Italian composer, pupil of Martini (q.v.) of Bologna, produced his first opera in Rome in 1759, had a great but brief success in Italy and Vienna.

Marcello, Benedetto (1686–1739), Italian composer, pupil of Lotti and Gasparini in Venice. Of noble birth, he held no musical posts, but important government appointments.

Martinez, Marianne (1744–1812), Austrian composer, singer and clavier player of Spanish descent, daughter of the master of ceremonies to the Pope's nuncio in Vienna; pupil of Porpora (q.v.) and Haydn.

Martini, Giovanni Battista (1706–84), Italian contrapuntist, teacher, composer and priest at Bologna, where he was *Maestro di cappella* at the church of San Francesco and established a reputation as the greatest theorist and teacher of the science of music in Europe.

Millico, Giuseppe (1739–1802), Italian male soprano and composer, had an immense success in Italy and went to the court opera in Vienna in 1772.

Mingotti, Regina (*née Valentin*) (1722–1808), Austrian soprano singer, married the impresario Pietro Mingotti at a tender age and became a pupil of Porpora (q.v.). Made her first important appearance at Naples in 1748.

Monticelli, Angelo Maria (*c.* 1710–64), Italian male soprano singer, made his first appearance in Rome in 1730, later sang in Venice, London, Naples, Vienna and Dresden, where he died.

Mysliveček, Josef (1737–81), Bohemian composer, mainly of Italian operas, with which he had a great success in Italy and in Munich.

Appendix C.—Personalia

Paisiello (or *Paesiello*), *Giovanni* (1740–1816), Italian opera composer, student at the Conservatorio di San Onofrio in Naples, had a great success all over Italy, went to the court of Catherine II of Russia, 1776–84, then made his reputation in Vienna and London, and returned to Naples.

Perez, *Davidde* (1711–78), Neapolitan composer of Spanish descent, produced his first opera at Naples in 1740.

Pergolesi, *Giovanni Battista* (1710–36), Italian composer, student at the Conservatorio dei Poveri at Naples, produced a sacred drama with a comic intermezzo in 1731 and several comic operas as well as church and instrumental music during his short career.

Peri, *Jacopo* (1561–1633), Florentine composer, who took an important share in originating opera.

Philidor, *François André Danican* (1726–95), French composer and chess player, did not begin to compose seriously until 1754 and produced his first comic opera in Paris in 1759.

Piccinni, *Niccolò* (1728–1800), Italian composer, pupil of Leo and Durante at Naples, produced his first opera there in 1754. Went to Paris in 1776 and returned to Naples in 1789 at the outbreak of the Revolution, but spent the last two years of his life in the French capital again.

Pockrich, *Richard* (*c*. 1690–1759), Irish musical amateur and player on the musical glasses.

Porpora, *Nicola Antonio* (1686–1768), Italian composer, theorist and singing teacher, went to London as Handel's rival in 1733. Master of Haydn in Vienna.

Predieri, *Luc'Antonio* (1688–1767), Italian composer, *maestro di cappella* of the cathedral at Bologna, went to the court chapel in Vienna in 1739 and became chief *Capellmeister* in 1746, but returned to Italy in 1751.

Reichardt, *Johann Friedrich* (1752–1814), German composer, critic and writer on music, appointed *Capellmeister* and court composer to Frederick the Great in 1776, dismissed from his Berlin appointment in 1794. Important precursor of Schubert as a composer of songs.

Reutter, *Johann Adam Carl Georg von* (1708–72), Austrian composer, chapel master of the cathedral of St. Stephen's in Vienna from 1738.

Rosa, *Salvatore* (1615–73), Italian painter, poet and musician, began his career as a lutenist, but afterwards devoted himself chiefly to painting.

Salieri, *Antonio* (1750–1825), Italian composer who settled in Vienna in 1766, studied under Gassmann, produced his first opera there in 1770 and succeeded Bonno as court *Capellmeister* in 1788.

Sammartini, Giovanni Battista (1698–1775), Italian composer, mainly of instrumental music, in Milan.

Scarlatti, Giuseppe (1723–77), Italian composer of the famous family to which Alessandro and Domenico Scarlatti belonged. Produced his first opera in Rome in 1740.

Scheibe, Johann Adolf (1708–76), German writer on music and critic, studied at Leipzig and settled in Hamburg as music teacher in 1736. Began to publish the weekly, *Der critische Musicus*, in 1737. He was also a prolific composer.

Schweitzer, Anton (1735–87), German composer, studied in Germany and Italy and was attached successively to the courts of Weimar and Gotha.

Senesino (Francesco Bernardi) (c. 1680–*c.* 1750), Italian male soprano singer, attached to the court opera at Dresden in 1719 and there invited by Handel to London, where he first appeared in 1720.

Sirmen, Maddalena (née Lombardini) (born *c.* 1735), Italian violinist and composer, who later became a singer.

Tesi-Tramontini, Vittoria (1700–75), Italian mezzo-soprano singer, who made her first stage appearance at a very early age. In 1719 she was at Dresden, later in Vienna.

Traetta, Tommaso Michele Francesco (1727–79), Italian opera composer, pupil of Durante at Naples, where he produced his first opera in 1751. Had a great success all over Italy and in Vienna.

Viardot-Garcia, Michelle Ferdinande Pauline (1821–1910), Franco-Spanish mezzo-soprano singer, daughter of Manuel Garcia and sister of Malibran, studied piano as well as singing and made her first appearance as a vocalist at Brussels in 1837.

Vinci, Leonardo (1690–1730), Italian composer, who studied at Naples and produced his first known comic opera there in 1719.

Wagenseil, Georg Christoph (1715–77), Austrian composer, pupil of Fux, music master to Maria Theresa and her daughters, composer of serious, chiefly instrumental music and the leading figure of the Viennese transitional symphonic school.

Waltz, Gustavus, German bass singer, who sang in several of Handel's oratorios.

Zumsteeg, Johann Rudolf (1760–1802), German composer, educated at Stuttgart, where he became *Capellmeister* to the Duke of Württemberg in 1792. Wrote many songs and ballads.

APPENDIX D

BIBLIOGRAPHY

Abert, Anna Amalie, 'Gluck.' (Munich, 1959.)

Arend, Max, 'Gluck, ein Biographie.' (Berlin, 1921.)

Barbedette, H., 'Gluck.' (Paris, 1882.)

Berlioz, Hector, 'À travers chants.' (Paris, 1862.)

—— 'Gluck and his Operas.' Translated by Edwin Evans, sen. (London, 1915.)

—— 'Voyage musical en Allemagne et en Italie.' (Paris, 1844.)

Bitter, C. H., 'Die Reform der Oper durch Gluck und Richard Wagner.' (Brunswick, 1884.)

Brandl, W., 'Christoph Willibald Ritter von Gluck.' (Wiesbaden, 1948.)

Cooper, Martin, 'Gluck.' (London, 1935.)

Della Corte, Andrea, 'Gluck e i suoi tempi.' (Florence, 1948.)

Desnoiresterres, Gustave, 'Gluck et Piccinni.' (2nd edition, Paris, 1875.)

Gerber, Rudolf, 'Christoph Willibald Gluck.' (2nd edition, Potsdam, 1950.)

Haas, Robert, 'Gluck und Durazzo im Burgtheater.' (Vienna, 1925.)

Hopkinson, Cecil, 'A Bibliography of the Works of C. W. von Gluck.' (London, 1959.)

Kinsky, Georg, 'Glucks Briefe an Franz Kruthoffer.' (Vienna, 1929.)

Kurth, Ernst, 'Die Jugendopern Glucks.' ('Studien zur Musikwissen-schaft,' i; Vienna, 1913.)

Landormy, Paul, 'Gluck.' (Paris, 1941.)

Lazzeri, G., 'La vita e l'opera letteraria di Ranieri Calzabigi.' (Città di Castello, 1907.)

[*Leblond, G. M.,*] 'Mémoires pour servir à l'histoire de la révolution opérée dans la musique par M. le chevalier Gluck.' (Naples, 1781.)

Liebeskind, Joseph, 'Ergänzungen und Nachträge zu Wotquennes Thema-tischem Verzeichnis.' (Leipzig, 1911.)

Loewenberg, Alfred, 'Gluck's Orfeo on the Stage' ('Musical Quarterly,' New York, July 1940.)

—— 'Annals of Opera, 1597–1940.' 2 vols. (2nd edition, Geneva, 1955.)

Marx, Adolf Bernhard, 'Gluck und die Oper.' 2 vols. (Berlin, 1863.)

Meyer, Ralph, 'Die Behandlung des Rezitativs in Glucks italienischen Reformopern.' (Halle, 1919.)

Miel, E. F. A. M., 'Notice sur Chr. Gluck.' (Paris, 1840.)

Moser, H. J., 'Christoph Willibald Gluck.' (Stuttgart, 1940.)

Mueller von Asow, Hedwig and E. H., eds., 'The Collected Correspondence and Papers of Christoph Willibald Gluck.' (London, 1962.)

Newman, Ernest, 'Gluck and the Opera.' (London, 1895.)

Piovano, Francesco, 'Un opéra inconnu de Gluck.' ('Sammelbände der Internationalen Musikgesellschaft,' Jan.–March 1908.)

Prod'homme, J. G., 'French Collaborators of Gluck.' ('Musical Quarterly,' New York, April, 1913.)

—— 'Gluck.' (Paris, 1948.)

Reissmann, A., 'Christoph Willibald von Gluck, sein Leben und seine Werke.' (Berlin & Leipzig, 1882.)

Riedel, C. H., 'Über die Musik des Ritters Christoph von Gluck: Verschie-dene Schriften.' (Vienna, 1775.)

Rolland, Romain, 'Musiciens d'autrefois.' (Paris, 1908.)

—— 'Some Musicians of Former Days.' Translated by Mary Blaiklock. (London, 1915.)

Schmid, Anton, 'Chr. W. Ritter von Gluck. Dessen Leben und ton-künstlerisches Wirken.' (Leipzig, 1854.)

Squire, W. Barclay, 'Gluck's London Operas.' ('Musical Quarterly,' New York, July 1915.)

Thoinan, Ernest, 'Notes bibliographiques sur la guerre musicale des Gluck-istes et Piccinistes.' (Paris, 1878.)

Tiersot, Julien, 'Gluck.' ('Les Maîtres de la Musique'; 4th edition, Paris, 1919.)

Tovey, Donald F., Essay on Gluck in 'The Heritage of Music,' edited by Hubert J. Foss, vol. ii. (Oxford and London, 1934.)

Udine, Jean d', 'Gluck.' ('Les Musiciens célèbres'; Paris, 1906.)

Welti, Heinrich, 'Gluck.' ('Musiker-Biographien'; Leipzig, 1888.)

Winterfeld, C. von, 'Alceste, 1674, 1726, 1769, 1776, von Lully, Händel und Gluck.' (Berlin, 1851.)

Wortsmann, Stephan, 'Die deutsche Gluck-Literatur.' (Nuremberg, 1914.)

Wotquenne, Alfred, 'Catalogue thématique des œuvres de Ch. W. Gluck.' (Leipzig, 1904.) See also under Liebeskind.

APPENDIX E

JE viens de recevoir, mon ami, votre lettre du 15 Janvier, par laquelle vous
m'exhortez à continuer de travailler sur les paroles de l'Opéra de *Roland*;
cela n'est plus faisable, parce que quand j'ai appris que l'Administration de
l'Opéra, qui n'ignoroit pas que je faisois *Roland*, avoit donné ce même
ouvrage à faire à M. Piccini, j'ai brûlé tout ce que j'en avois déjà fait, qui
peut-être ne valoit pas grand'chose, et en ce cas, le Public doit avoir obligation à M. Marmontel d'avoir empêché qu'on ne lui fit entendre une mauvaise
Musique. D'ailleurs, je ne suis plus un homme fait pour entrer en con-
currence. M. Piccini auroit trop d'avantage sur moi, car, outre son mérite
personnel, qui est assûrément très-grand, il auroit celui de la nouveauté,
moi ayant donné à Paris quatre Ouvrages bons ou mauvais, n'importe;
cela use la fantaisie et puis je lui ai frayé le chemin, il n'a qu'à me suivre.
Je ne vous parle pas de ses protections. Je suis sûr qu'un certain Politique
de ma connoissance, donnera à diner et à souper aux trois quarts de Paris,
pour lui faire des prosélites, et que Marmontel, qui sait si bien faire des
Contes, contera à tout le Royaume le mérite exclusif du sieur Piccini. Je
plains, en vérité, M. Hébert, d'être tombé dans les griffes de tels personnages,
l'un Amateur exclusif de Musique Italienne, l'autre Auteur Dramatique
d'Opéras prétendus Comiques. Ils lui feront voir la Lune à midi. J'en
suis vraiment fâché; car c'est un galant homme que ce M. Hébert, et c'est
la raison pour laquelle je ne m'éloigne pas de lui donner mon *Armide,* aux
conditions cependant que je vous ai marquées dans ma précédente Lettre,
et dont les essentielles, je vous le répète, sont qu'on me donnera au moins
deux mois, quand je serai à Paris, pour former mes Acteurs et Actrices;
que je serai le maître de faire autant de répétitions que je croirai nécessaires;
qu'on ne laissera doubler aucun Rôle, et qu'on tiendra un autre Opéra tout
prêt, au cas que quelque Acteur ou Actrice soit incommodé. Voilà mes
conditions, sans lesquelles je garderai l'*Armide* pour mon plaisir. J'en ai
fait la Musique de manière qu'elle ne vieillira pas sitôt.

Vous me dites, mon cher ami, dans votre Lettre, que rien ne vaudra
jamais l'*Alceste*; mais moi, je ne souscris pas encore à votre prophétie.
Alceste est une Tragédie complette, et je vous avoue que je crois qu'il

manque très-peu de chose à sa perfection; mais vous n'imaginez pas de combien de nuances et de routes différentes la Musique est susceptible; l'ensemble de l'*Armide* est si différent de celui de l'*Alceste,* que vous croirez qu'ils ne sont pas du même Compositeur. Aussi ai-je employé le peu de suc qui me restoit pour achever l'*Armide*; j'ai tâché d'y être plus Peintre et plus Poète que Musicien; enfin, vous en jugerez, si on veut l'entendre. Je vous confesse qu'avec cet Opéra, j'aimerai à finir ma carrière. Il est vrai que pour le Public, il faudra au moins autant de temps pour le comprendre, qu'il lui en a fallu pour comprendre l'*Alceste.* Il y a une espèce de délicatesse dans l'*Armide* qui n'est pas dans l'*Alceste*: car j'ai trouvé le moyen de faire parler les personnages de manière que vous connaîtrez d'abord à leur façon de s'exprimer, quand ce sera Armide qui parlera, ou une suivante, etc., etc. Il faut finir, autrement vous croirez que je suis devenu fou ou Charlatan. Rien ne fait un si mauvais effet que de se louer soi-même, cela ne convenoit qu'au grand Corneille; mais quand Marmontel ou moi nous nous louons, on se moque de nous, et on nous rit au nez. Au reste, vous avez grande raison de dire qu'on a trop négligé les Compositeurs François; car, ou je me trompe fort, je crois que Gossec et Philidor, qui connoissent la coupe de l'Opéra Françoise, serviroient infiniment mieux le Public que les meilleurs Auteurs Italiens, si l'on ne s'enthousiasmoit pas pour tout ce qui a l'air de nouveauté. Vous me dites encore, mon ami, qu'*Orphée* perd par la comparaison avec *Alceste.* Eh mon Dieu! comment peut-on comparer ces deux ouvrages qui n'ont rien de comparable? L'un peut plaire davantage que l'autre; mais faites exécuter l'*Alceste* avec vos mauvais Acteurs et toute autre Actrice que Mlle Le Vasseur, et *Orphée* avec ce que vous avez de meilleur, et vous verrez qu'*Orphée* emportera la balance: les choses les mieux faites, mal exécutées, deviennent d'autant plus insupportables. Une comparaison ne peut subsister entre deux ouvrages de différente nature. Que si, par exemple, Piccini et moi, nous faisons chacun pour notre compte l'Opéra de *Roland,* alors on pourrait juger lequel des deux l'auroit le mieux fait; mais les divers Poèmes doivent nécessairement produire différentes Musiques, lesquelles peuvent être pour l'expression des paroles, tout ce qu'on peut trouver de plus sublime chacune dans son genre; mais alors toute comparaison *claudicat.* Je tremble presque qu'on ne veuille comparer l'*Armide* et l'*Alceste,* poèmes si différens dont l'un doit faire pleurer, et l'autre faire éprouver une voluptueuse sensation; si cela arrive, je n'aurai pas d'autre ressource que de faire prier Dieu pour que la bonne ville de Paris retrouve son bon-sens.

Adieu, mon cher ami, je vous embrasse, etc., etc.

INDEX

INDEX

Catalog

If you are interested in a list of fine Paperback
books, covering a wide range of subjects
and interests, send your name and address,
requesting your free catalog, to:

McGraw-Hill Paperbacks
1221 Avenue of Americas
New York, N.Y. 10020